Andrews McMeel
PUBLISHING®

I left the house today!

Comics by Cassandra Calin

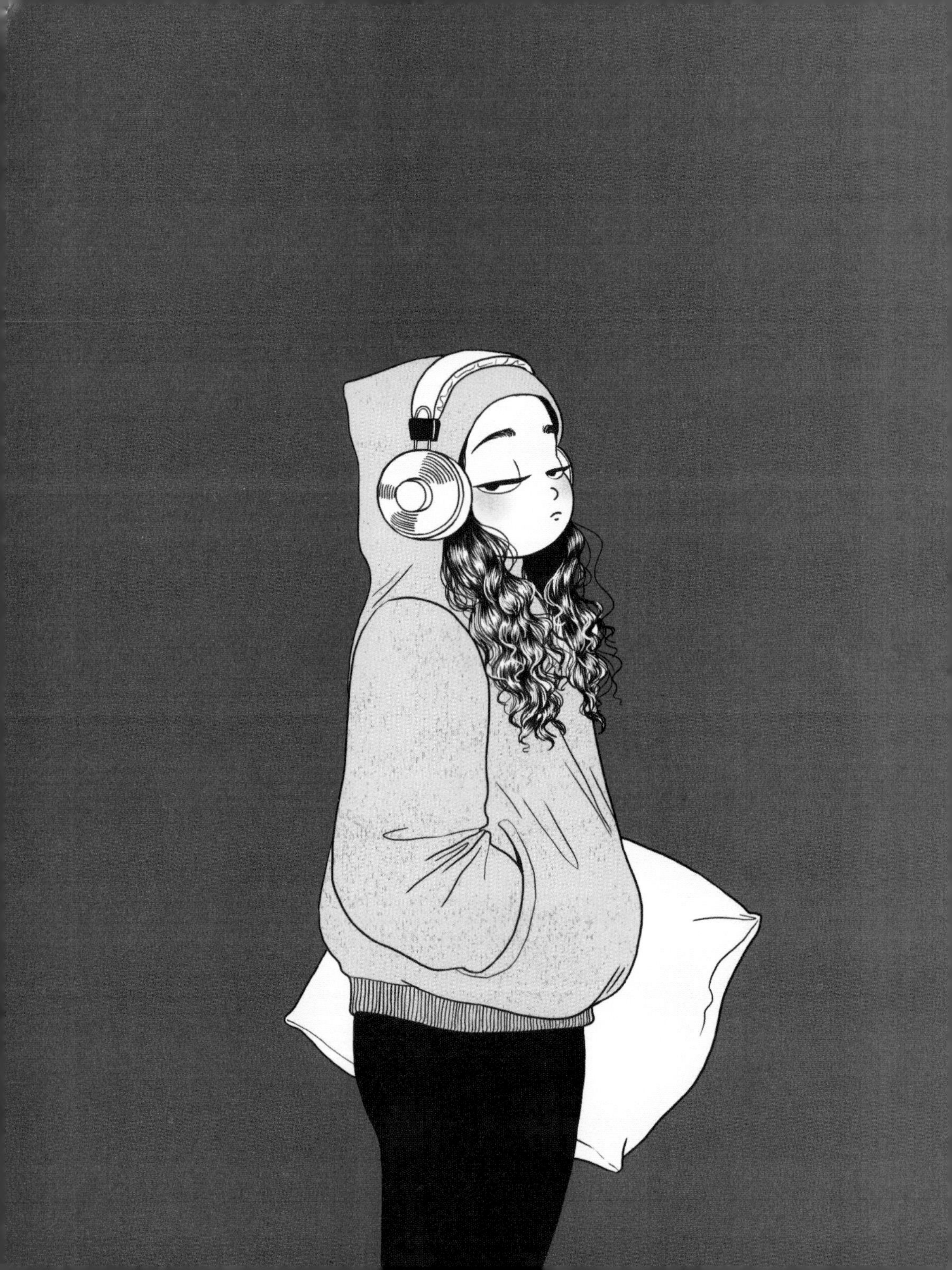

Introduction

I left the house today! . . . Not really. But I do leave occasionally, I swear! My name is Cassandra and I draw a semi-autobiographical webcomic series about my life with curly hair and high expectations. In this series, I like to borrow some aspects from daily life and my personal experiences while also finding humor in the most basic first-world problems.

I Left the House Today! is a collection of short comics depicting the simple and, most times, unglamorous parts of everyday life. This book will give you an insight on what it's like to try your best to be a normal human being—and actually leaving your house from time to time.

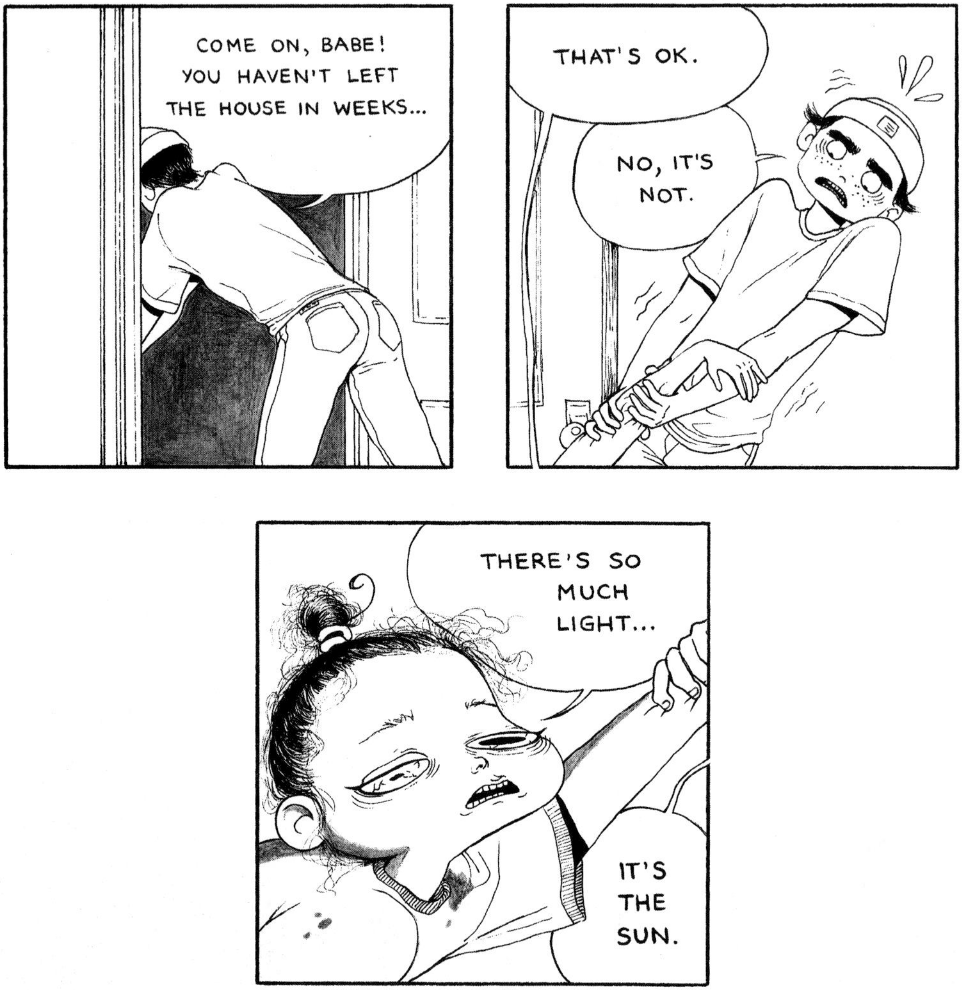
COME ON, BABE! YOU HAVEN'T LEFT THE HOUSE IN WEEKS...
THAT'S OK.
NO, IT'S NOT.
THERE'S SO MUCH LIGHT...
IT'S THE SUN.

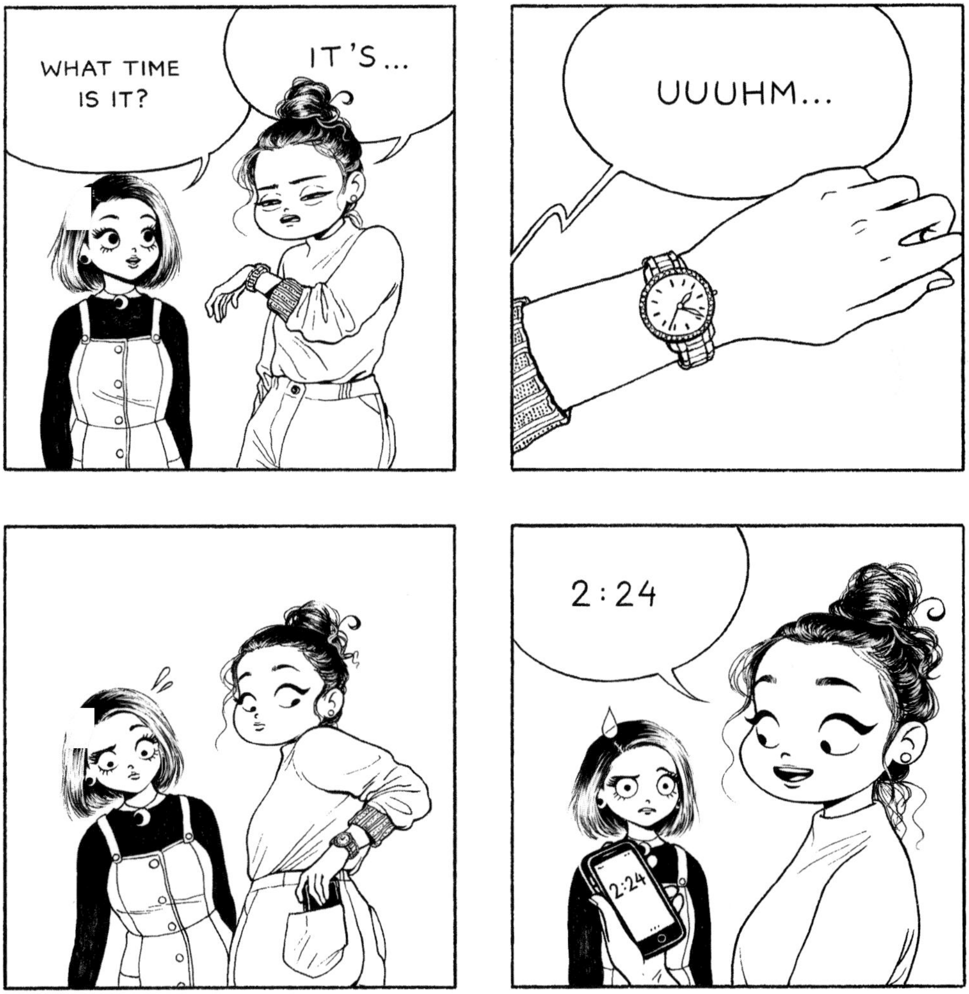
WHAT TIME IS IT?
IT'S...
UUUHM...
2:24
2:24

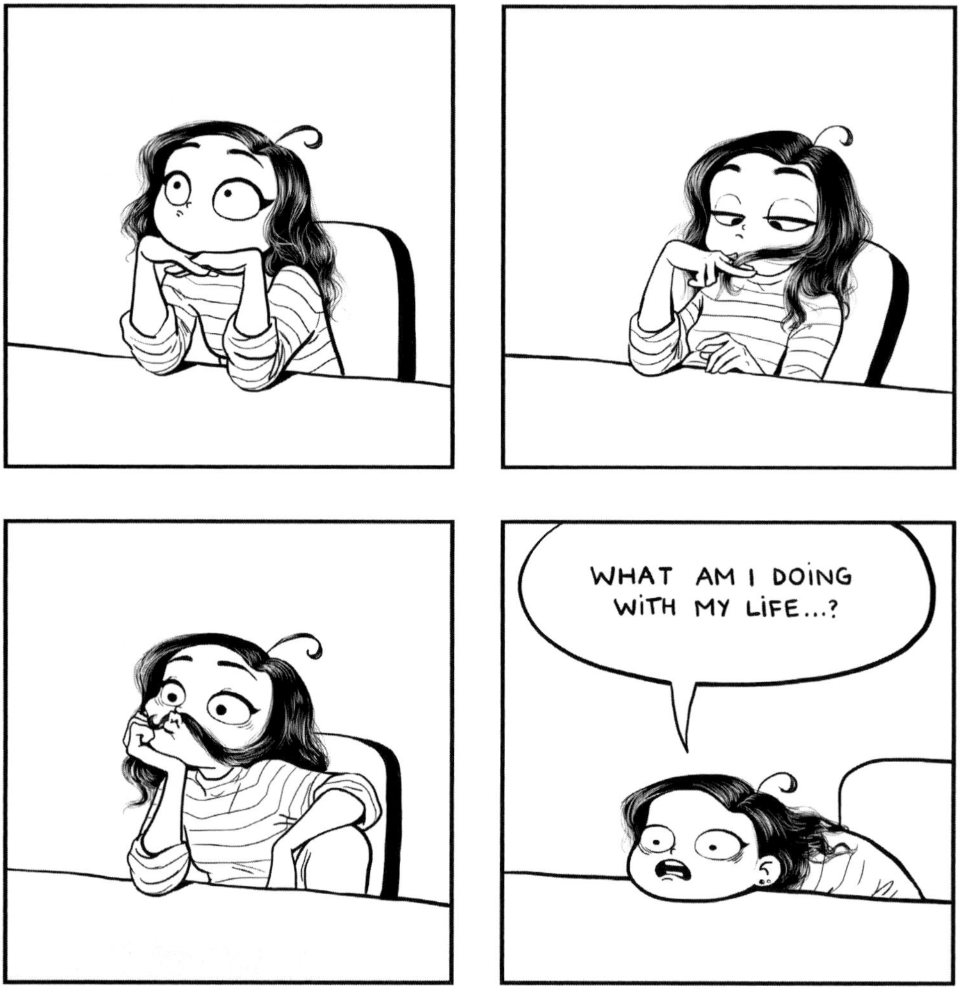
WHAT AM I DOING WITH MY LIFE...?

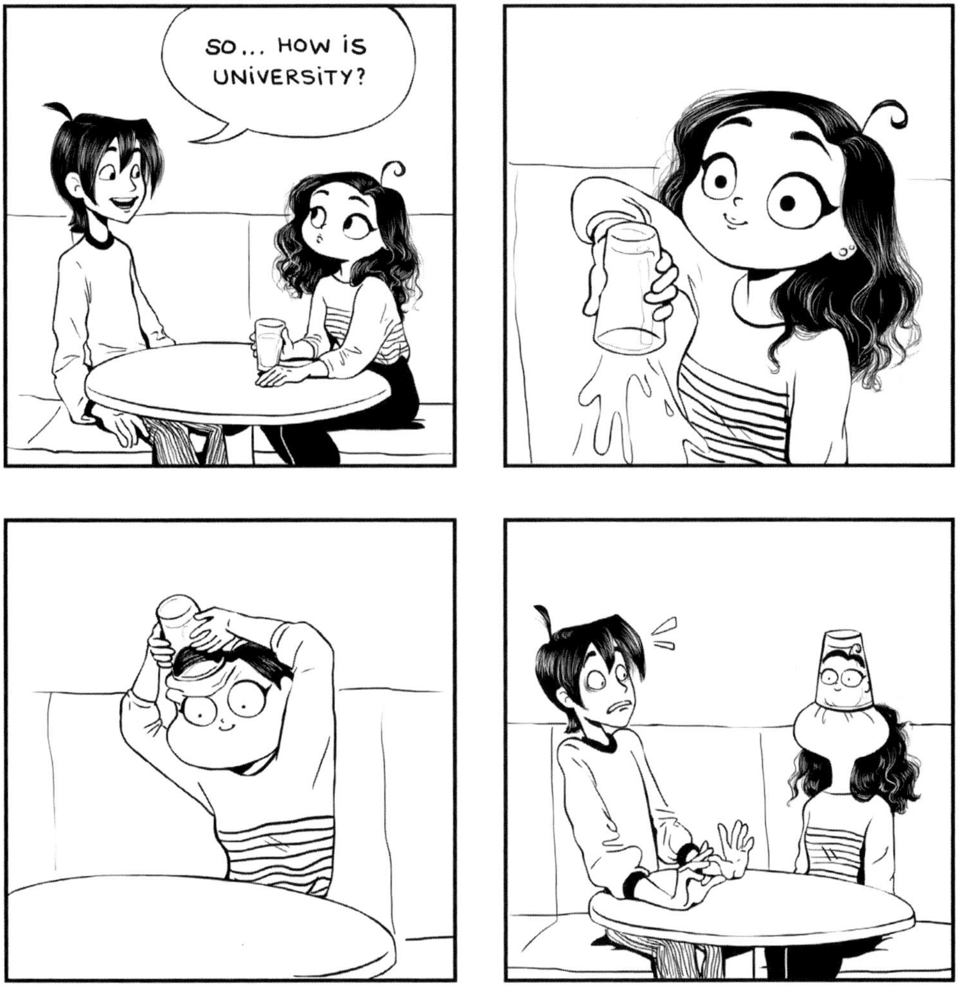
SO... HOW IS UNIVERSITY?

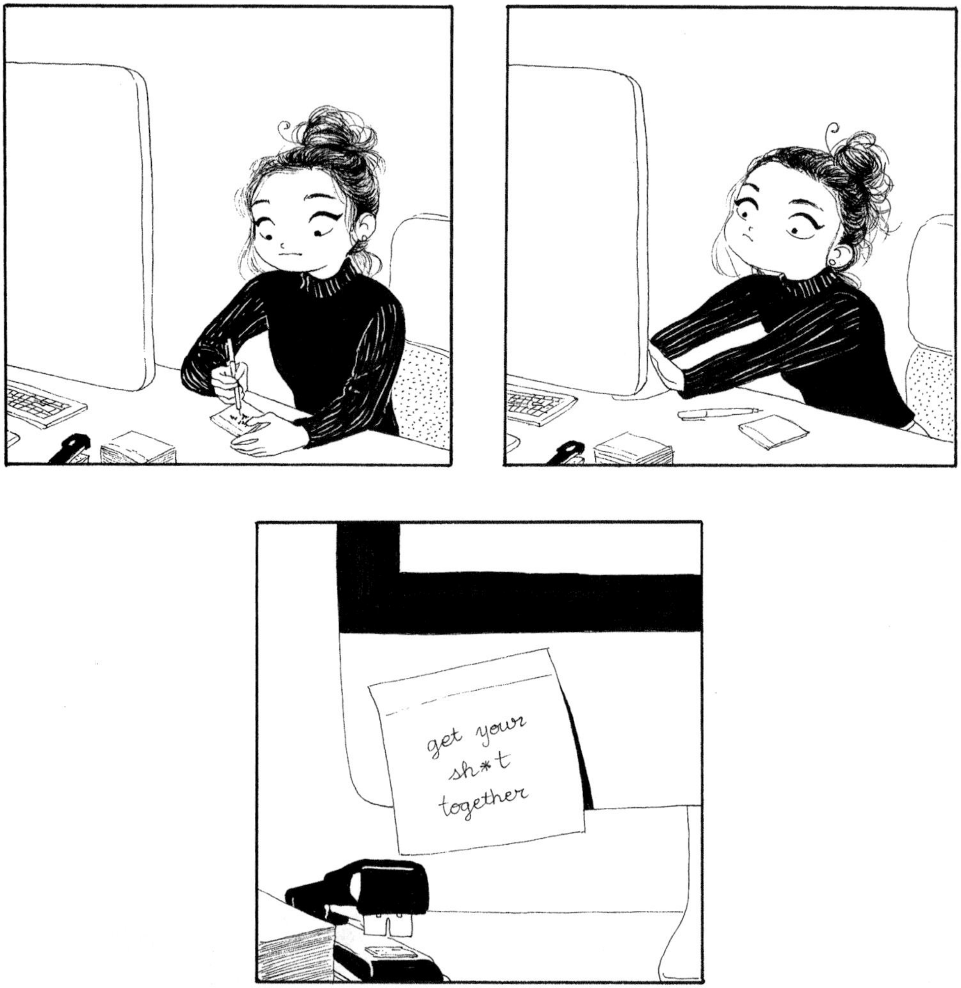
get your
sh*t
together

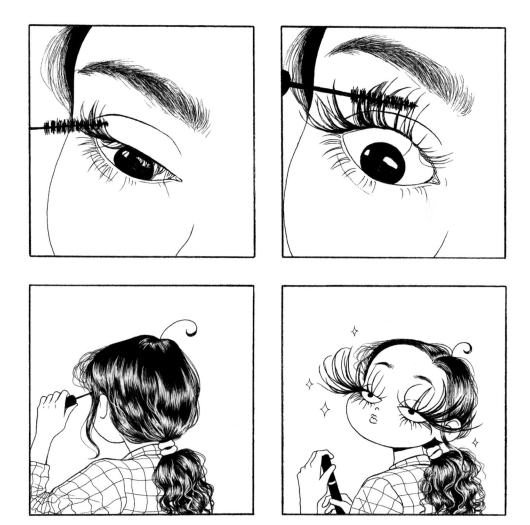

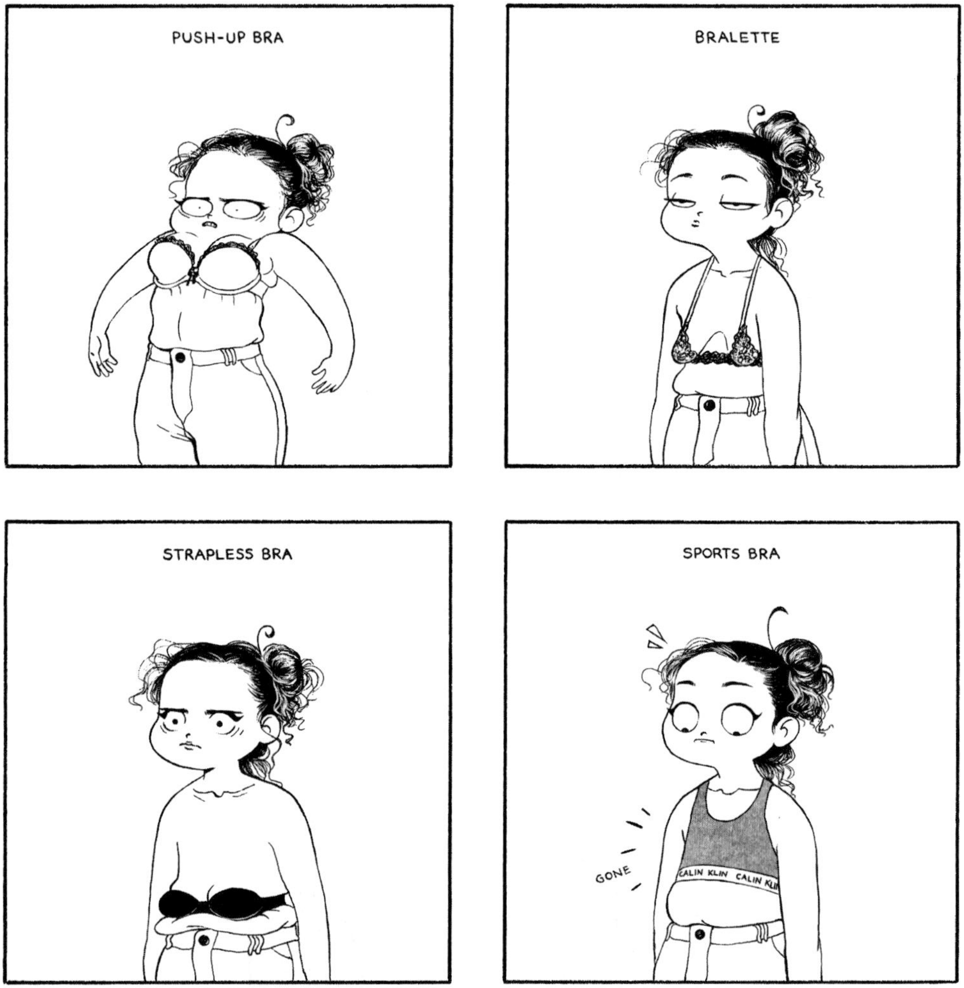
PUSH-UP BRA
BRALETTE
STRAPLESS BRA
SPORTS BRA
GONE
CALIN KLIN

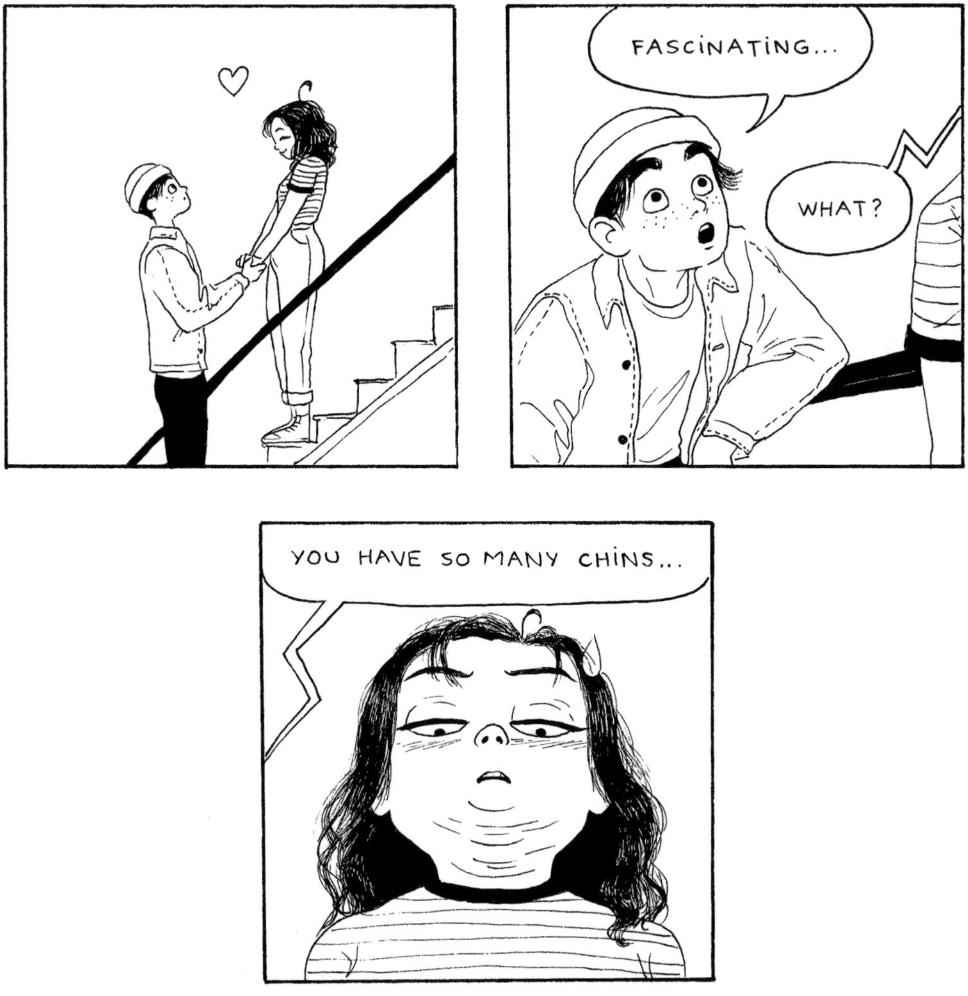
FASCINATING...
WHAT?
YOU HAVE SO MANY CHINS...

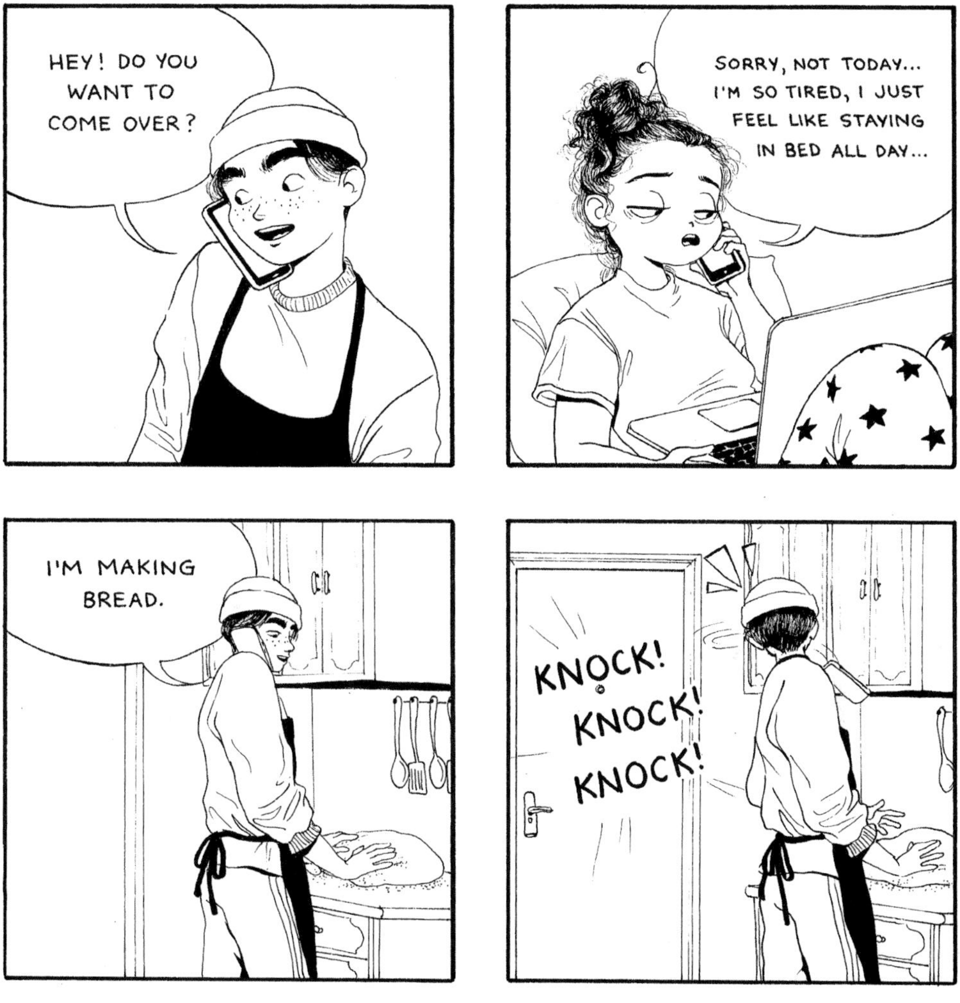
HEY! DO YOU WANT TO COME OVER?
SORRY, NOT TODAY... I'M SO TIRED, I JUST FEEL LIKE STAYING IN BED ALL DAY...
I'M MAKING BREAD.
KNOCK! KNOCK! KNOCK!

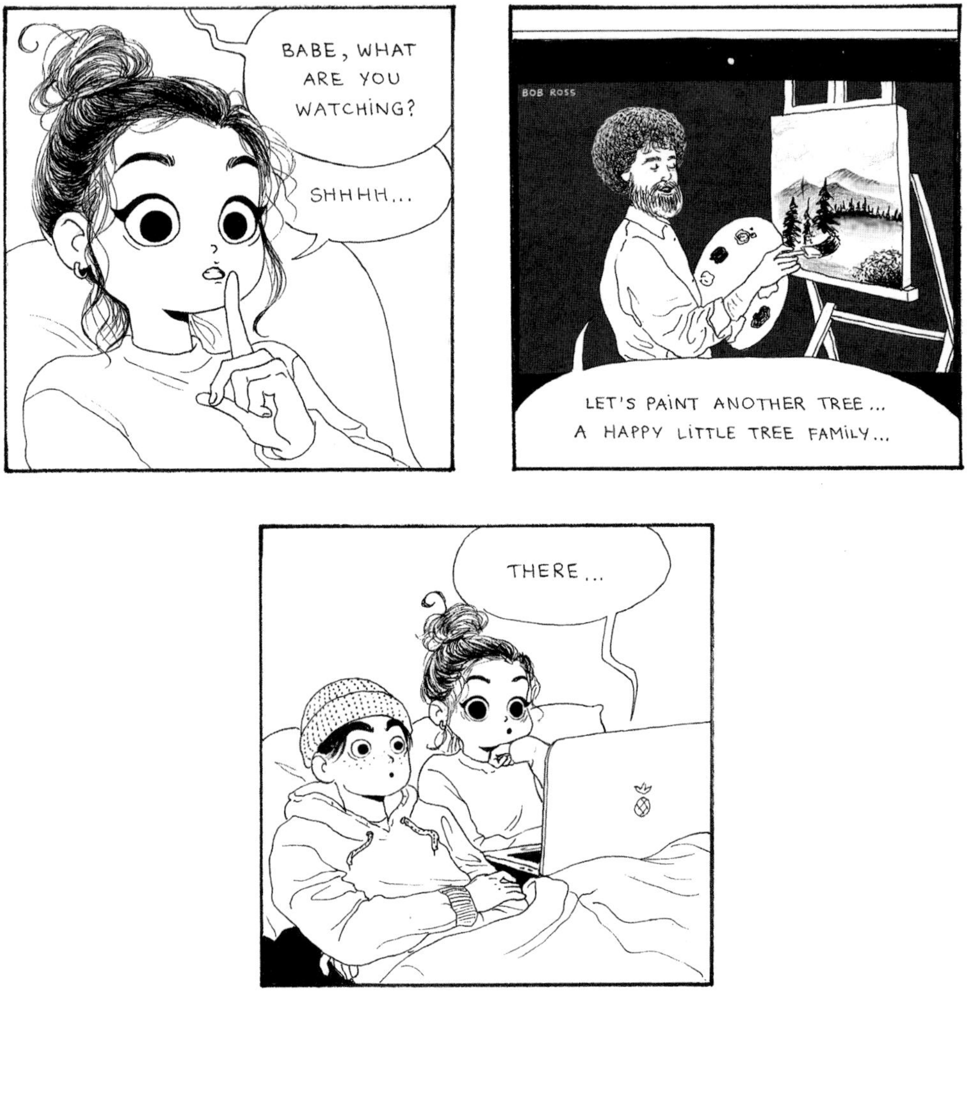
BABE, WHAT ARE YOU WATCHING?
SHHHH...
BOB ROSS
LET'S PAINT ANOTHER TREE...
A HAPPY LITTLE TREE FAMILY...
THERE...

BRUSHED HAIR

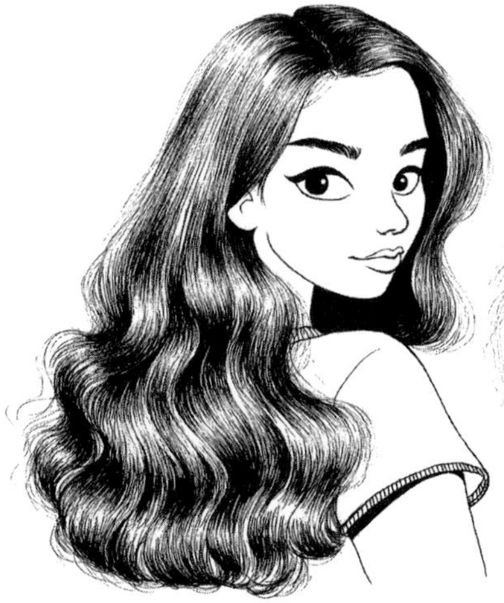

EXPECTATIONS

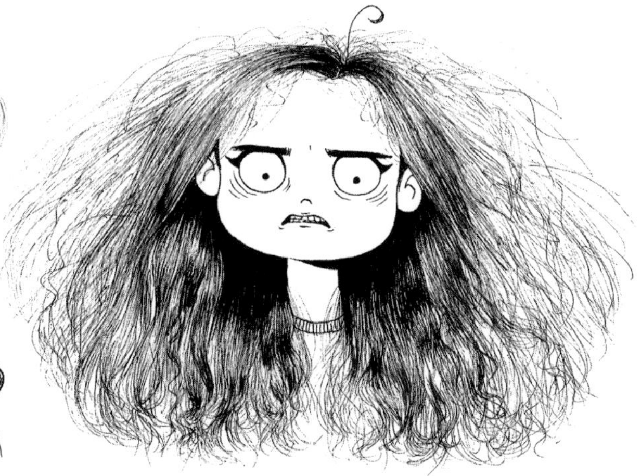

REALITY

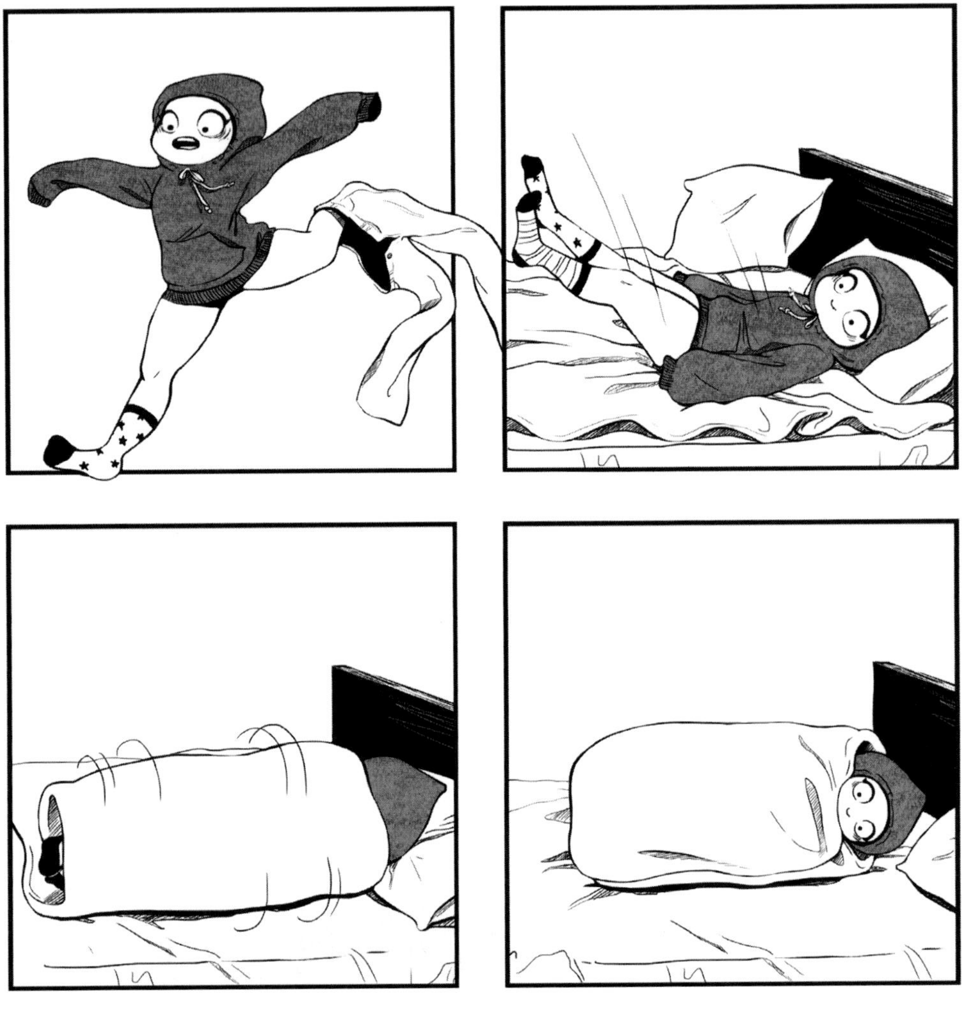

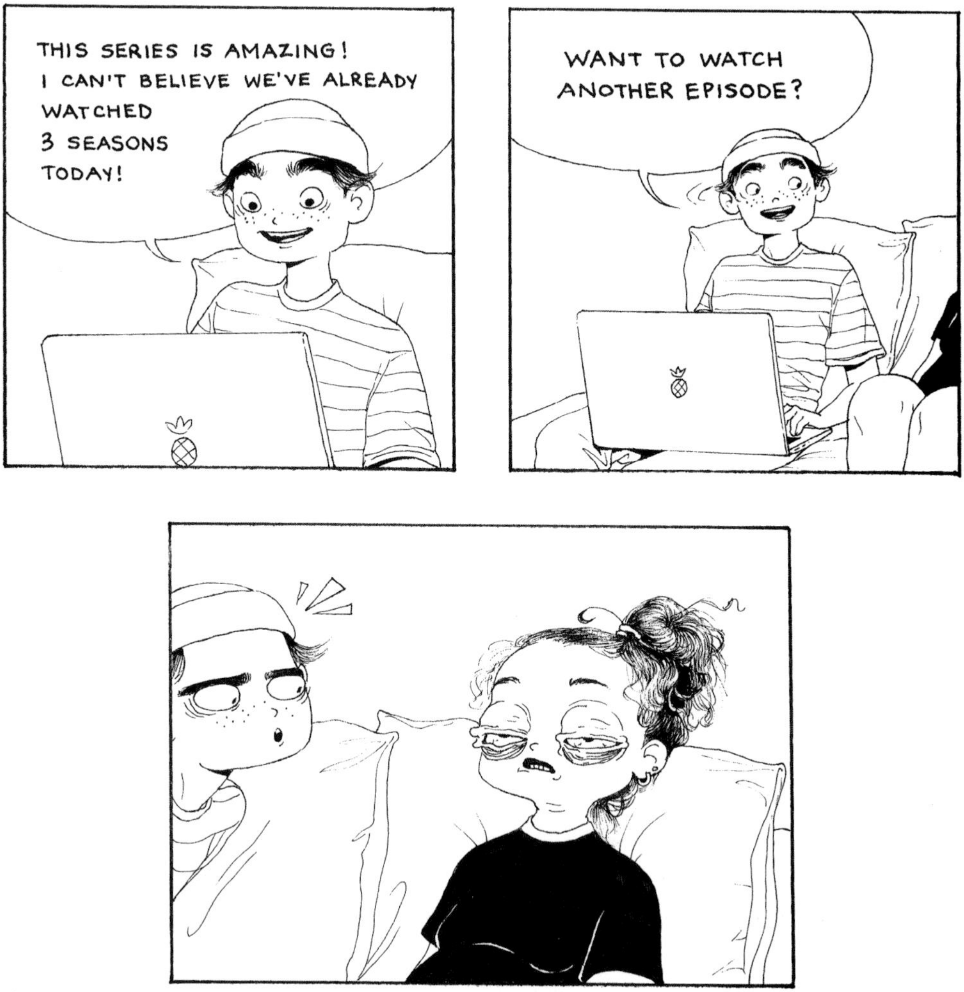
THIS SERIES IS AMAZING! I CAN'T BELIEVE WE'VE ALREADY WATCHED 3 SEASONS TODAY!
WANT TO WATCH ANOTHER EPISODE?

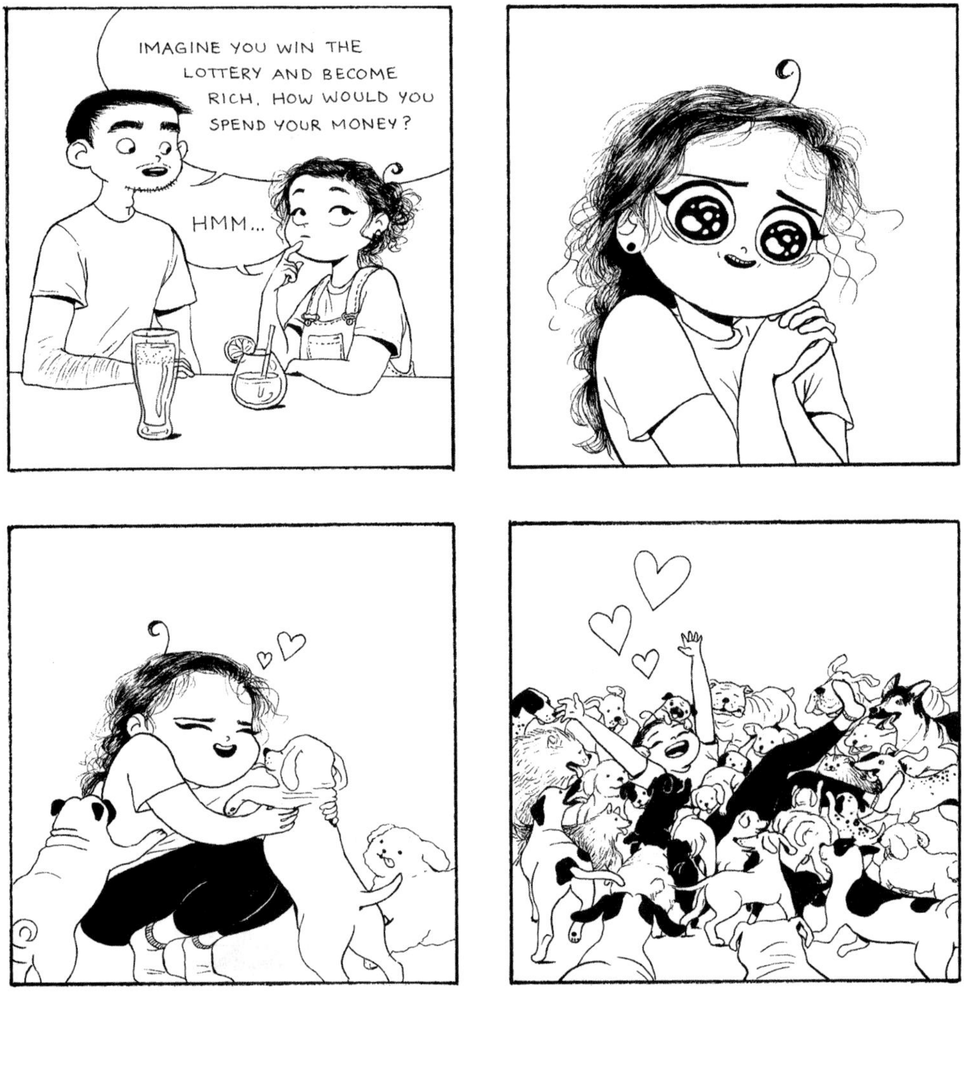
IMAGINE YOU WIN THE LOTTERY AND BECOME RICH, HOW WOULD YOU SPEND YOUR MONEY?
HMM...

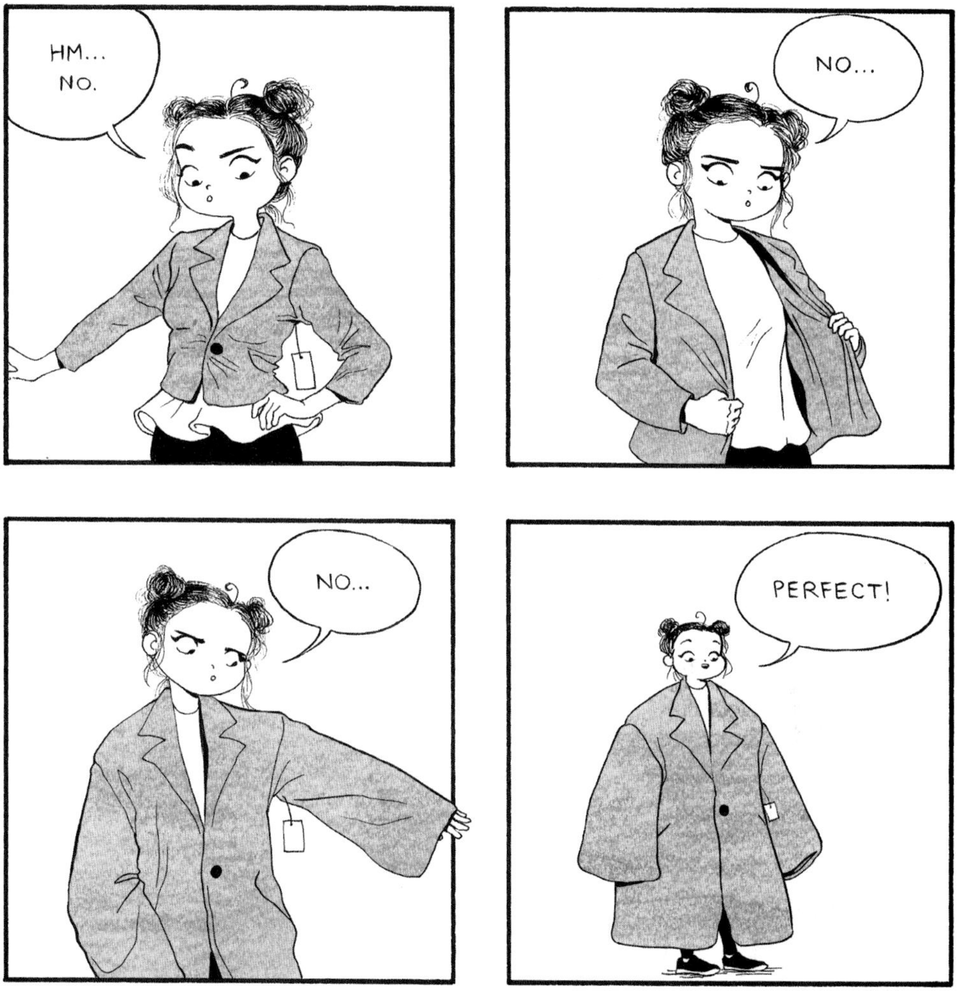
HM... NO.
NO...
NO...
PERFECT!

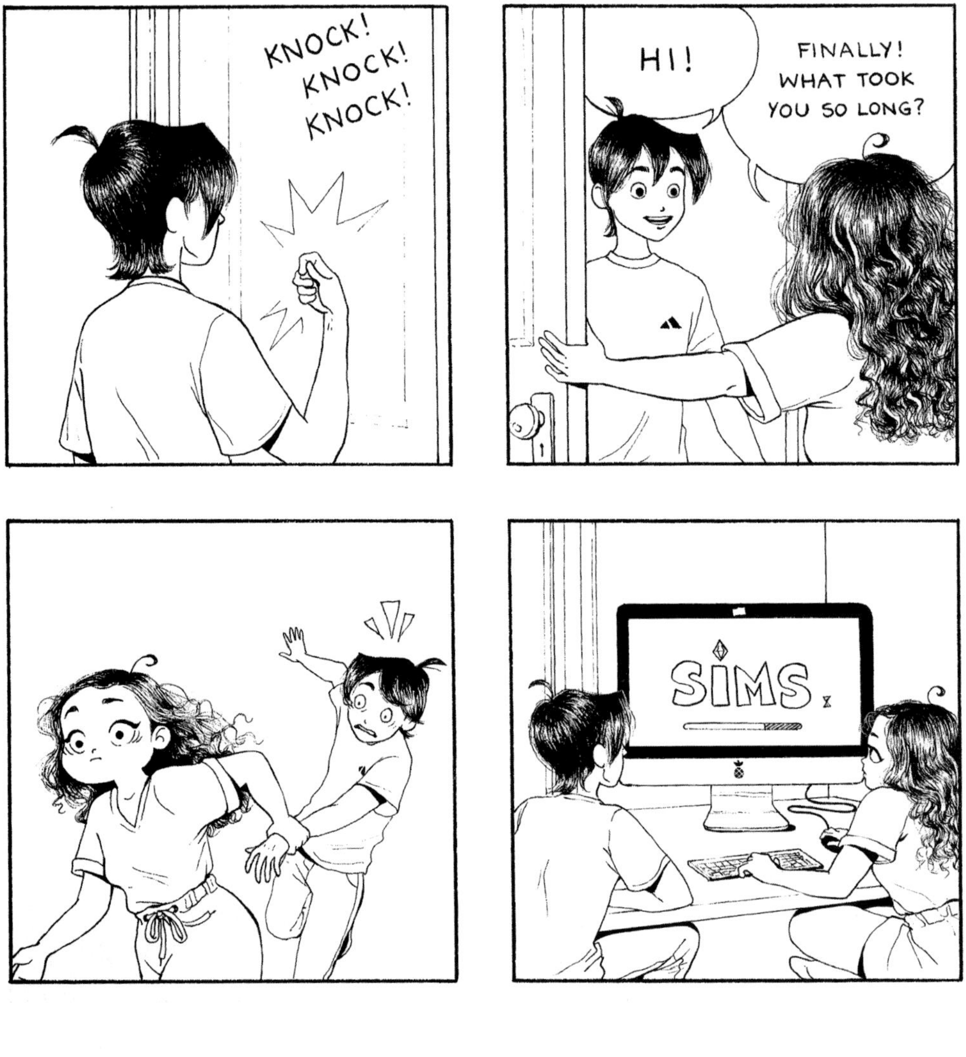
KNOCK!
KNOCK!
KNOCK!
HI!
FINALLY! WHAT TOOK YOU SO LONG?
SIMS

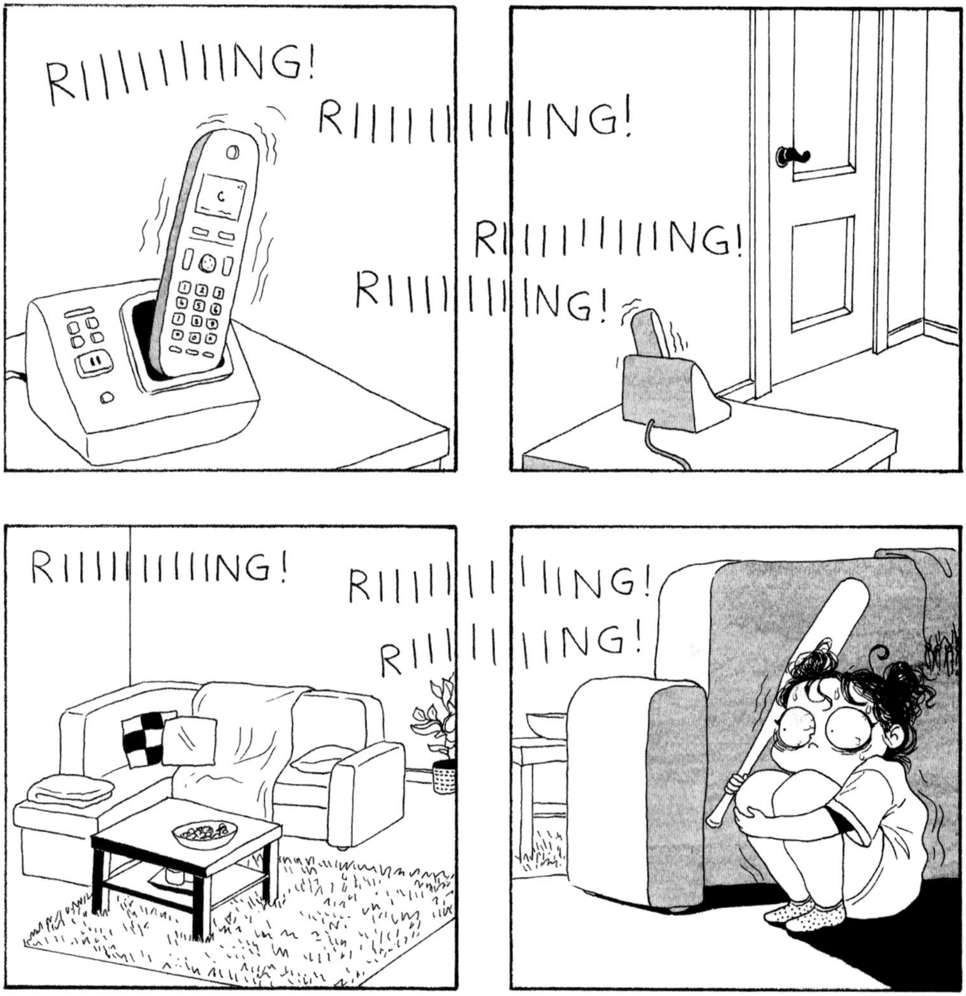
RIIIIIIIING!
RIIIIIIIIIING!
RIIIIIIIIING!
RIIIIIIIING!
RIIIIIIIIIING!
RIIIIIIIIIING!
RIIIIIIING!

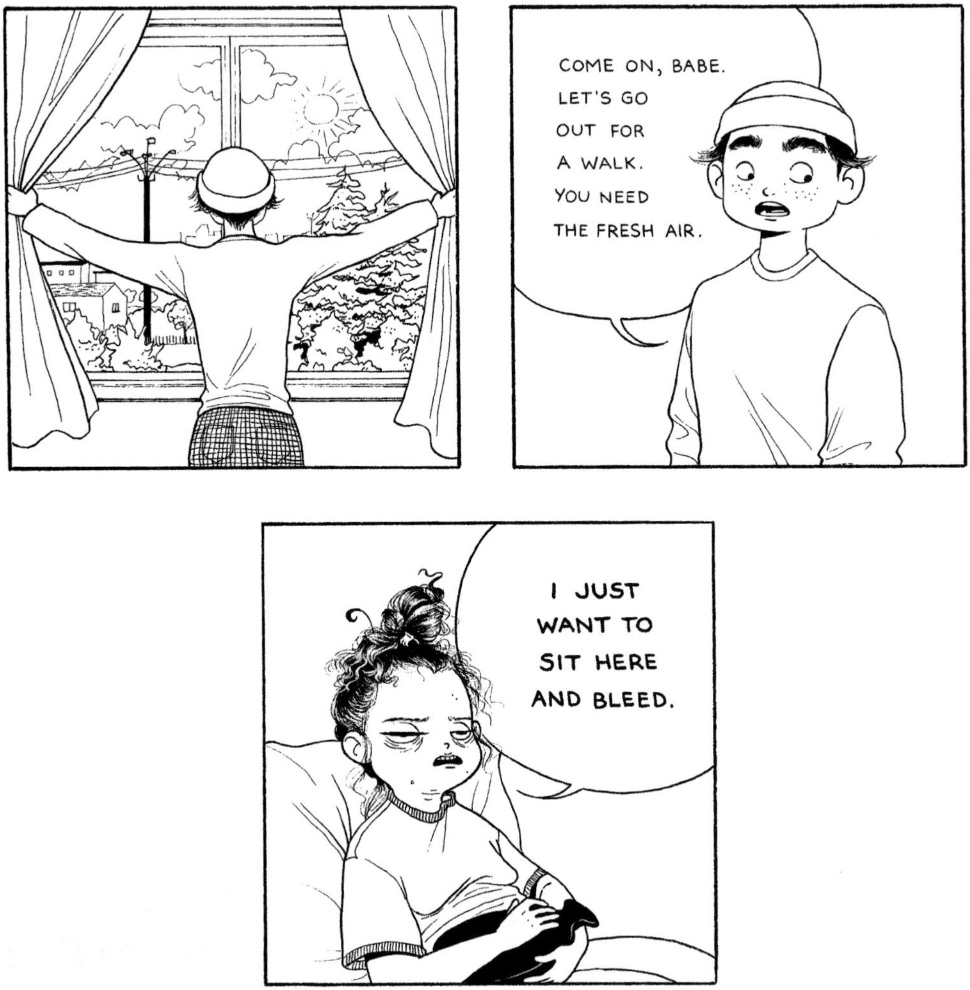
COME ON, BABE. LET'S GO OUT FOR A WALK. YOU NEED THE FRESH AIR.
I JUST WANT TO SIT HERE AND BLEED.

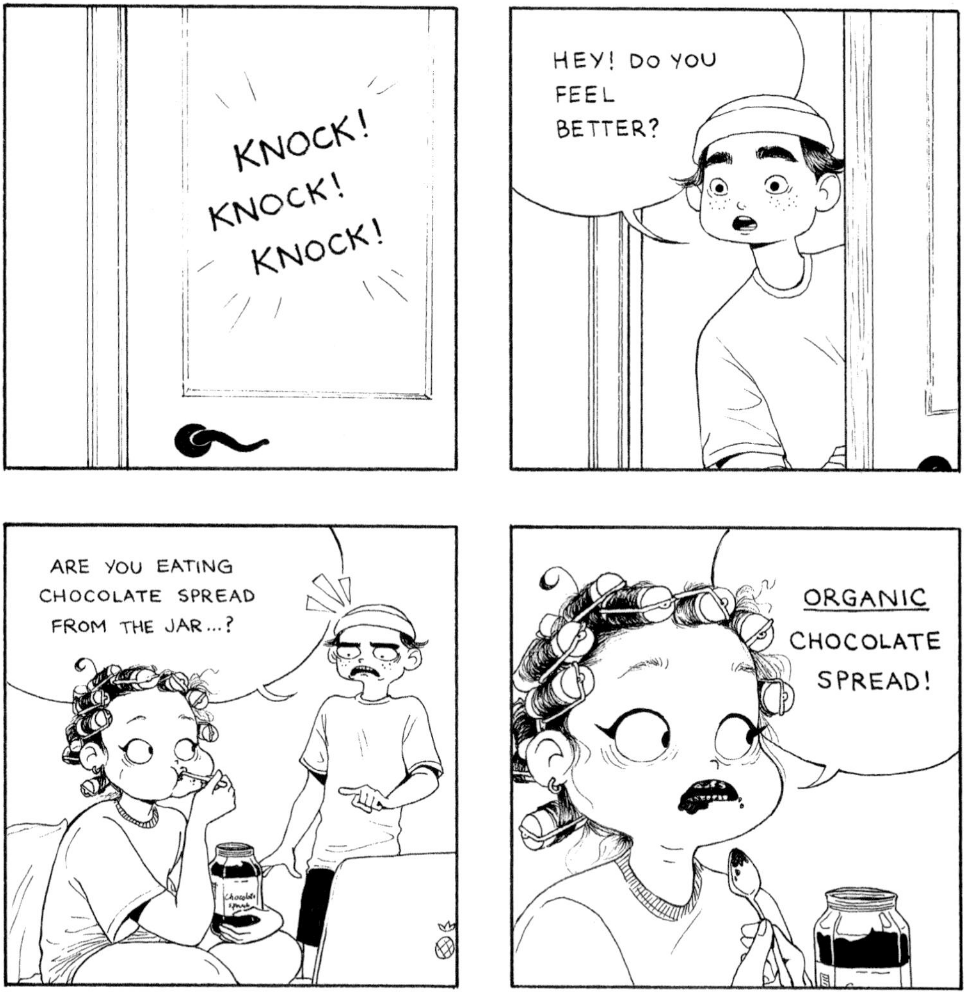
KNOCK! KNOCK! KNOCK!
HEY! DO YOU FEEL BETTER?
ARE YOU EATING CHOCOLATE SPREAD FROM THE JAR...?
ORGANIC CHOCOLATE SPREAD!

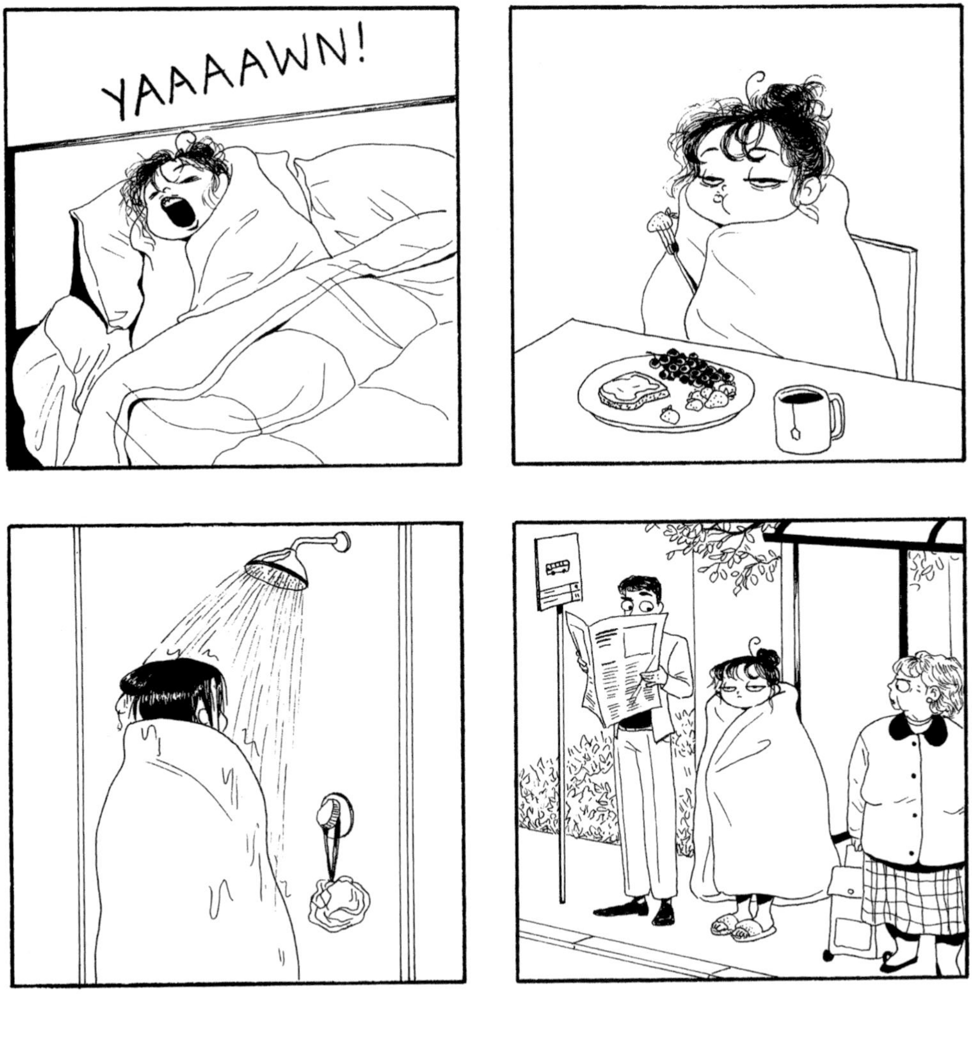
YAAAAWN!

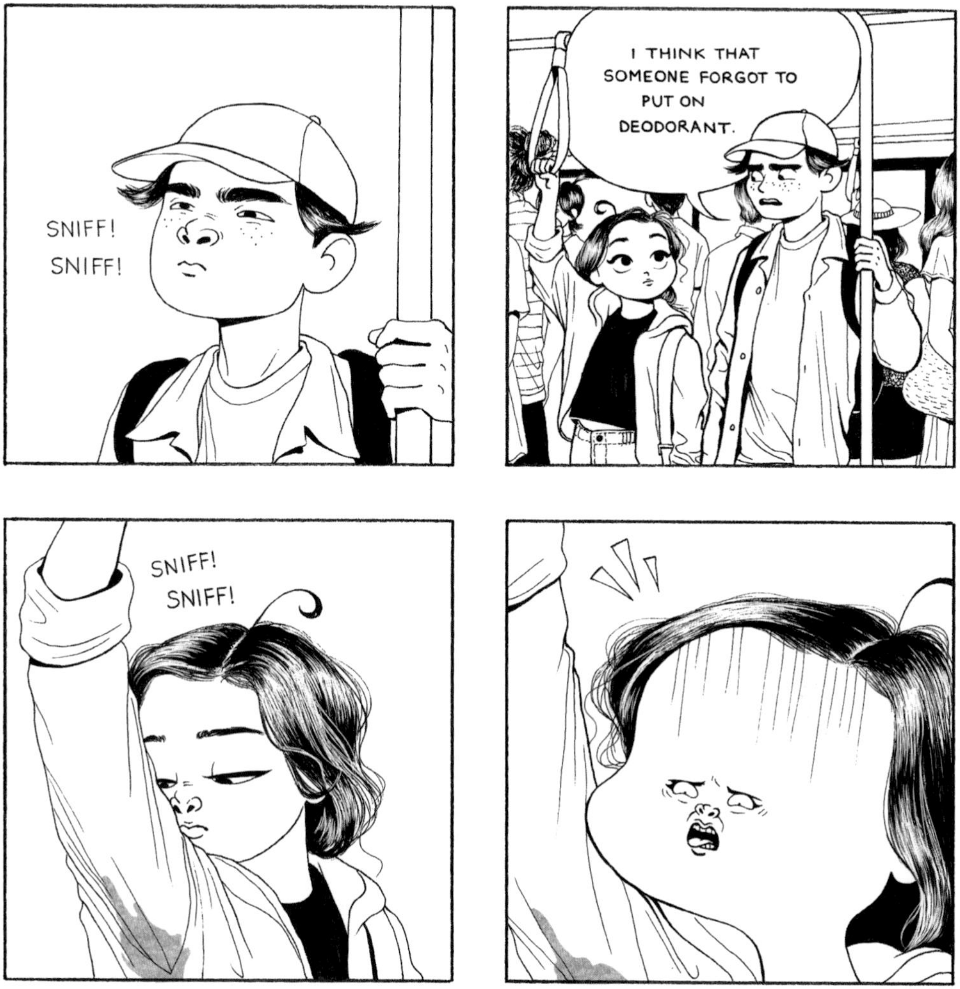
SNIFF!
SNIFF!
I THINK THAT SOMEONE FORGOT TO PUT ON DEODORANT.
SNIFF!
SNIFF!

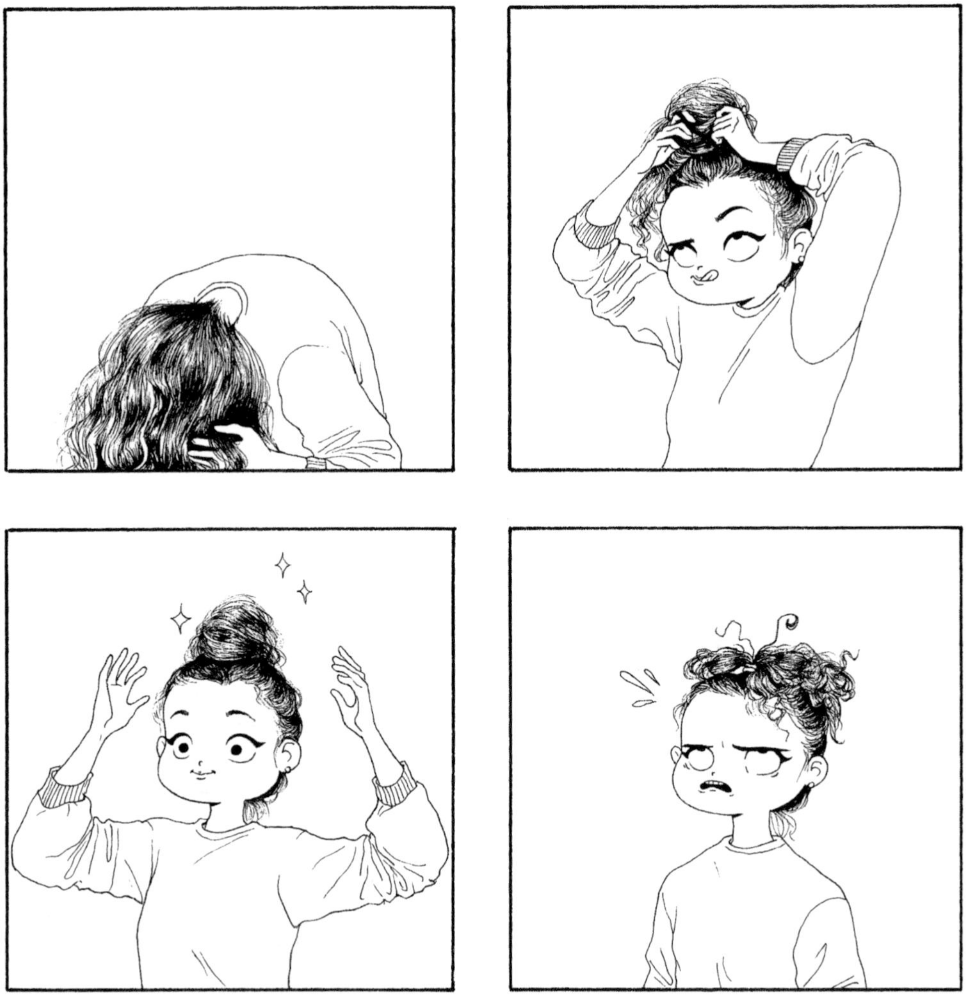

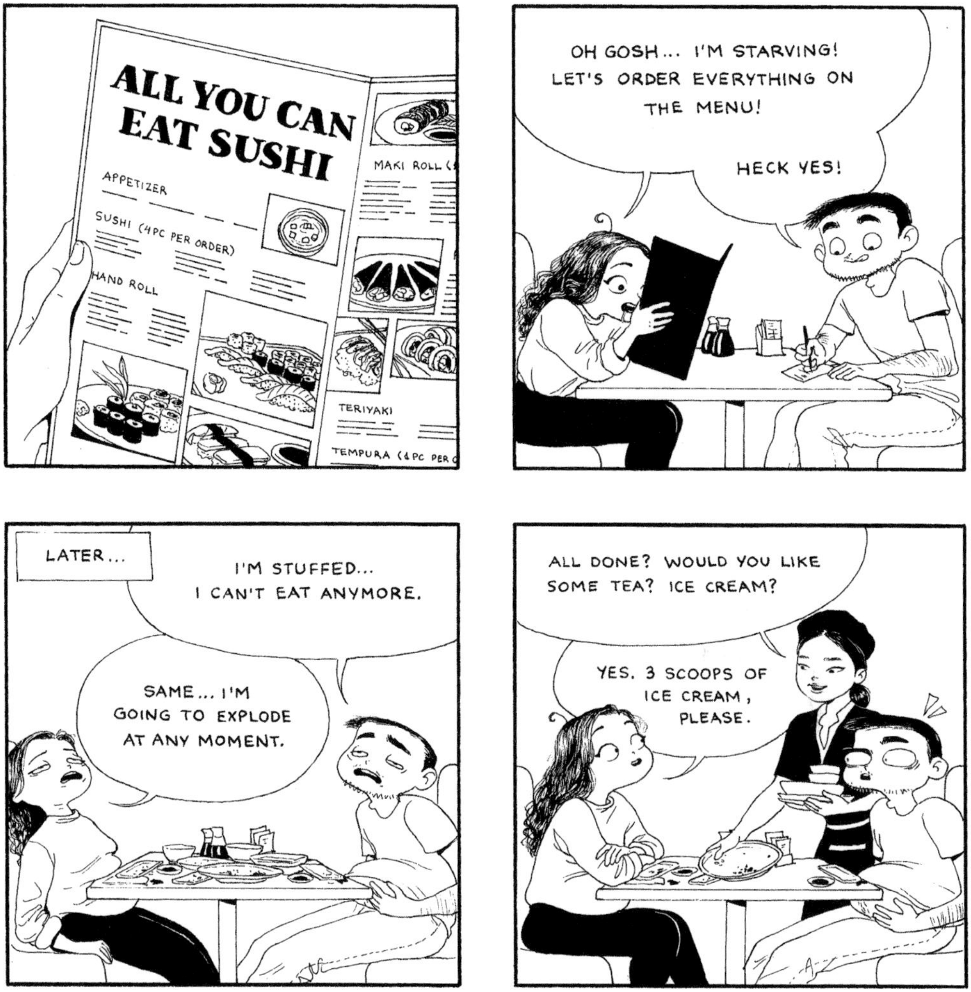
ALL YOU CAN EAT SUSHI
APPETIZER
SUSHI (4PC PER ORDER)
HAND ROLL
MAKI ROLL
TERIYAKI
TEMPURA
OH GOSH... I'M STARVING! LET'S ORDER EVERYTHING ON THE MENU!
HECK YES!
LATER...
I'M STUFFED... I CAN'T EAT ANYMORE.
SAME... I'M GOING TO EXPLODE AT ANY MOMENT.
ALL DONE? WOULD YOU LIKE SOME TEA? ICE CREAM?
YES. 3 SCOOPS OF ICE CREAM, PLEASE.

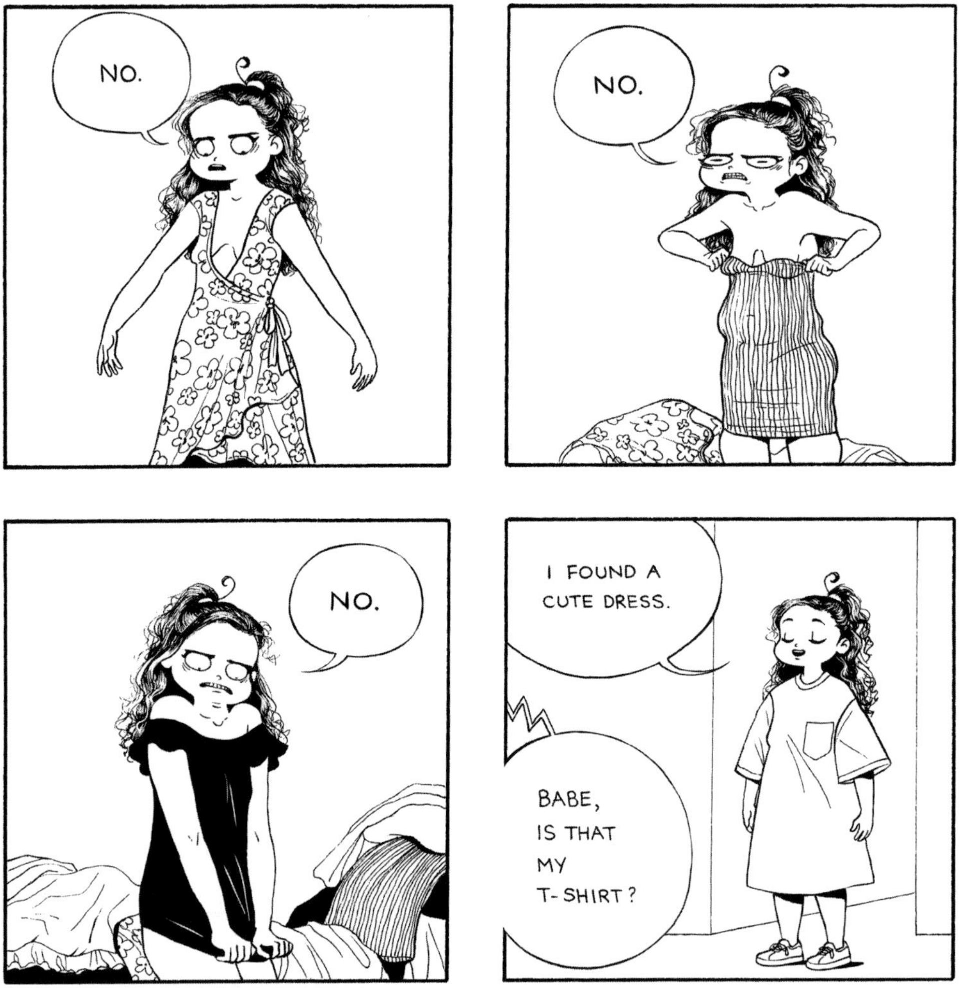
NO.
NO.
NO.
I FOUND A CUTE DRESS.
BABE, IS THAT MY T-SHIRT?

MIDI SKIRT

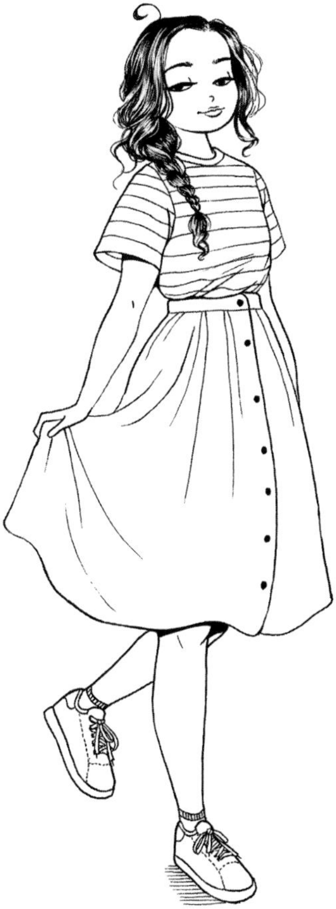

EXPECTATIONS

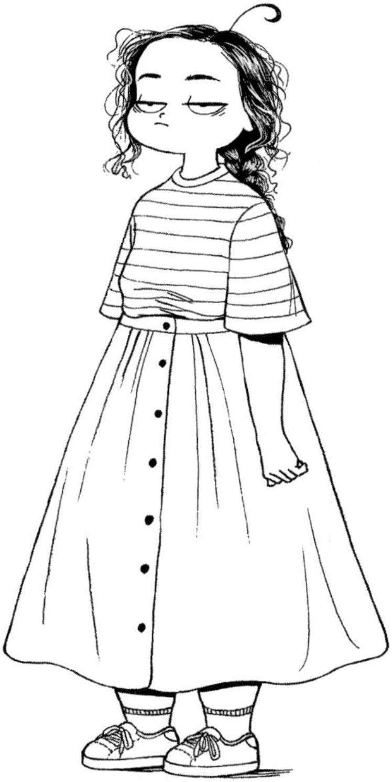

REALITY

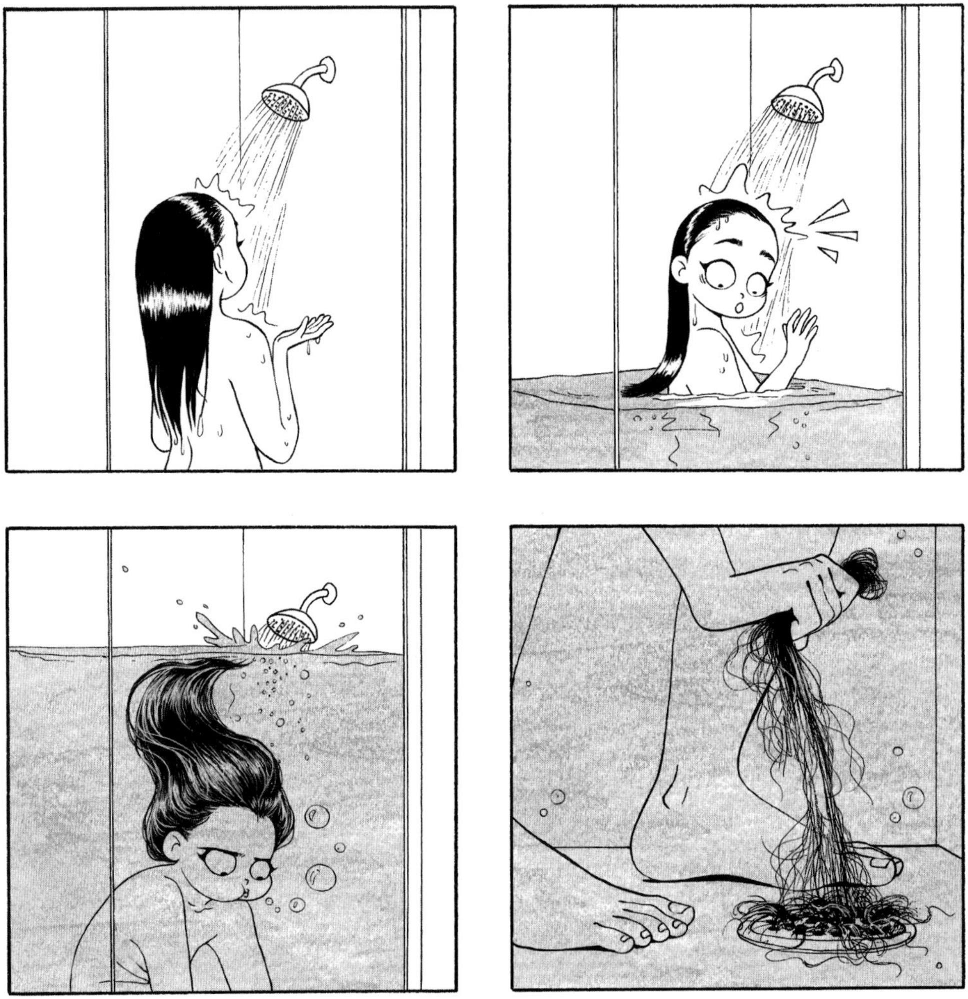

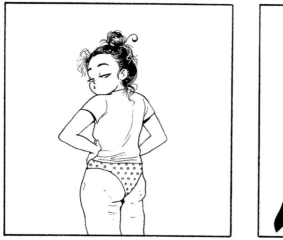

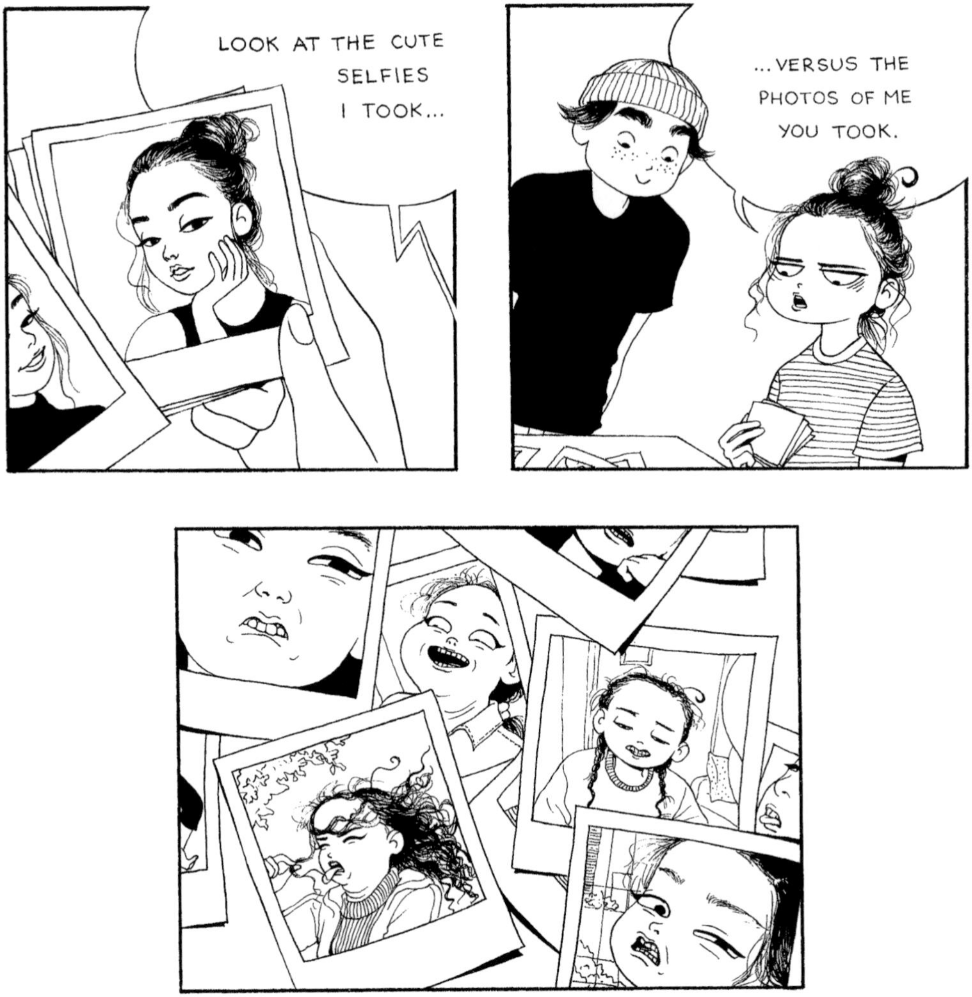
LOOK AT THE CUTE SELFIES I TOOK...
...VERSUS THE PHOTOS OF ME YOU TOOK.

THE AWKWARD STEPS OF
GROWING OUT BANGS

WEEK 4

WEEK 6

WEEK 8

WEEK ???

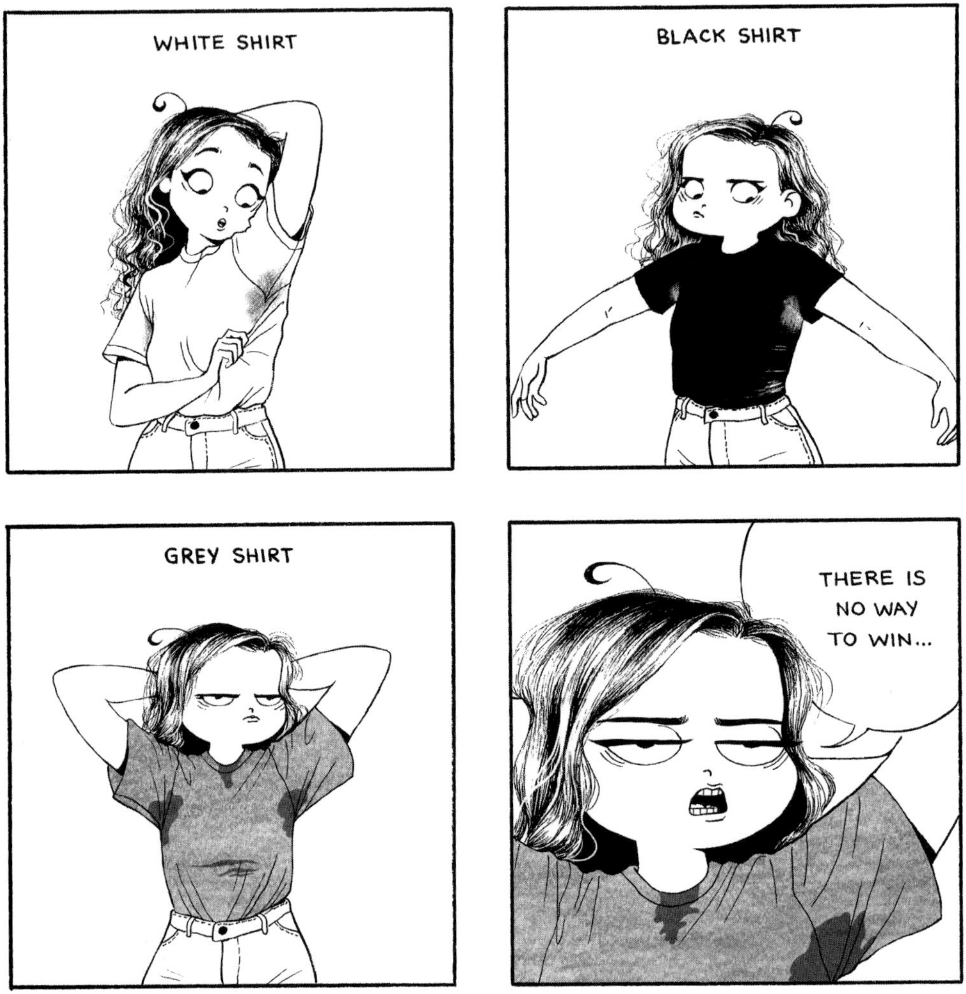
WHITE SHIRT
BLACK SHIRT
GREY SHIRT
THERE IS NO WAY TO WIN...

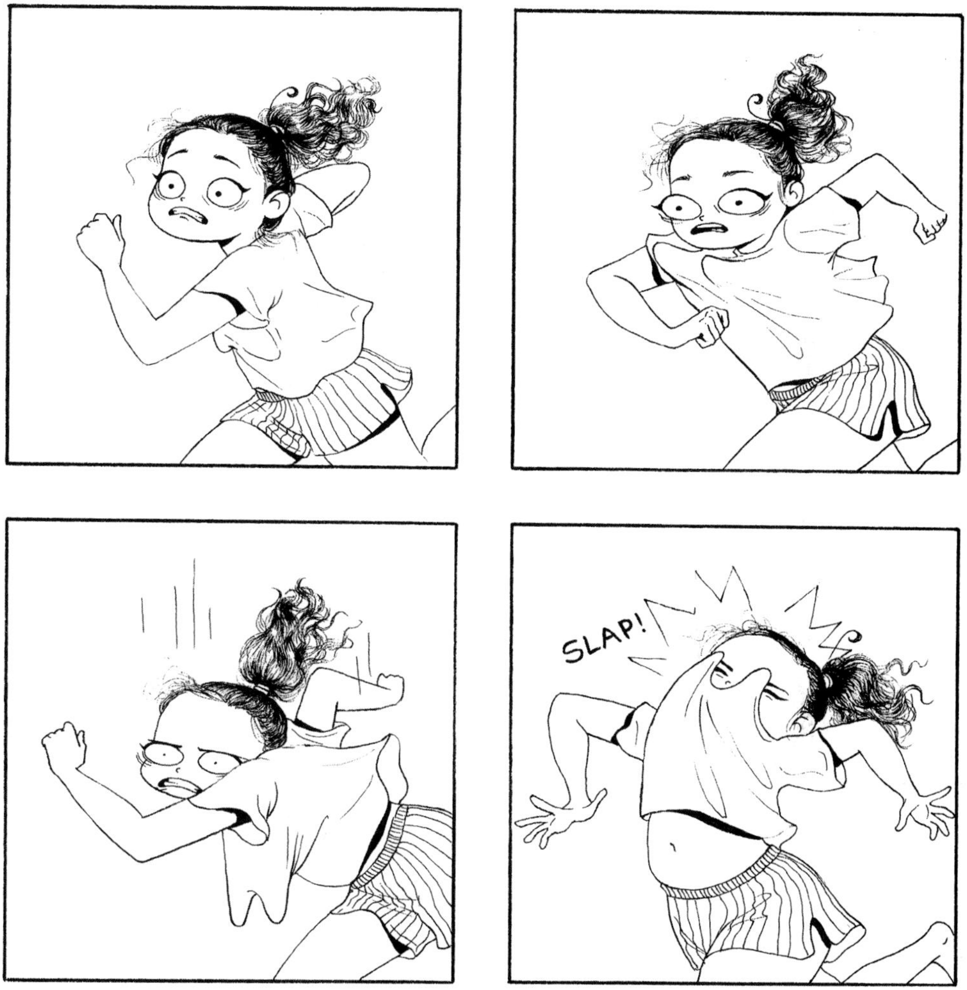
SLAP!

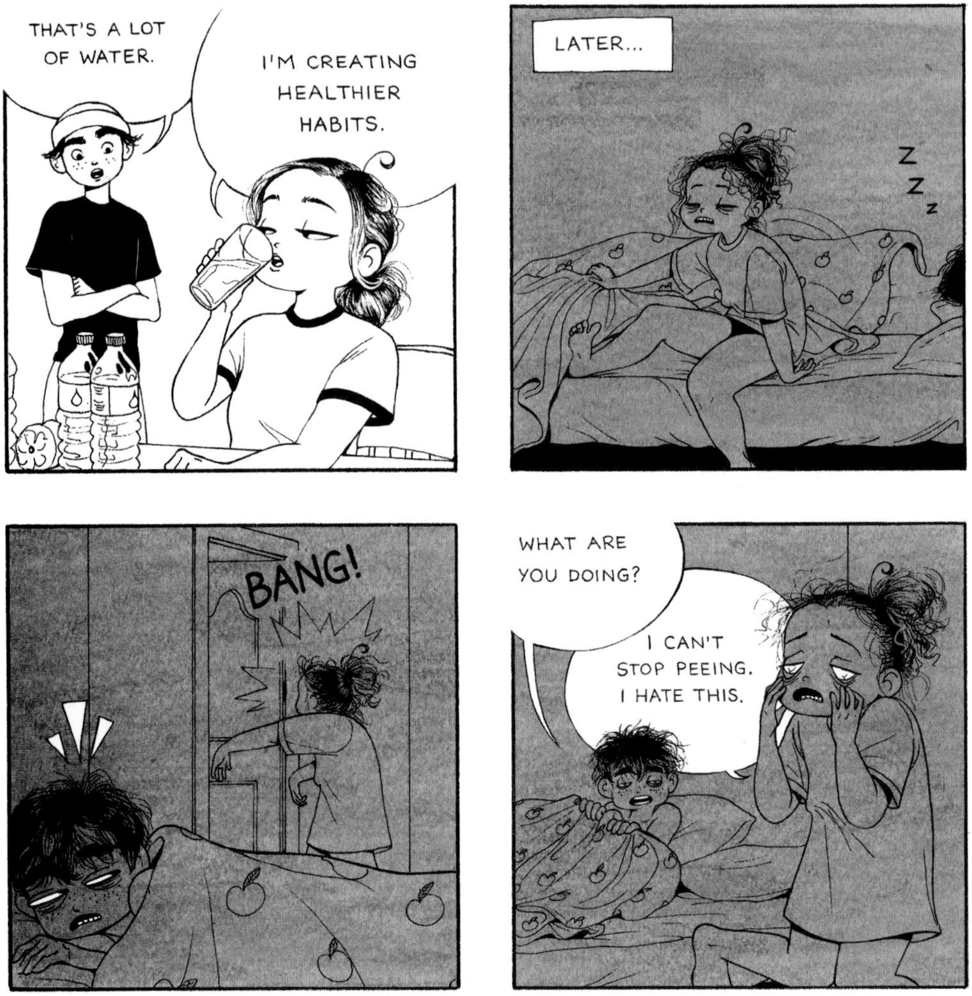
THAT'S A LOT OF WATER.
I'M CREATING HEALTHIER HABITS.
LATER...
Z Z z
BANG!
WHAT ARE YOU DOING?
I CAN'T STOP PEEING. I HATE THIS.

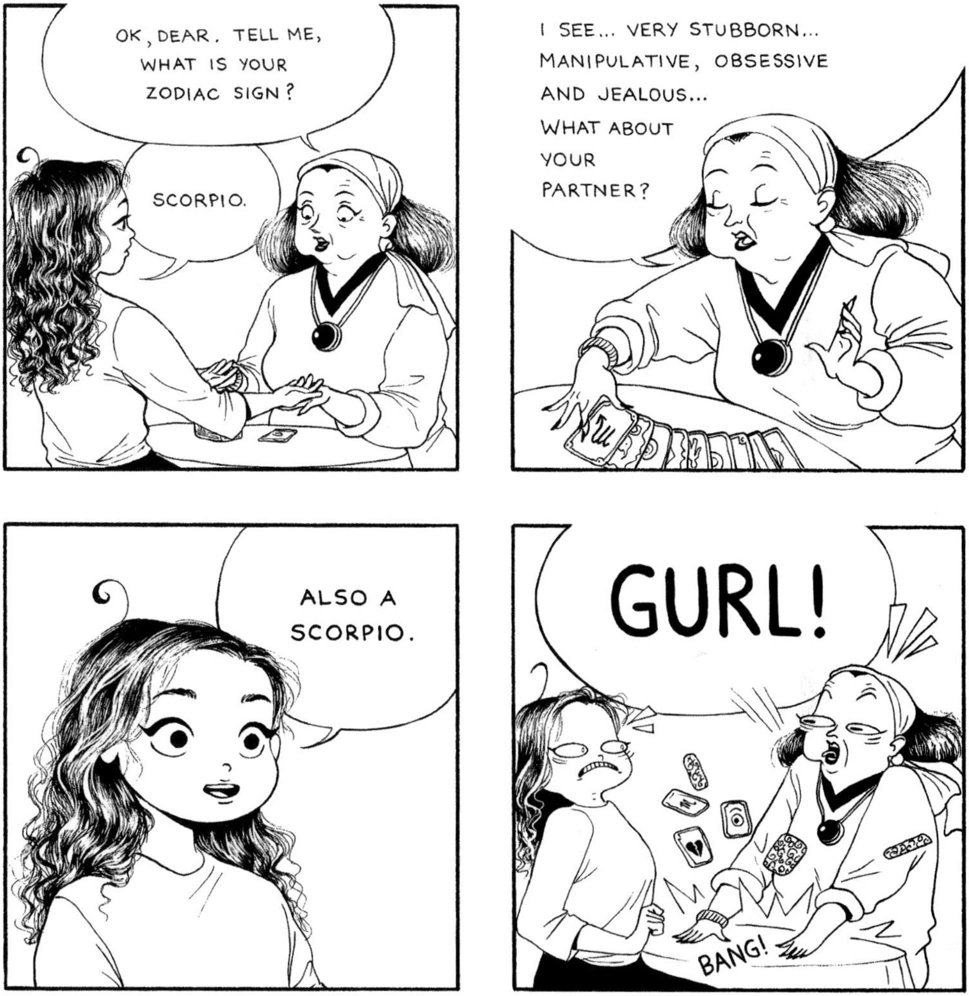
OK, DEAR. TELL ME, WHAT IS YOUR ZODIAC SIGN?
SCORPIO.
I SEE... VERY STUBBORN... MANIPULATIVE, OBSESSIVE AND JEALOUS... WHAT ABOUT YOUR PARTNER?
ALSO A SCORPIO.
GURL!
BANG!

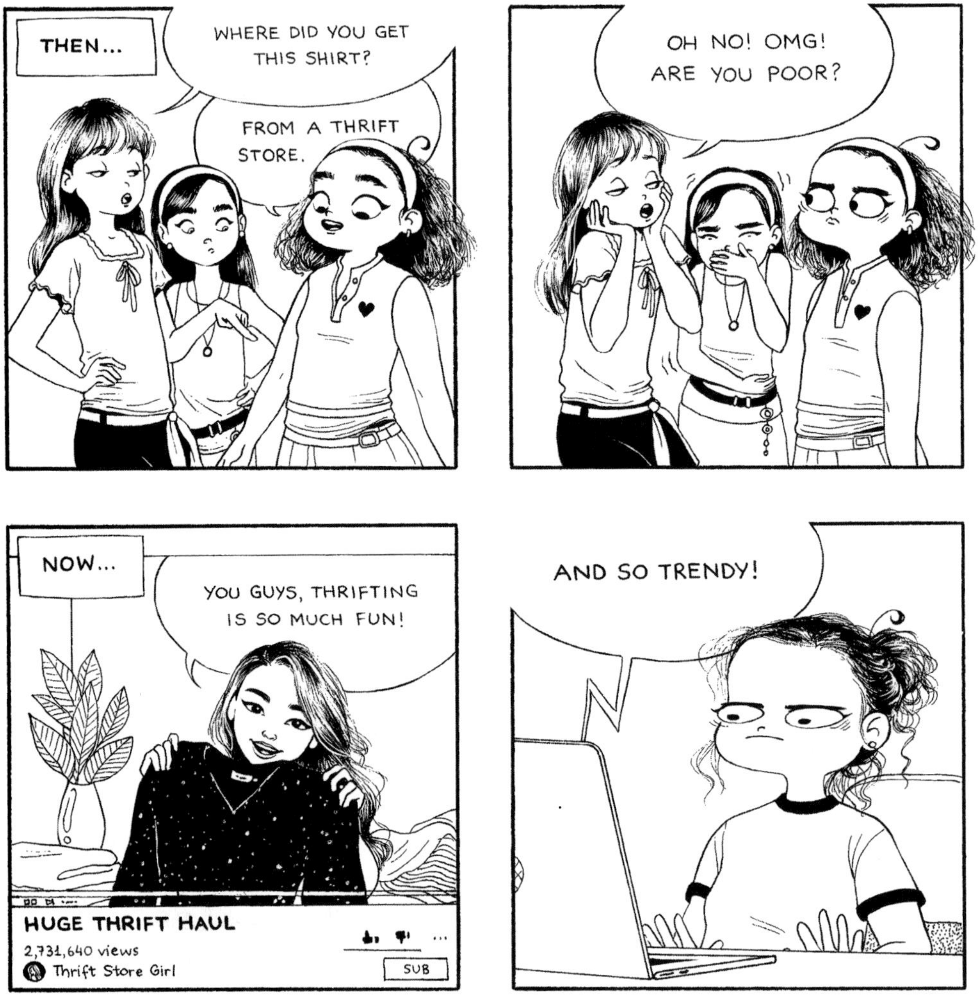
THEN...
WHERE DID YOU GET THIS SHIRT?
FROM A THRIFT STORE.
OH NO! OMG! ARE YOU POOR?
NOW...
YOU GUYS, THRIFTING IS SO MUCH FUN!
HUGE THRIFT HAUL
2,731,640 views
Thrift Store Girl
SUB
AND SO TRENDY!

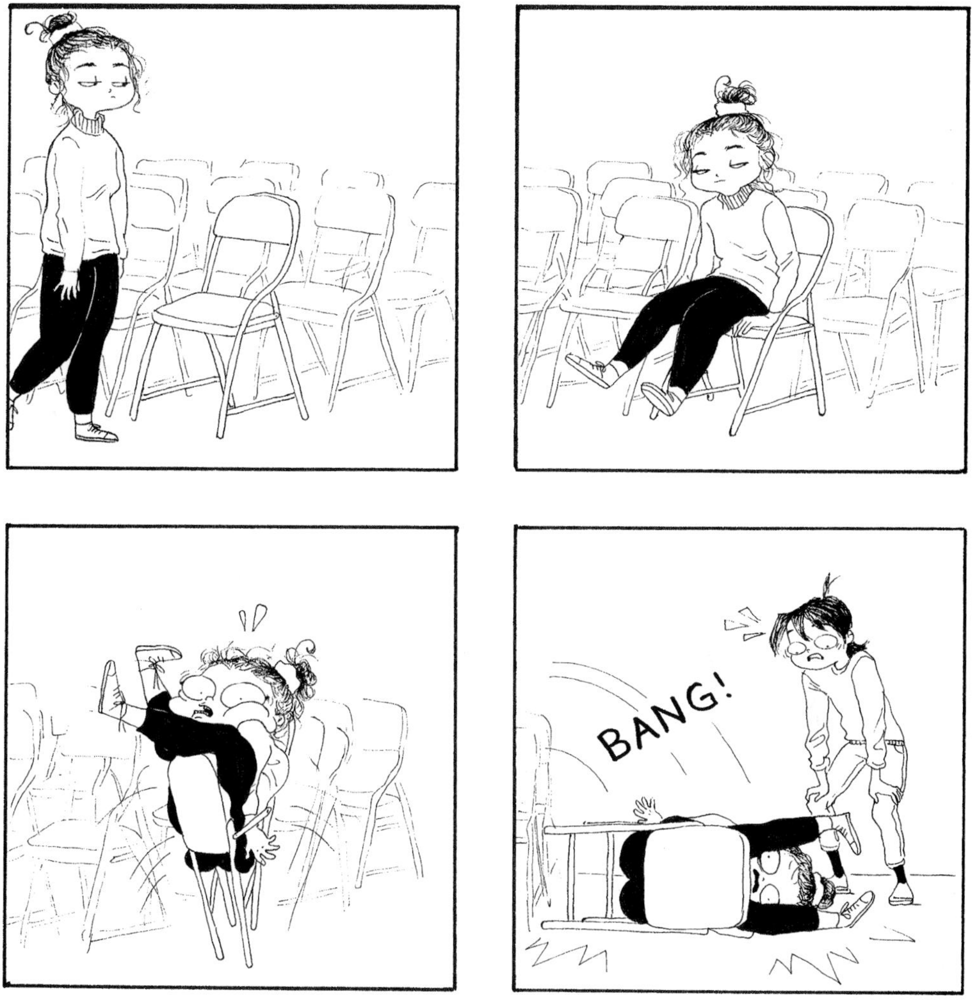
BANG!

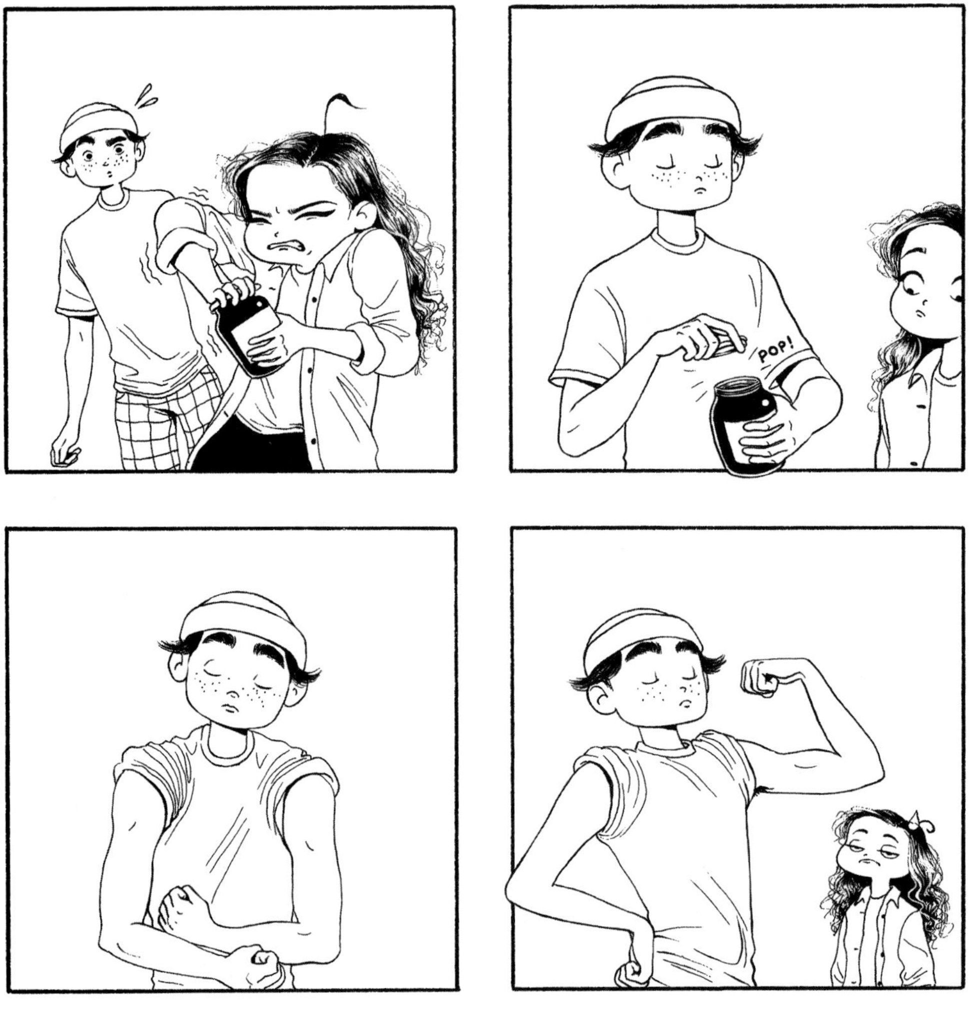
POP!

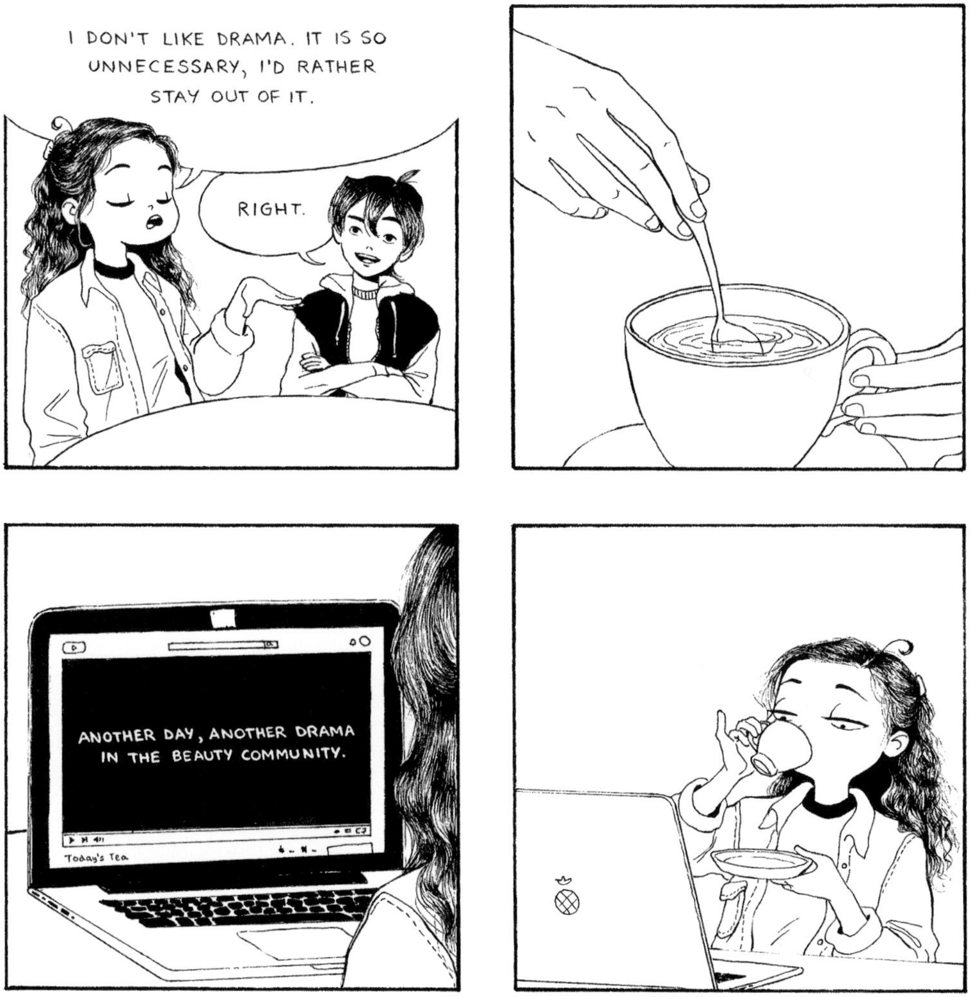
I DON'T LIKE DRAMA. IT IS SO UNNECESSARY, I'D RATHER STAY OUT OF IT.
RIGHT.
ANOTHER DAY, ANOTHER DRAMA IN THE BEAUTY COMMUNITY.
Today's Tea

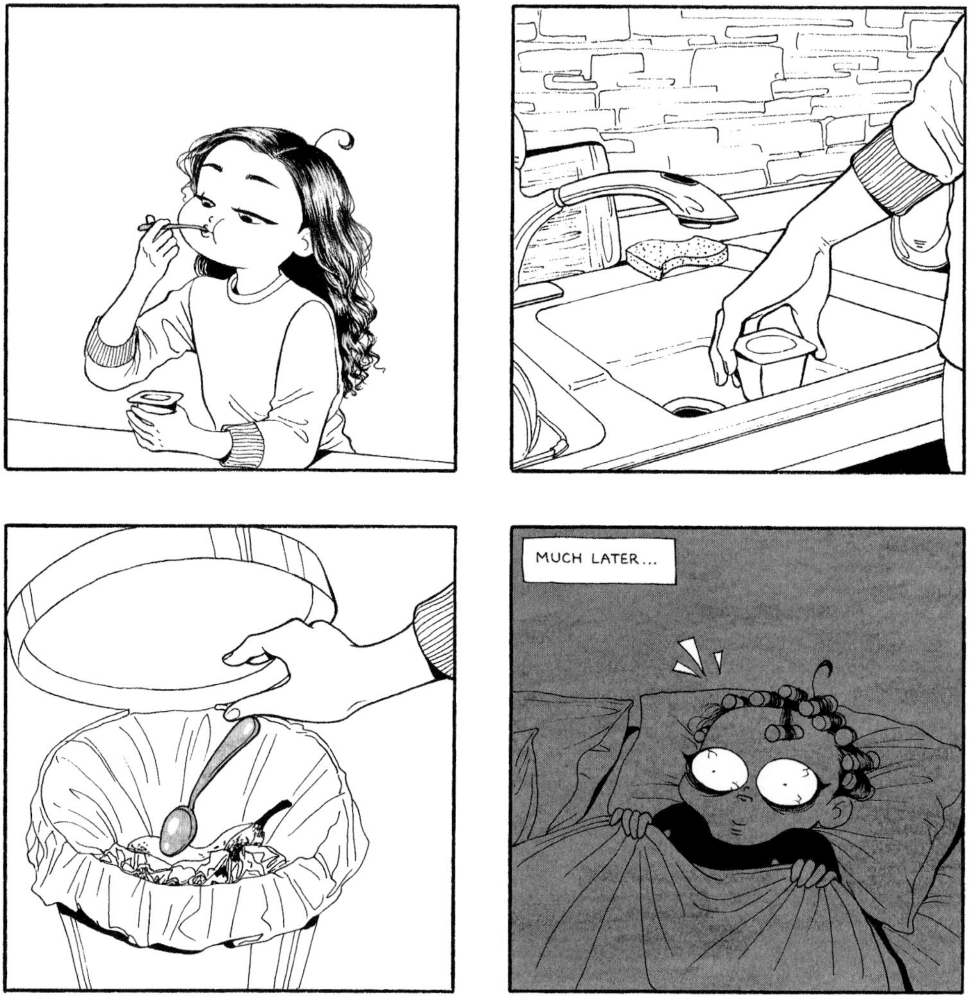
MUCH LATER...

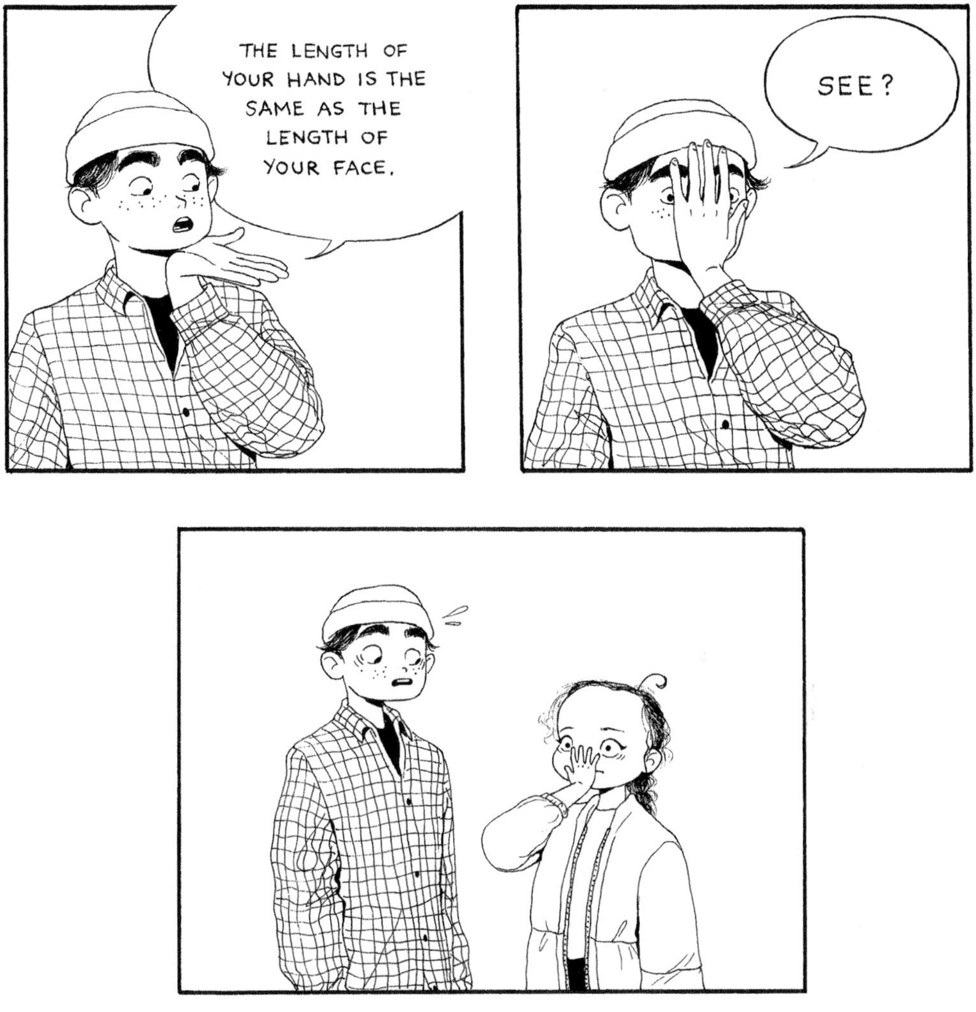
THE LENGTH OF YOUR HAND IS THE SAME AS THE LENGTH OF YOUR FACE.
SEE?

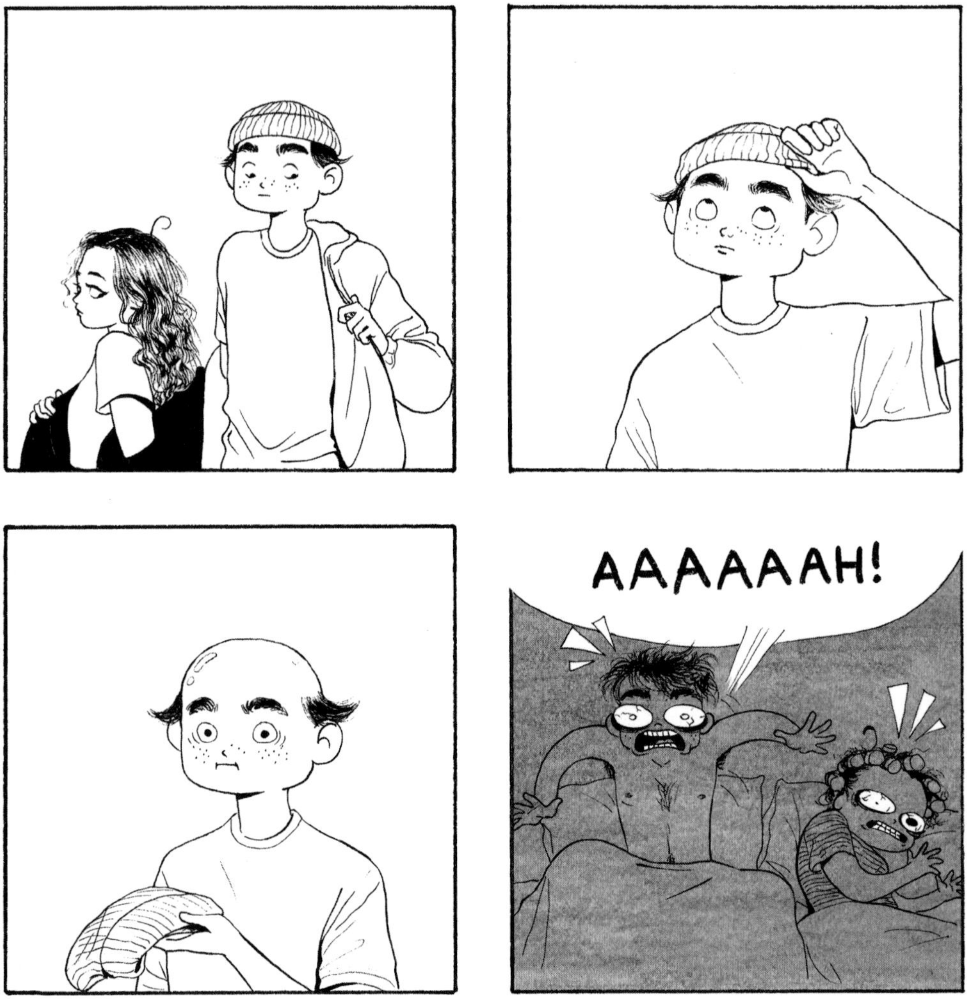
AAAAAAH!

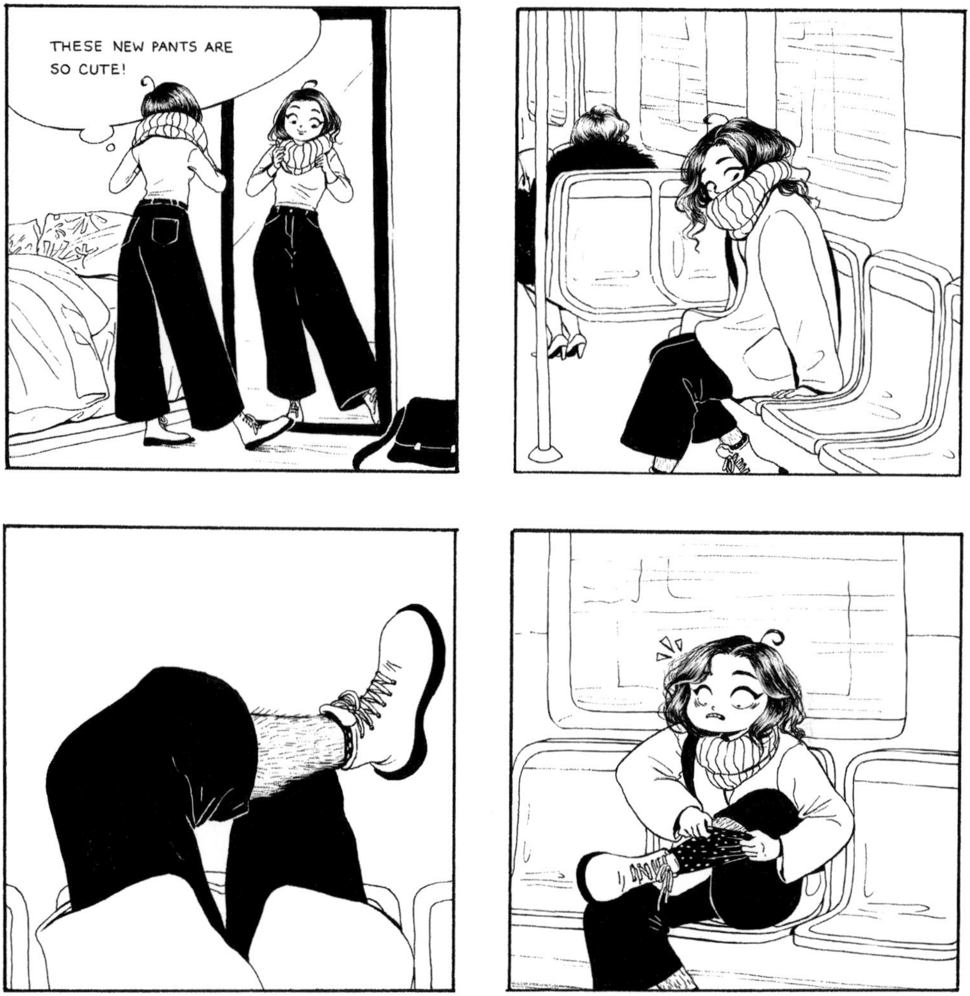
THESE NEW PANTS ARE SO CUTE!

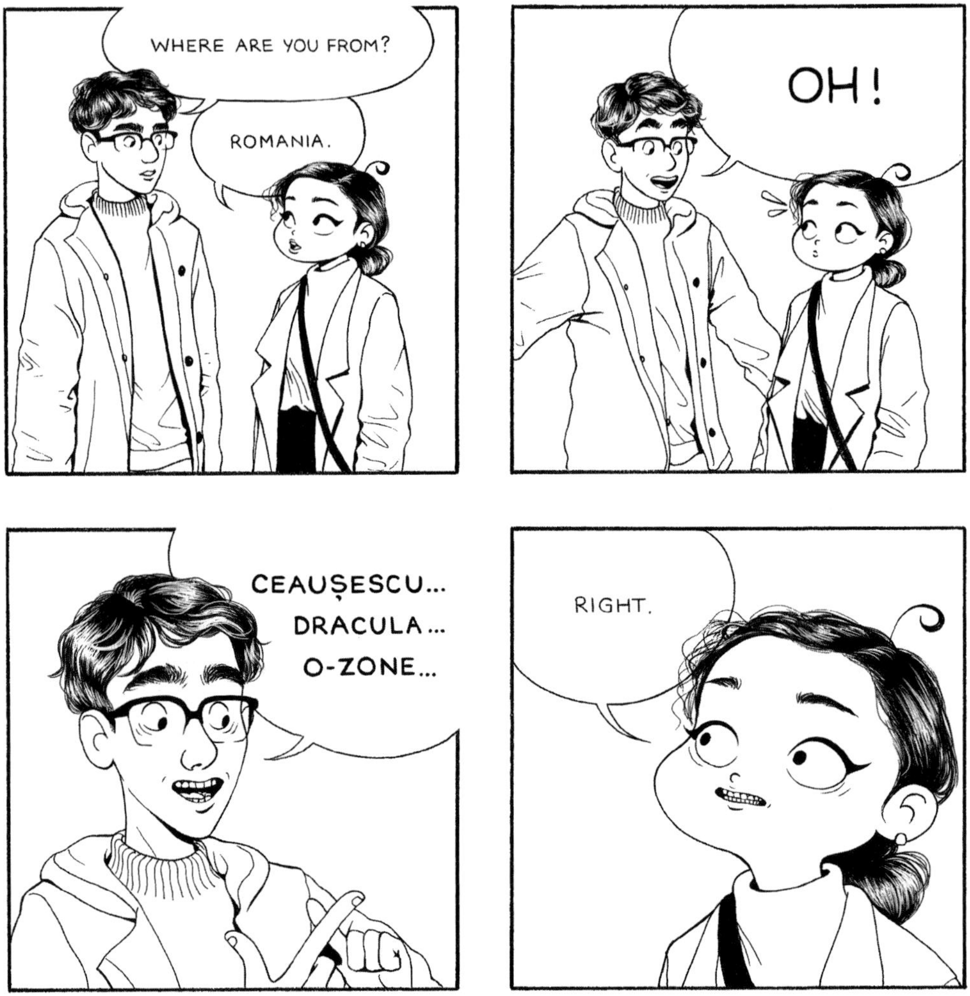
WHERE ARE YOU FROM?
ROMANIA.
OH!
CEAUȘESCU... DRACULA... O-ZONE...
RIGHT.

DUTCH BRAIDS

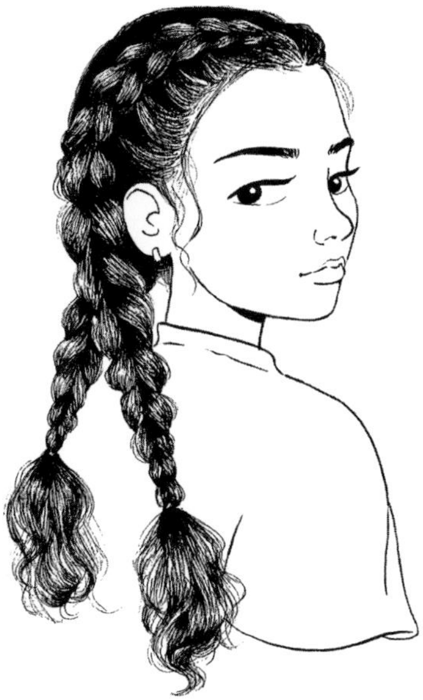

EXPECTATIONS

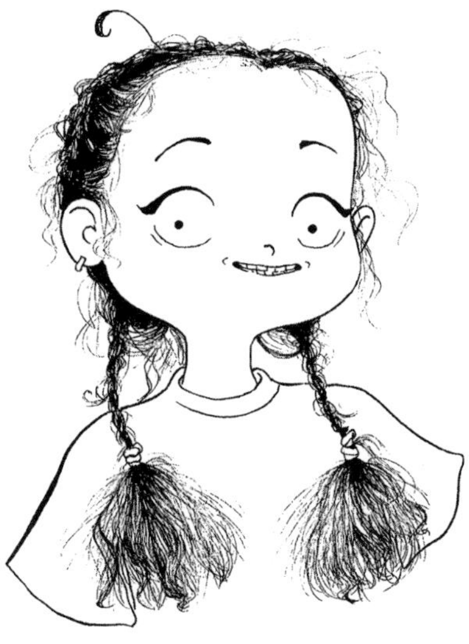

REALITY

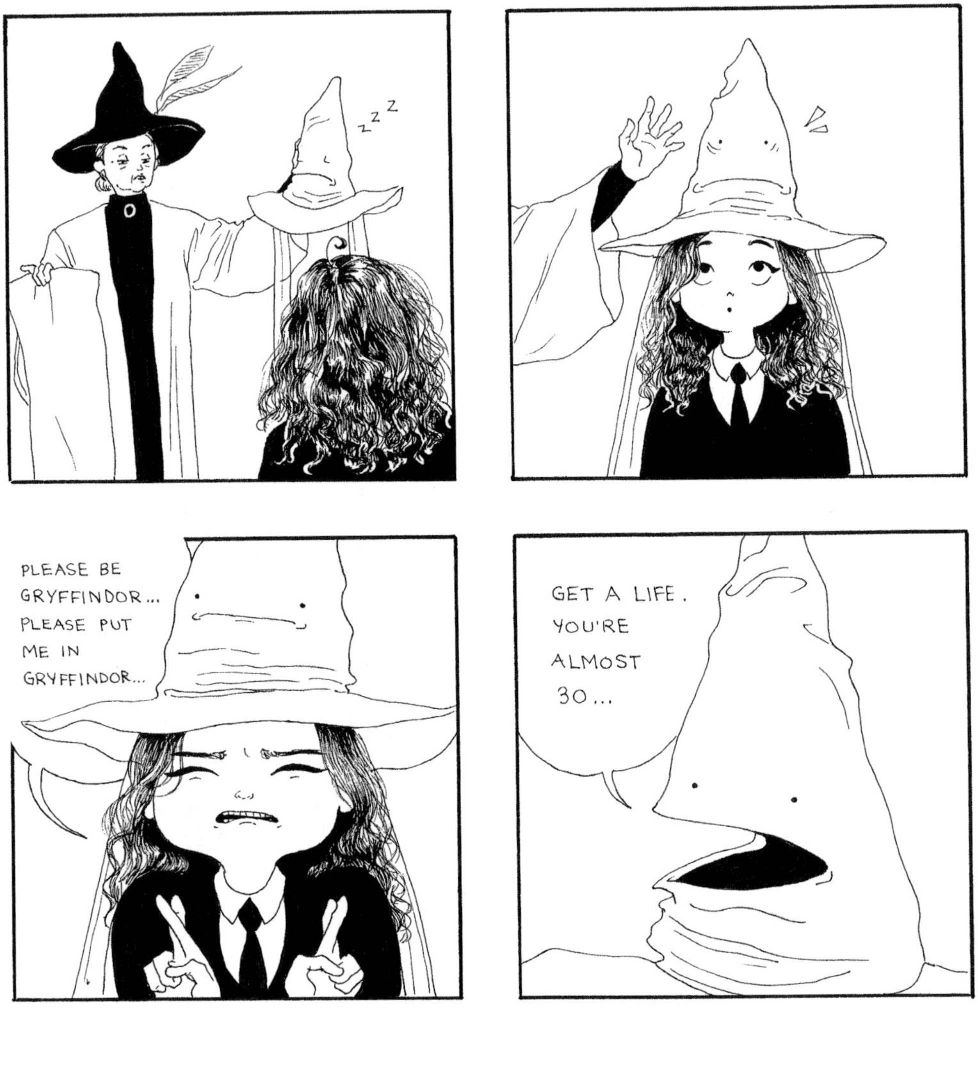
Z Z Z
PLEASE BE GRYFFINDOR... PLEASE PUT ME IN GRYFFINDOR...
GET A LIFE. YOU'RE ALMOST 30...

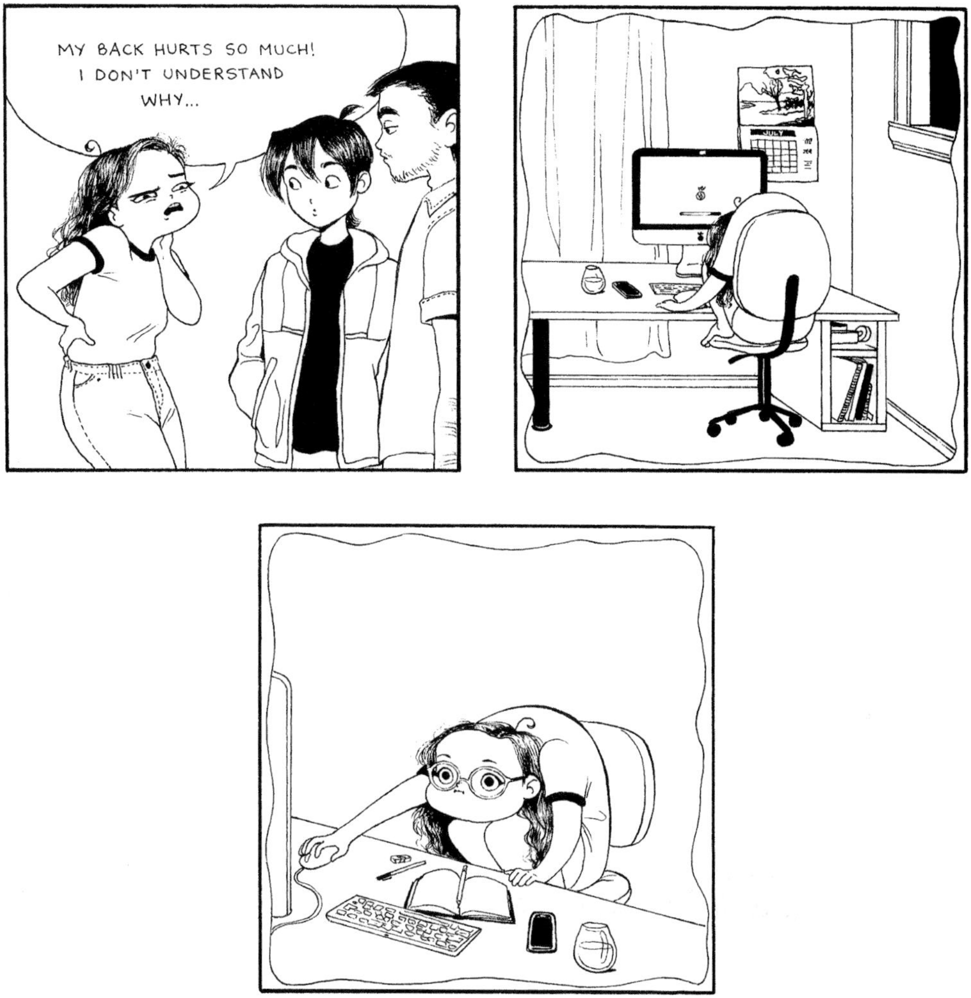

MY BACK HURTS SO MUCH! I DON'T UNDERSTAND WHY...

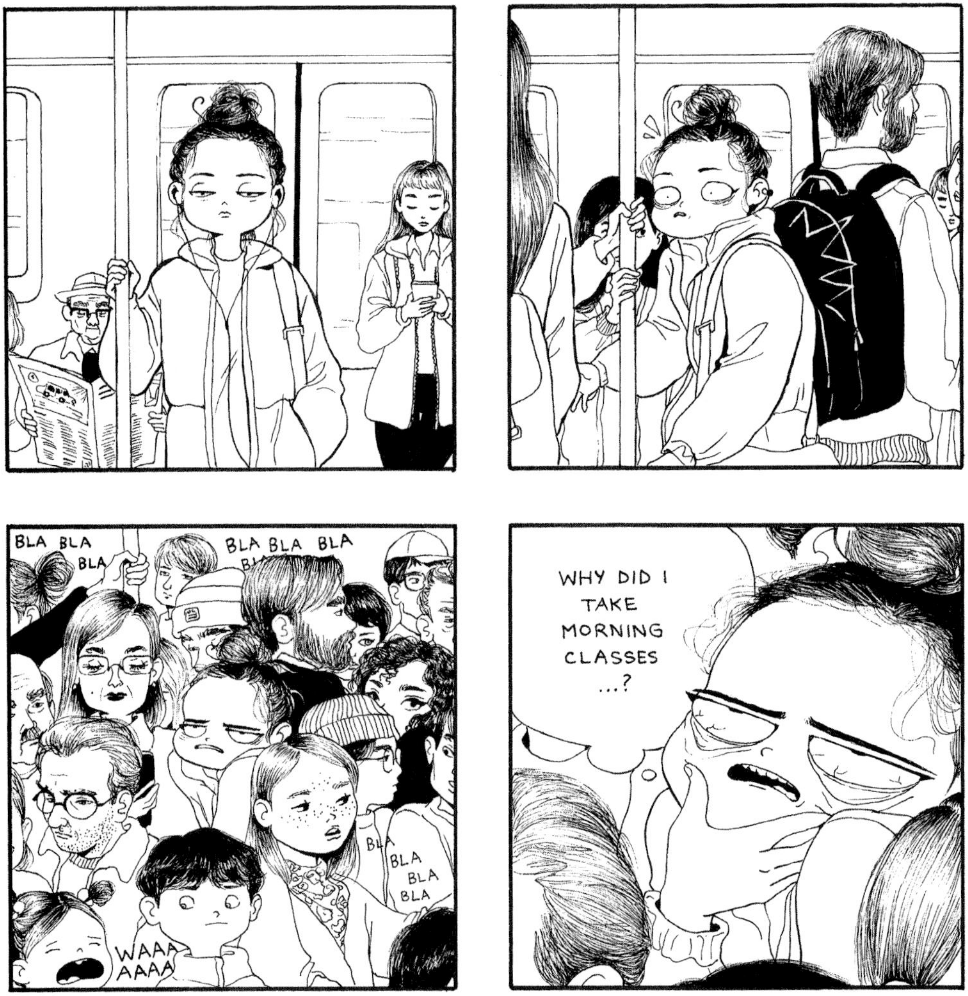
BLA BLA BLA
BLA BLA BLA
BLA BLA BLA BLA
WAAA AAAA
WHY DID I TAKE MORNING CLASSES ...?

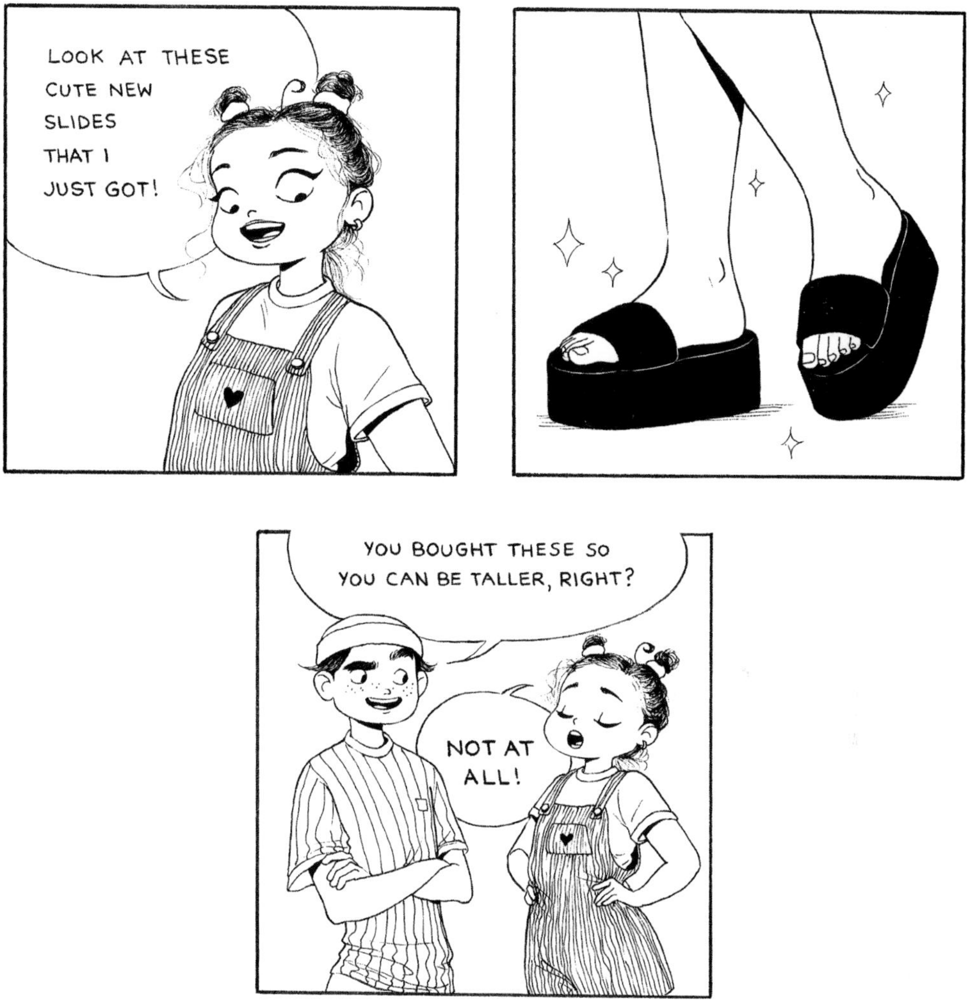
LOOK AT THESE CUTE NEW SLIDES THAT I JUST GOT!
YOU BOUGHT THESE SO YOU CAN BE TALLER, RIGHT?
NOT AT ALL!

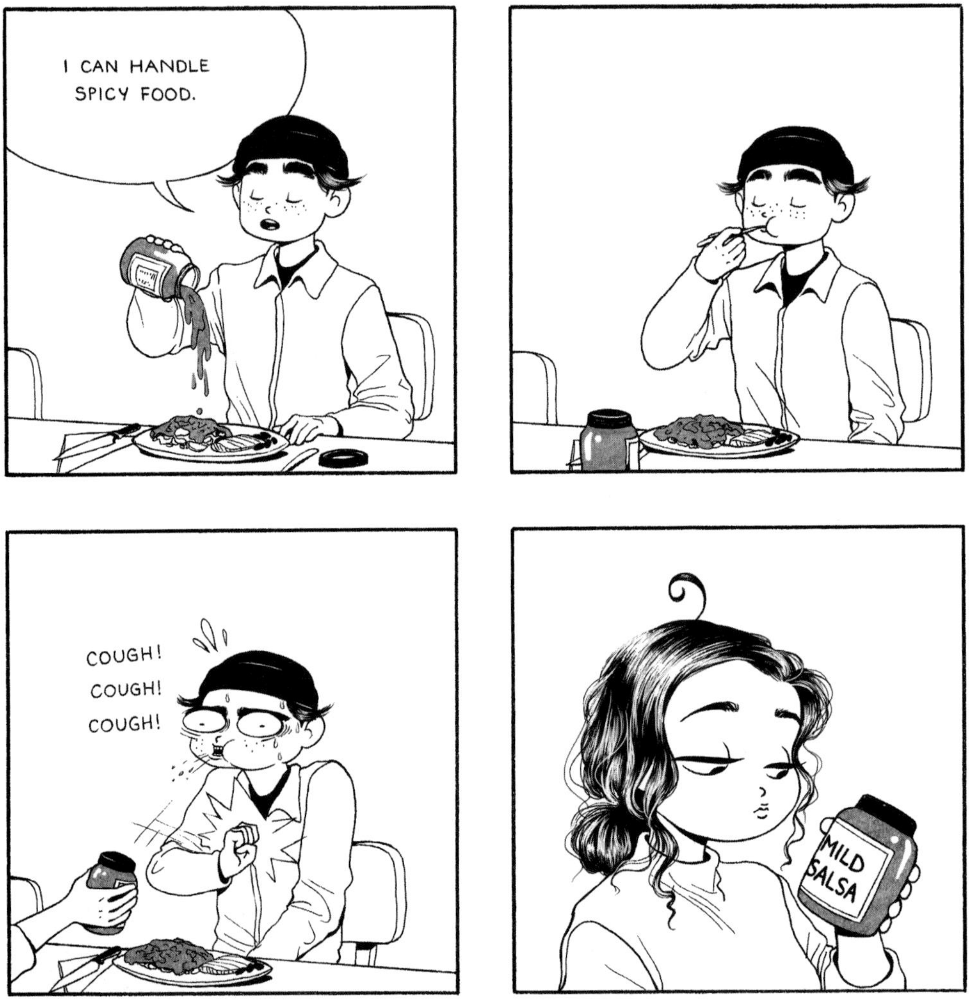
I CAN HANDLE SPICY FOOD.
COUGH!
COUGH!
COUGH!
MILD SALSA

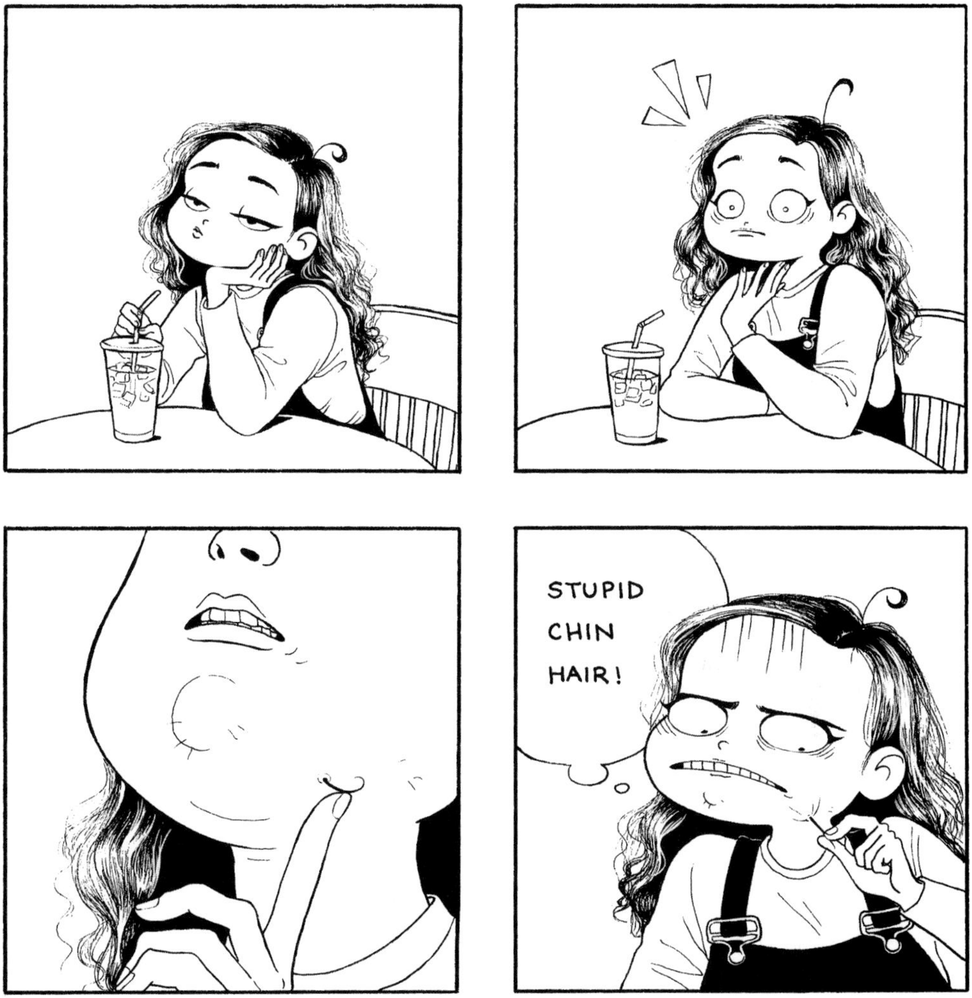
STUPID
CHIN
HAIR!

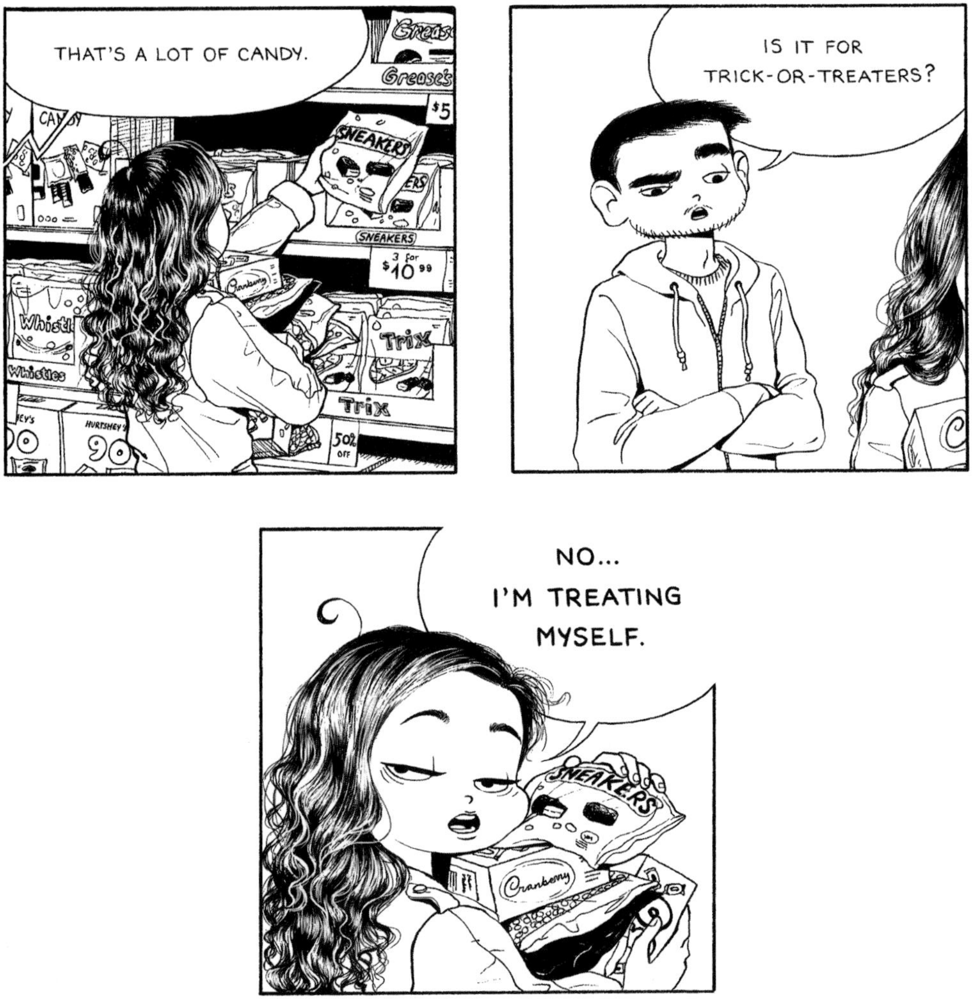
THAT'S A LOT OF CANDY.
SNEAKERS
3 for $10.99
Trix
Whistles
50% OFF
IS IT FOR TRICK-OR-TREATERS?
NO... I'M TREATING MYSELF.
SNEAKERS
Cranberry

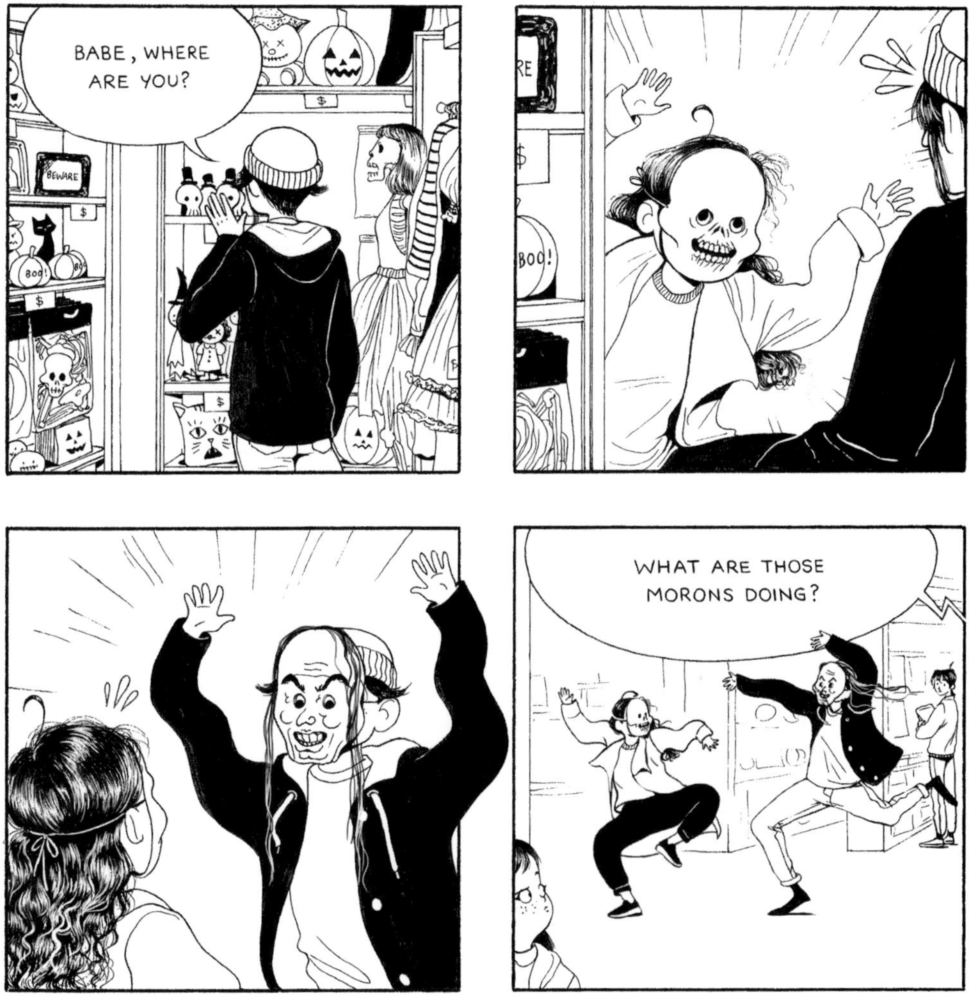
BABE, WHERE ARE YOU?
BEWARE
BOO!
WHAT ARE THOSE MORONS DOING?

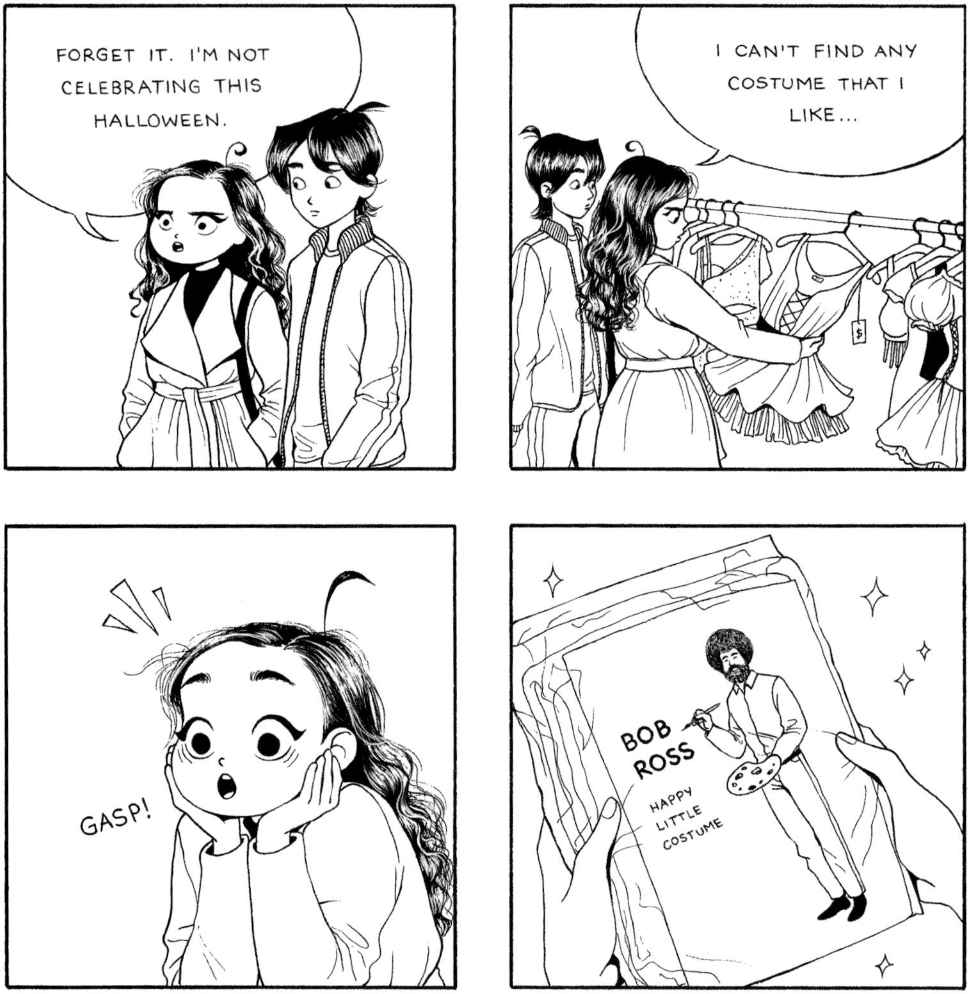
FORGET IT. I'M NOT CELEBRATING THIS HALLOWEEN.
I CAN'T FIND ANY COSTUME THAT I LIKE...
GASP!
BOB ROSS
HAPPY LITTLE COSTUME

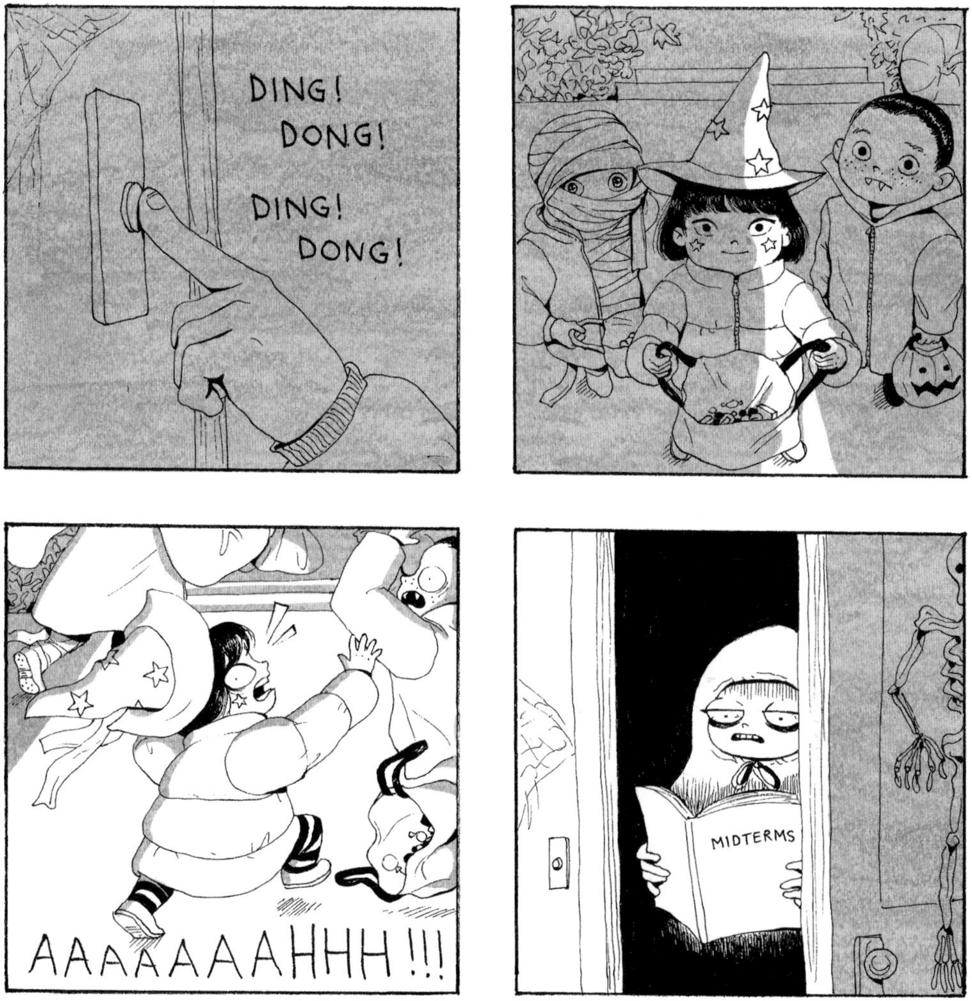
DING! DONG!
DING! DONG!
AAAAAAAHHH!!!
MIDTERMS

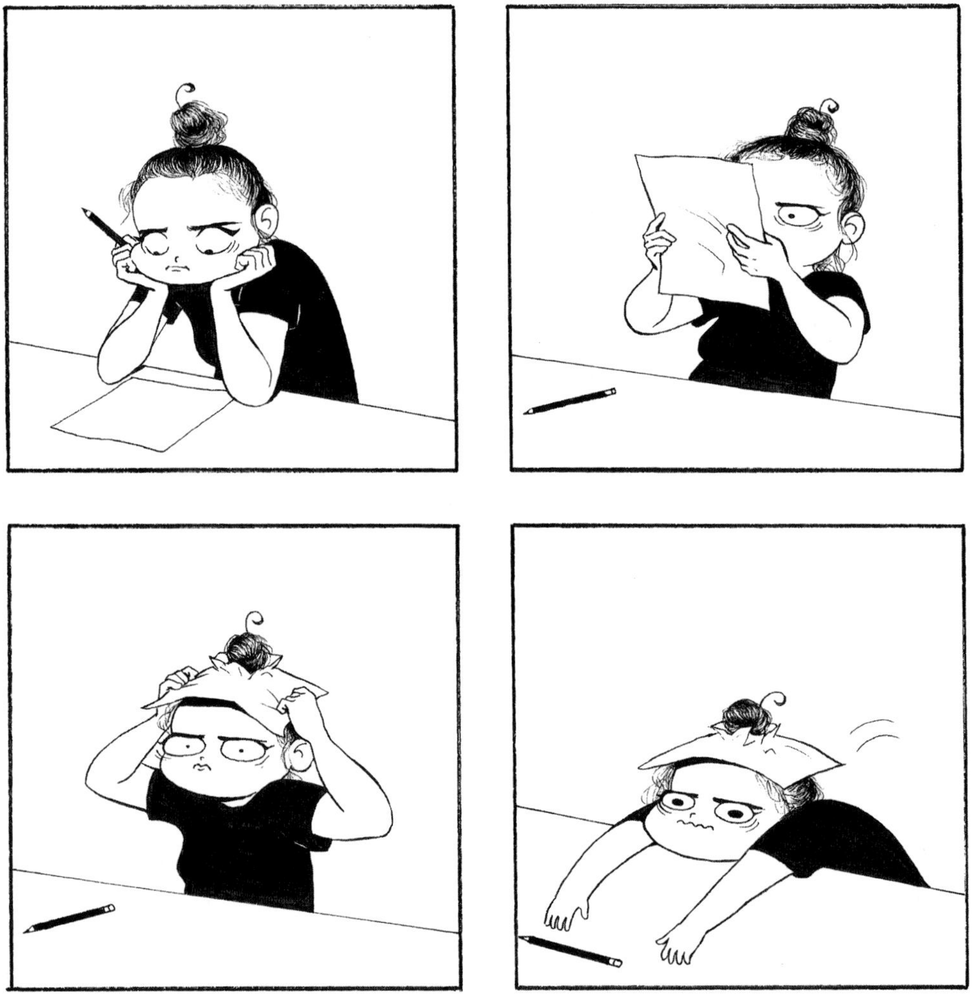

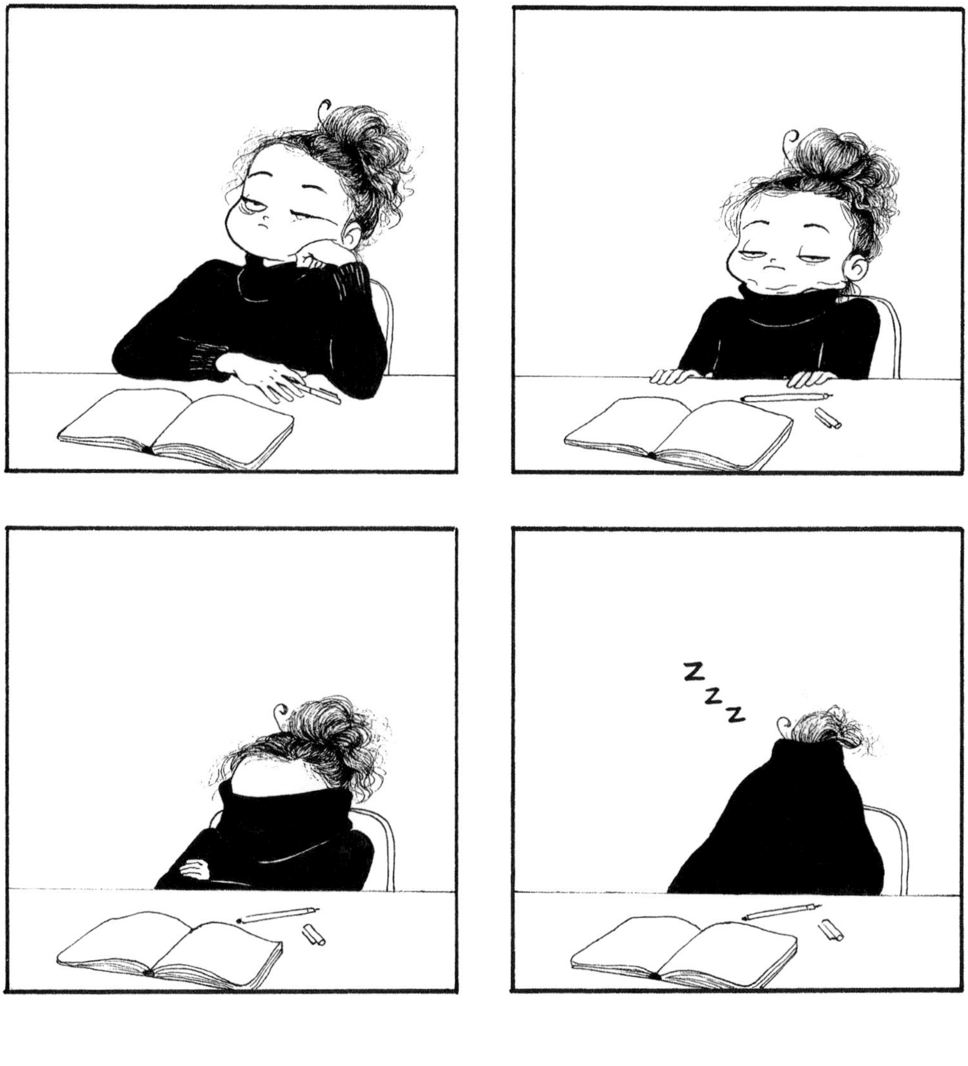
Z Z Z

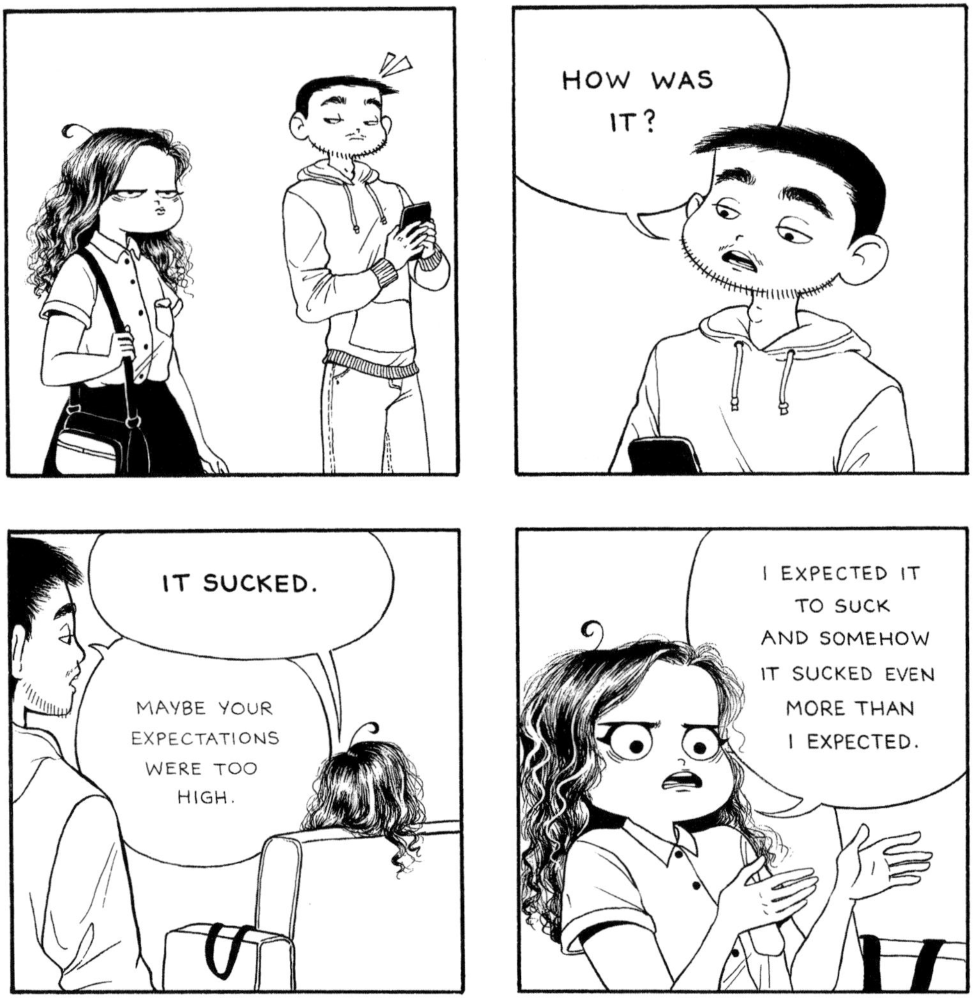
HOW WAS IT?
IT SUCKED.
MAYBE YOUR EXPECTATIONS WERE TOO HIGH.
I EXPECTED IT TO SUCK AND SOMEHOW IT SUCKED EVEN MORE THAN I EXPECTED.

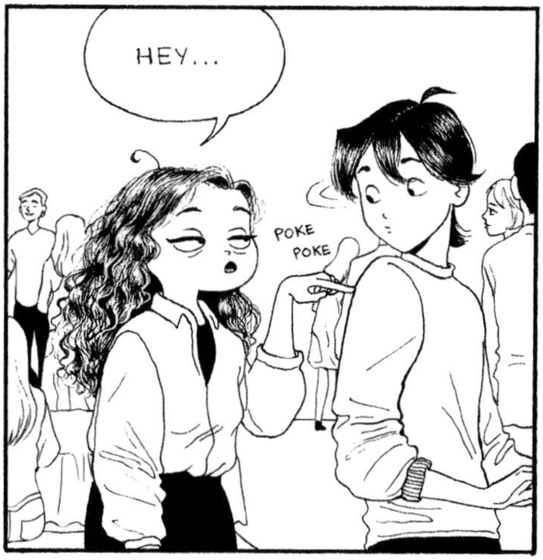
HEY...
POKE
POKE

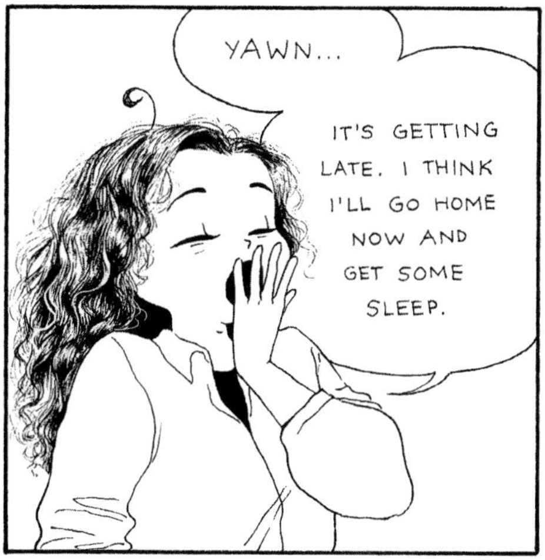
YAWN...
IT'S GETTING LATE. I THINK I'LL GO HOME NOW AND GET SOME SLEEP.

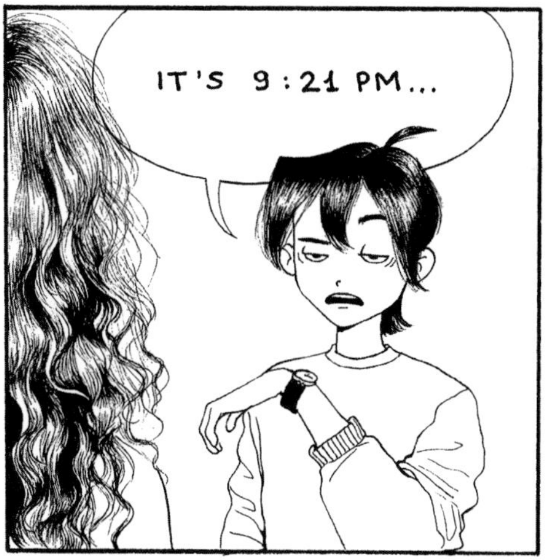
IT'S 9:21 PM...

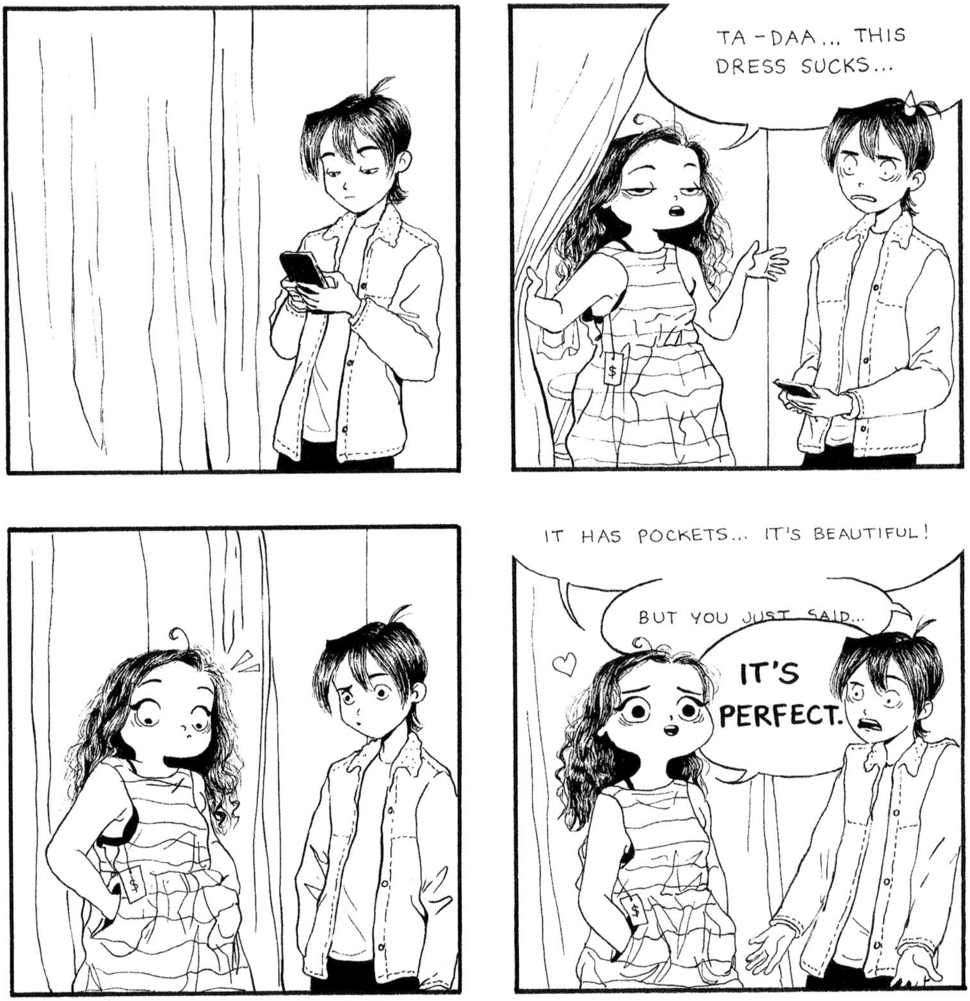
TA-DAA... THIS DRESS SUCKS...
IT HAS POCKETS... IT'S BEAUTIFUL!
BUT YOU JUST SAID...
IT'S PERFECT.

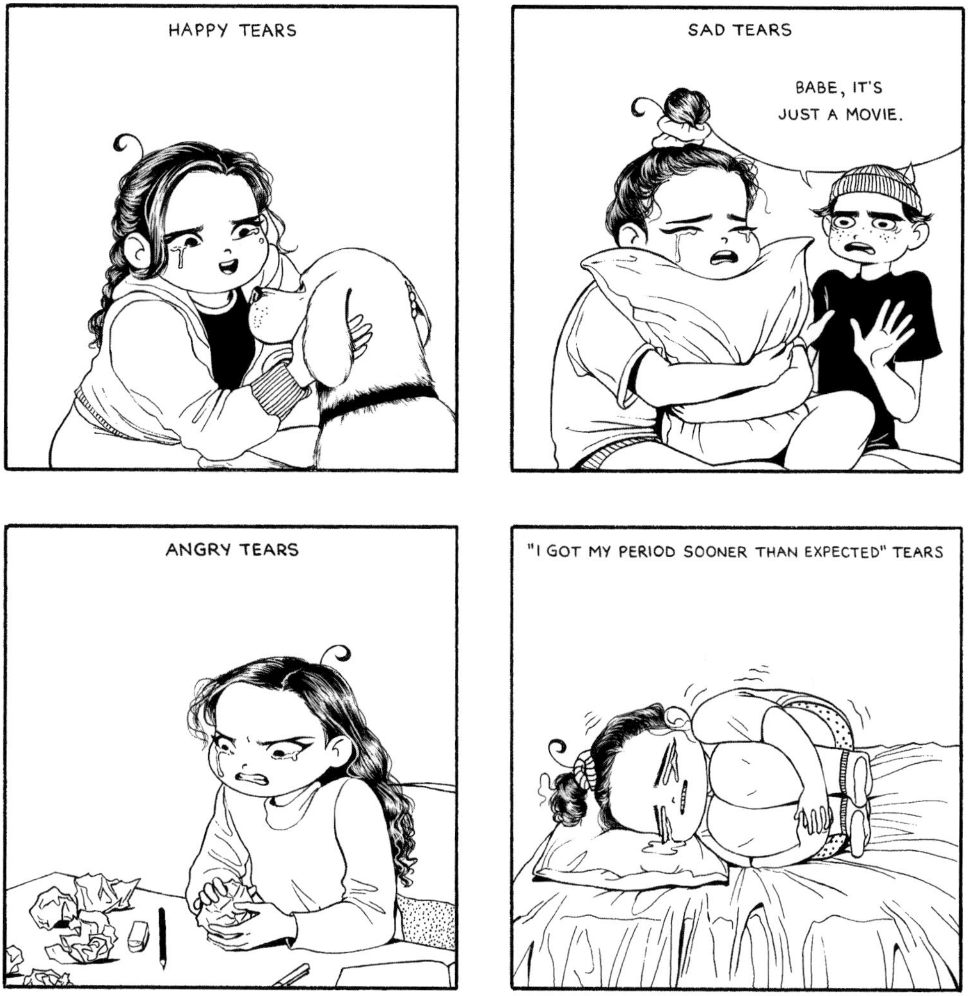
HAPPY TEARS
SAD TEARS
BABE, IT'S JUST A MOVIE.
ANGRY TEARS
"I GOT MY PERIOD SOONER THAN EXPECTED" TEARS

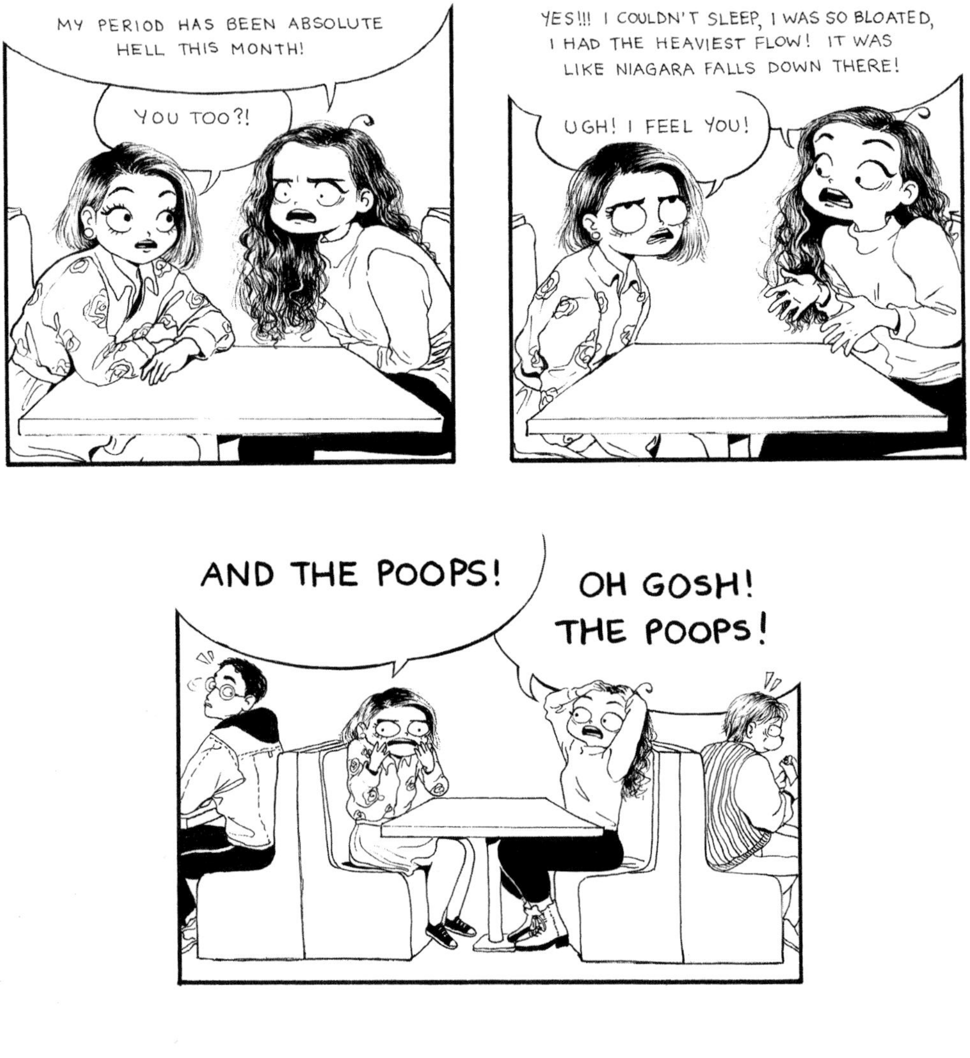
MY PERIOD HAS BEEN ABSOLUTE HELL THIS MONTH!
YOU TOO?!
YES!!! I COULDN'T SLEEP, I WAS SO BLOATED, I HAD THE HEAVIEST FLOW! IT WAS LIKE NIAGARA FALLS DOWN THERE!
UGH! I FEEL YOU!
AND THE POOPS!
OH GOSH! THE POOPS!

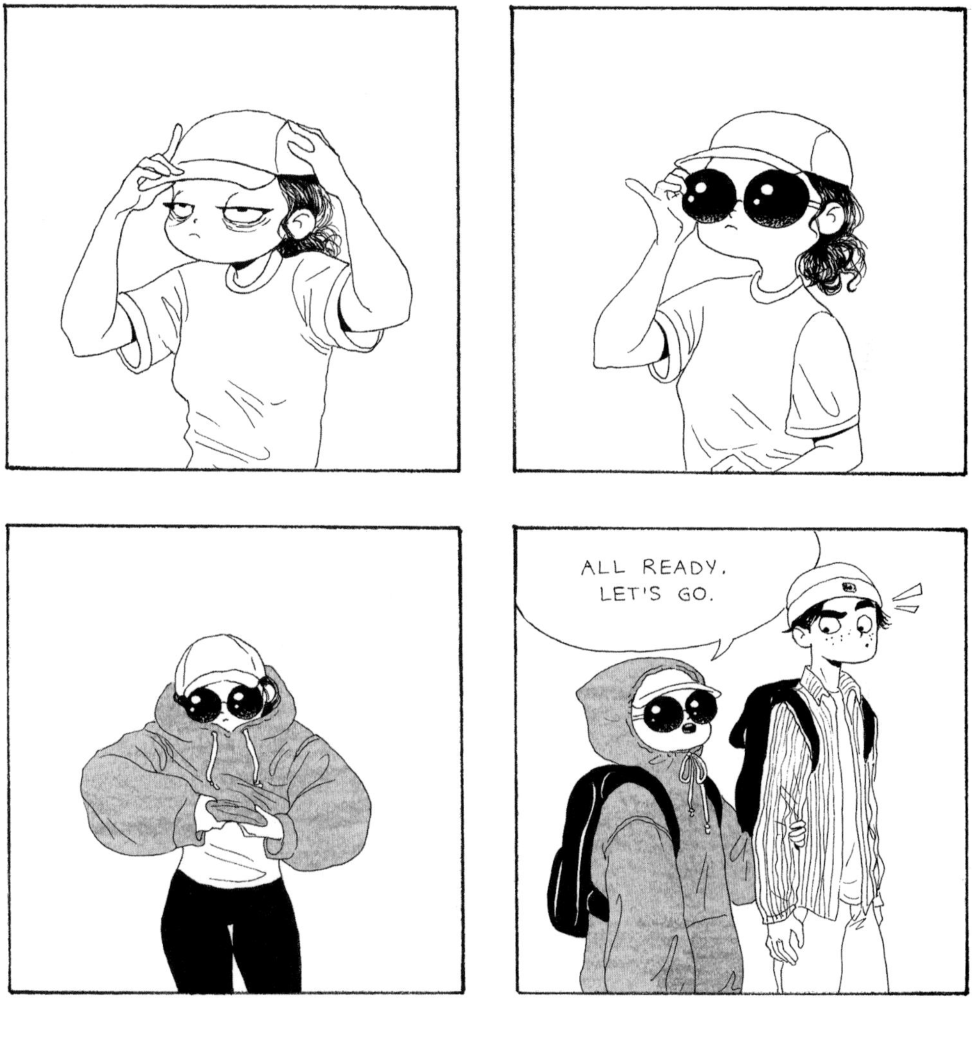
ALL READY.
LET'S GO.

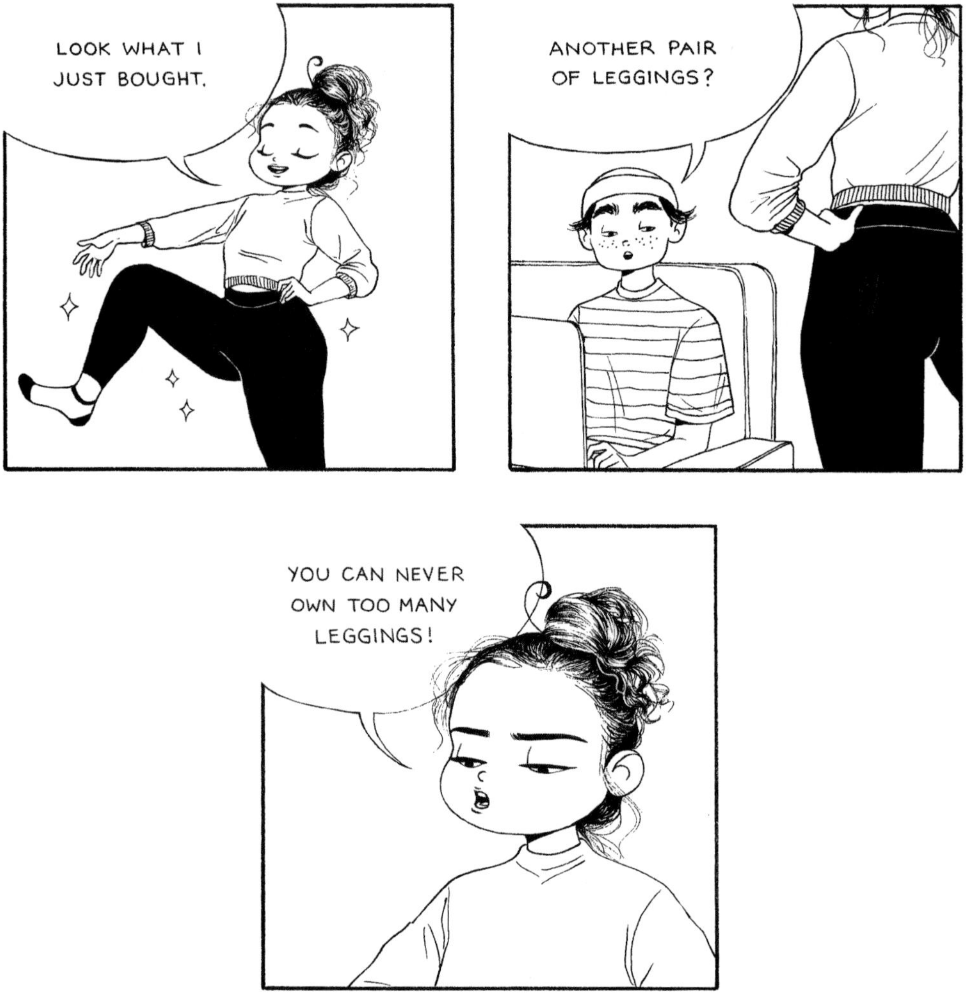
LOOK WHAT I JUST BOUGHT.
ANOTHER PAIR OF LEGGINGS?
YOU CAN NEVER OWN TOO MANY LEGGINGS!

BABY BANGS

EXPECTATIONS   REALITY

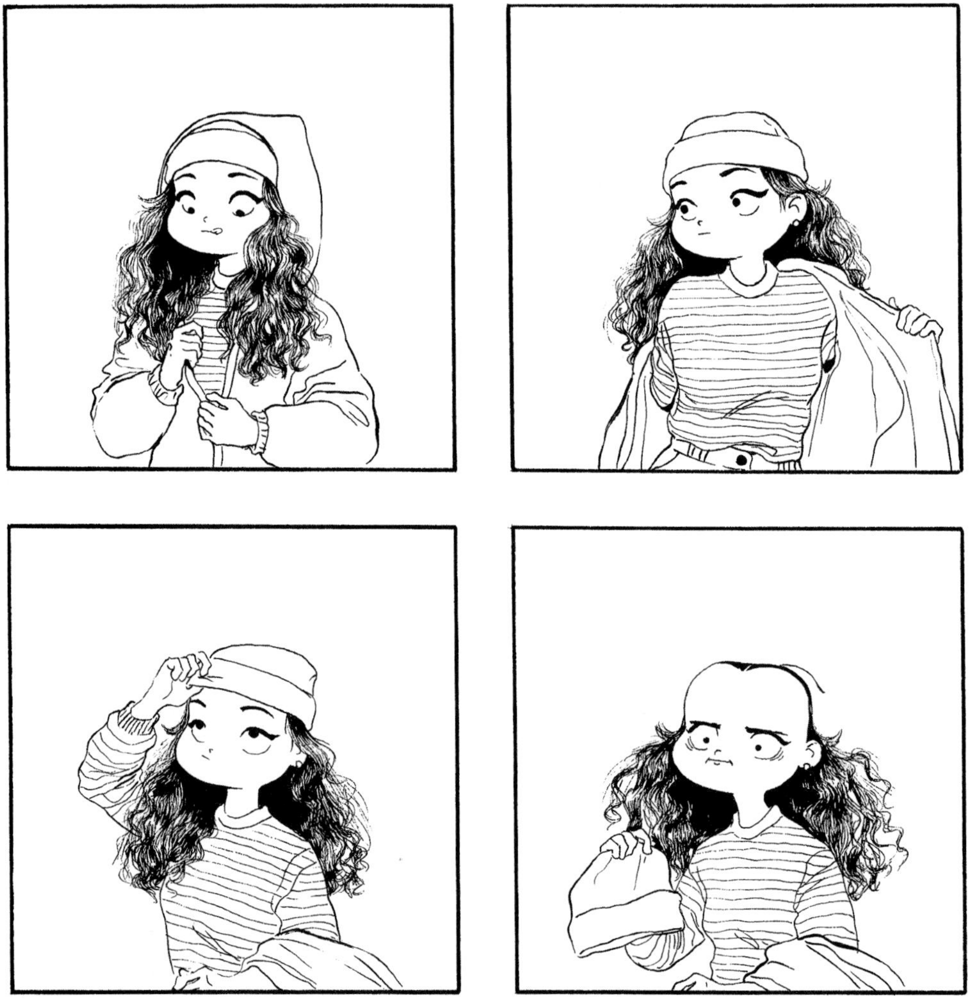

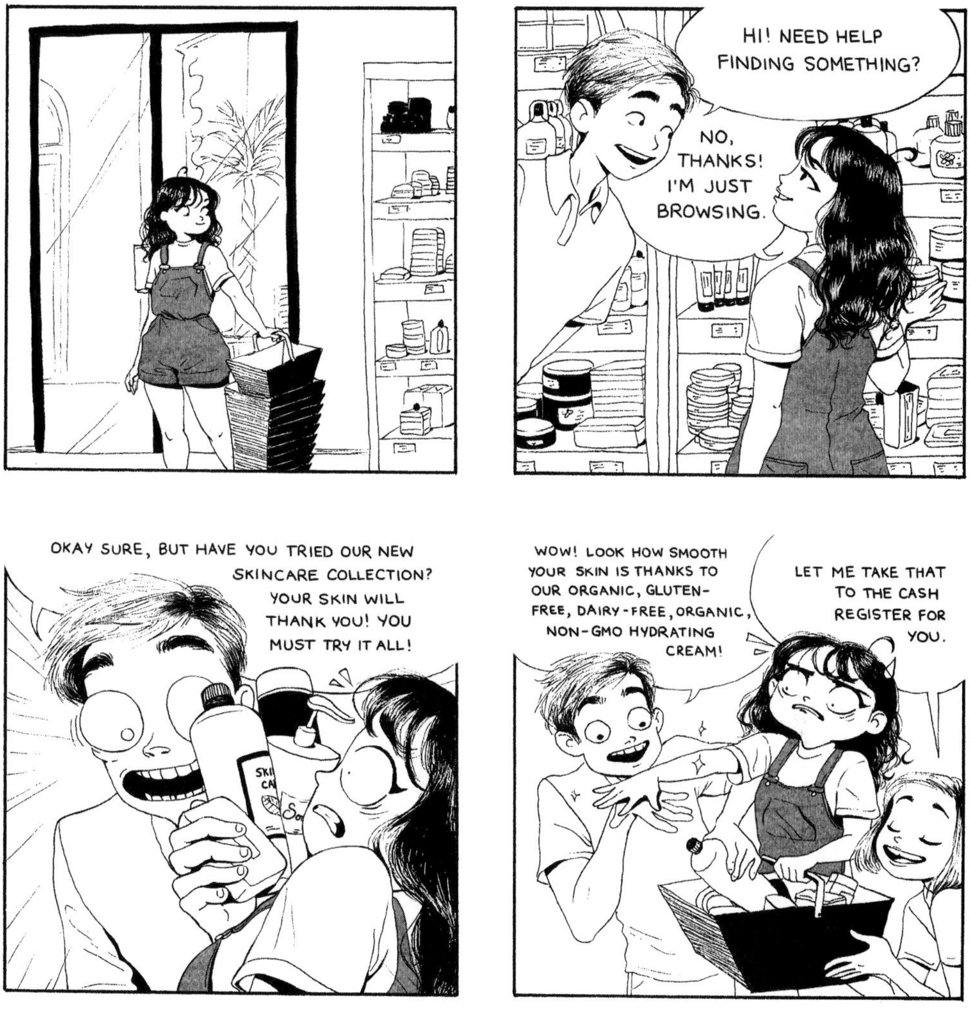
HI! NEED HELP FINDING SOMETHING?
NO, THANKS! I'M JUST BROWSING.
OKAY SURE, BUT HAVE YOU TRIED OUR NEW SKINCARE COLLECTION? YOUR SKIN WILL THANK YOU! YOU MUST TRY IT ALL!
WOW! LOOK HOW SMOOTH YOUR SKIN IS THANKS TO OUR ORGANIC, GLUTEN-FREE, DAIRY-FREE, ORGANIC, NON-GMO HYDRATING CREAM!
LET ME TAKE THAT TO THE CASH REGISTER FOR YOU.

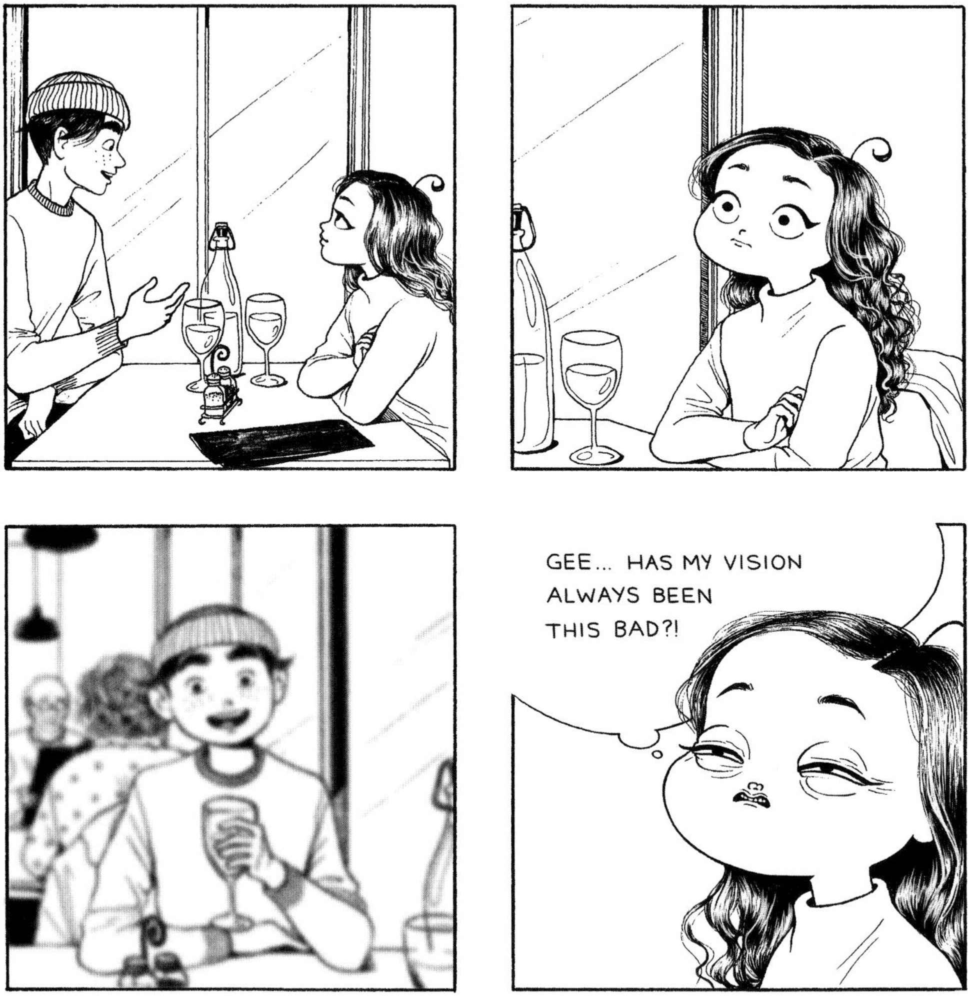
GEE... HAS MY VISION
ALWAYS BEEN
THIS BAD?!

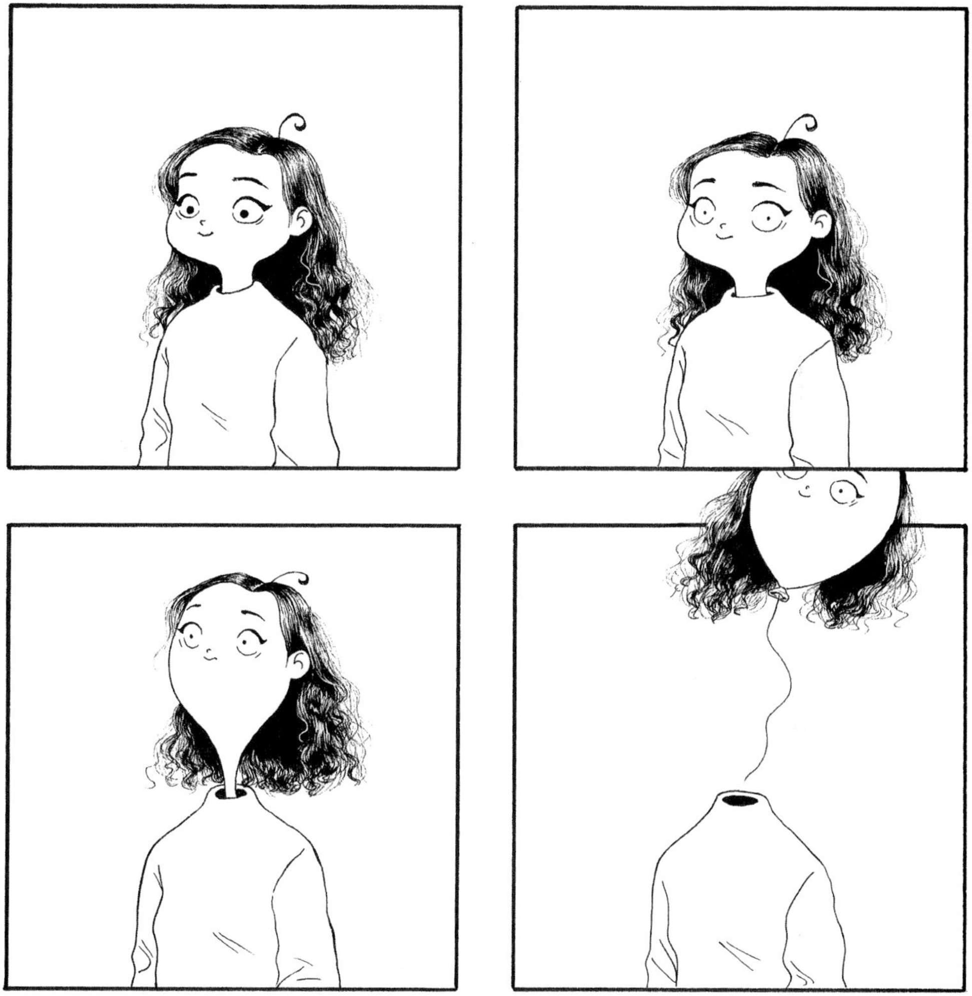

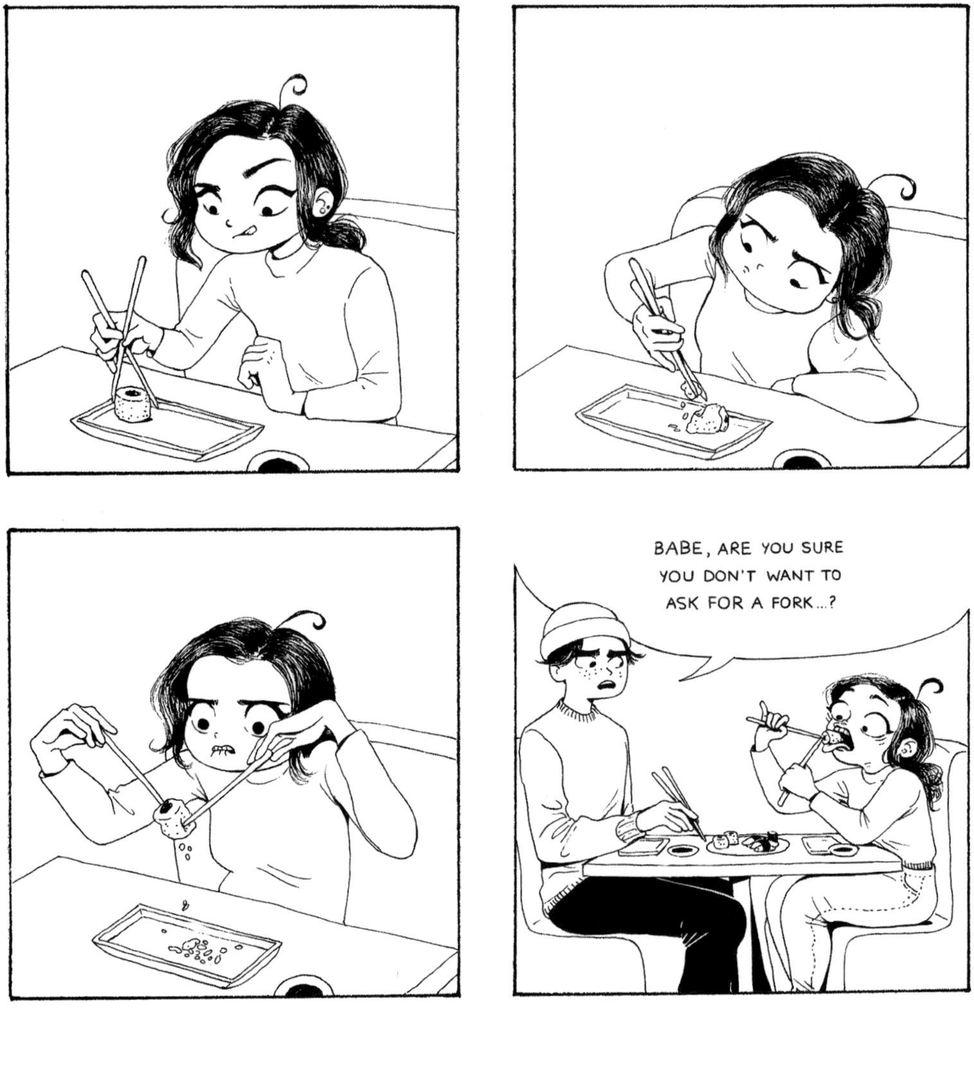
BABE, ARE YOU SURE
YOU DON'T WANT TO
ASK FOR A FORK...?

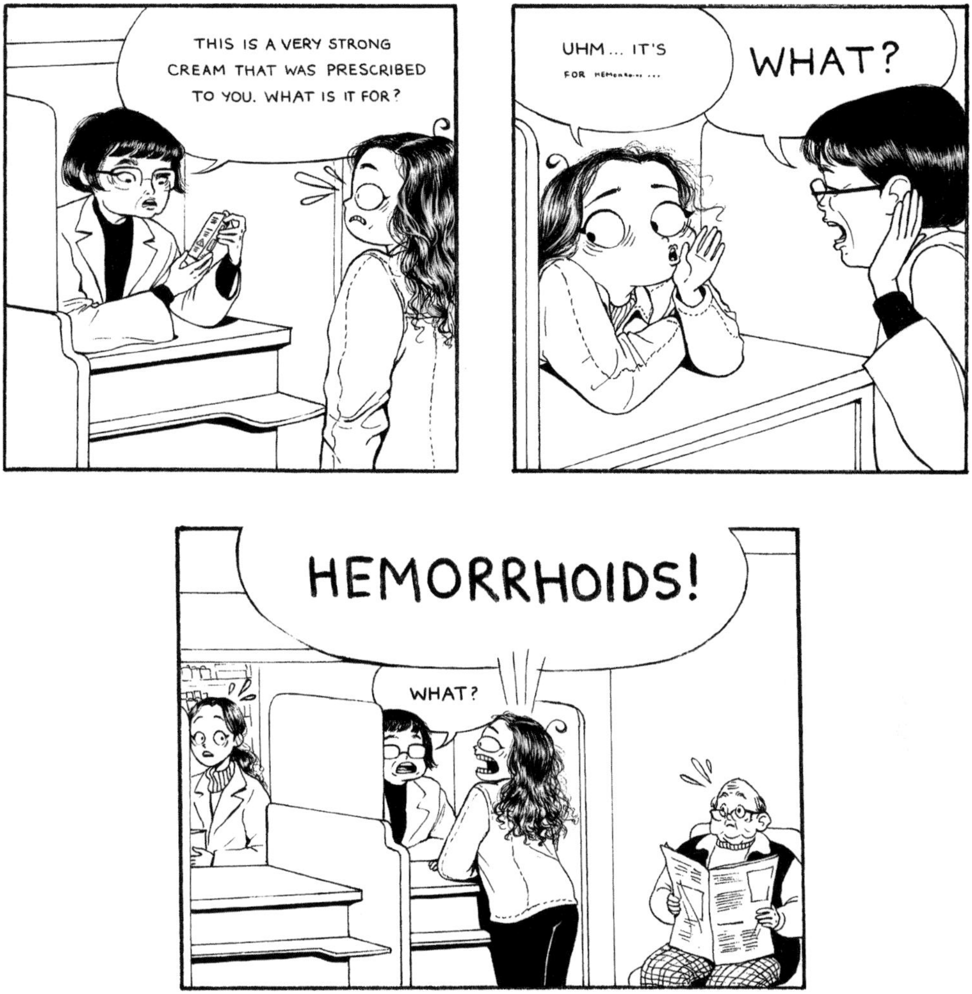
THIS IS A VERY STRONG CREAM THAT WAS PRESCRIBED TO YOU. WHAT IS IT FOR?
UHM... IT'S FOR ...
WHAT?
HEMORRHOIDS!
WHAT?

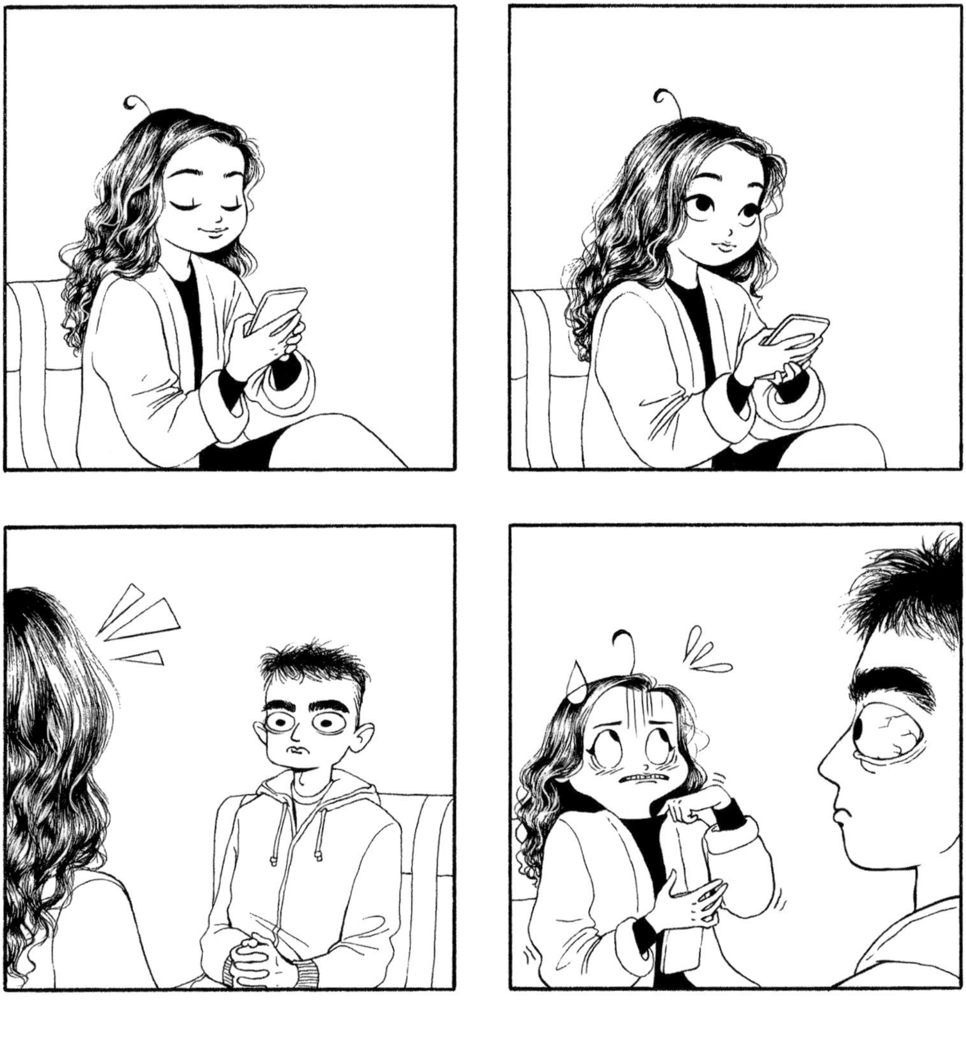

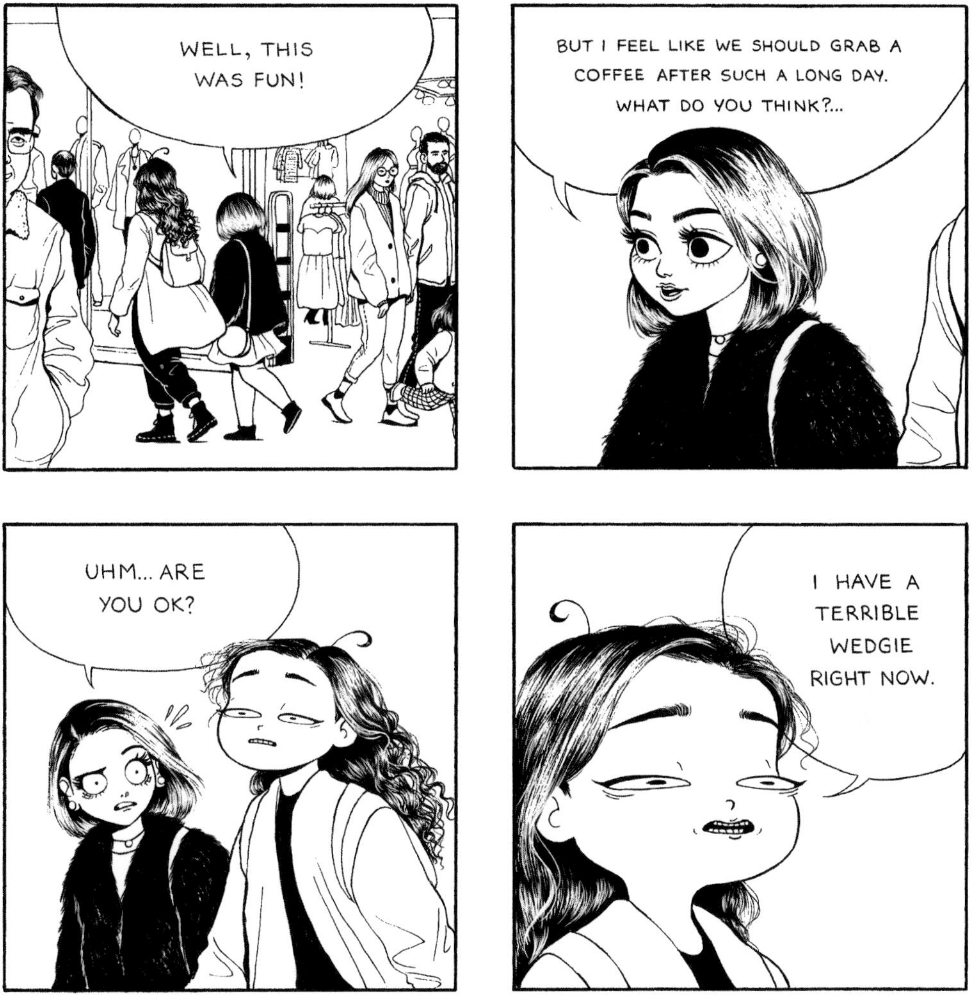
WELL, THIS WAS FUN!
BUT I FEEL LIKE WE SHOULD GRAB A COFFEE AFTER SUCH A LONG DAY. WHAT DO YOU THINK?...
UHM... ARE YOU OK?
I HAVE A TERRIBLE WEDGIE RIGHT NOW.

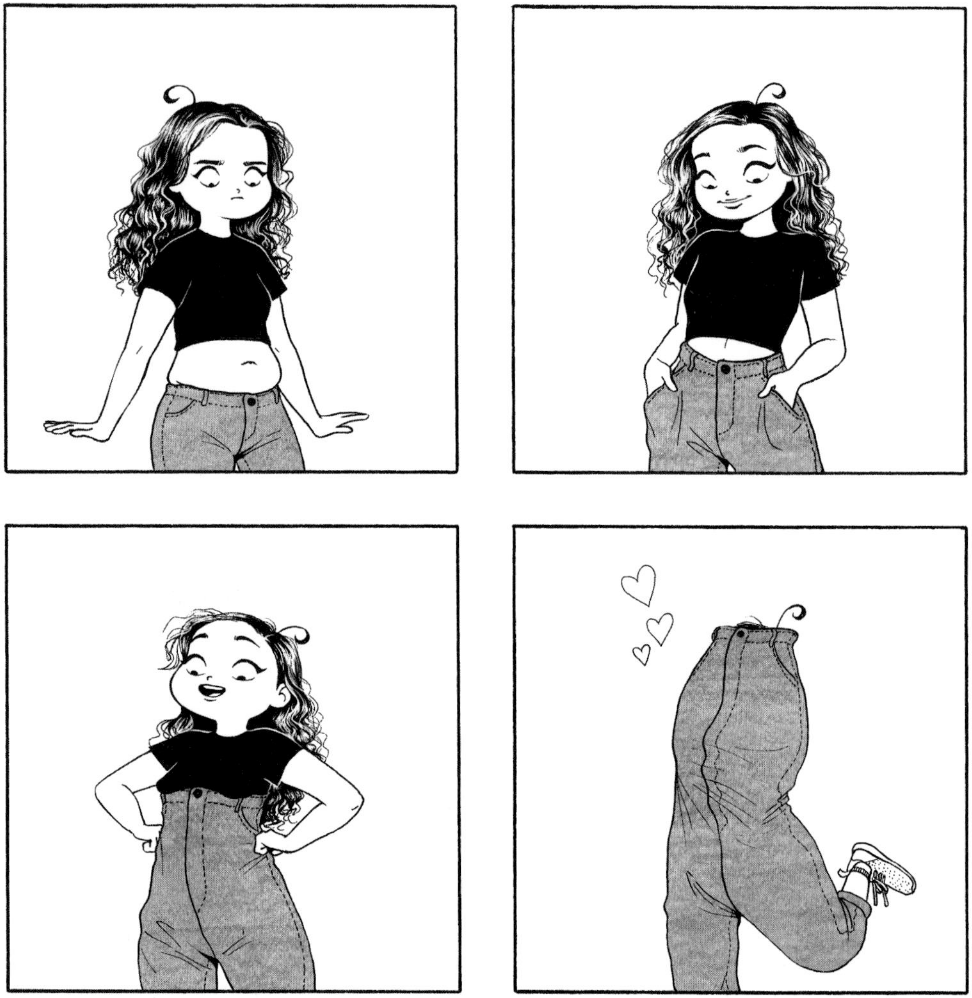

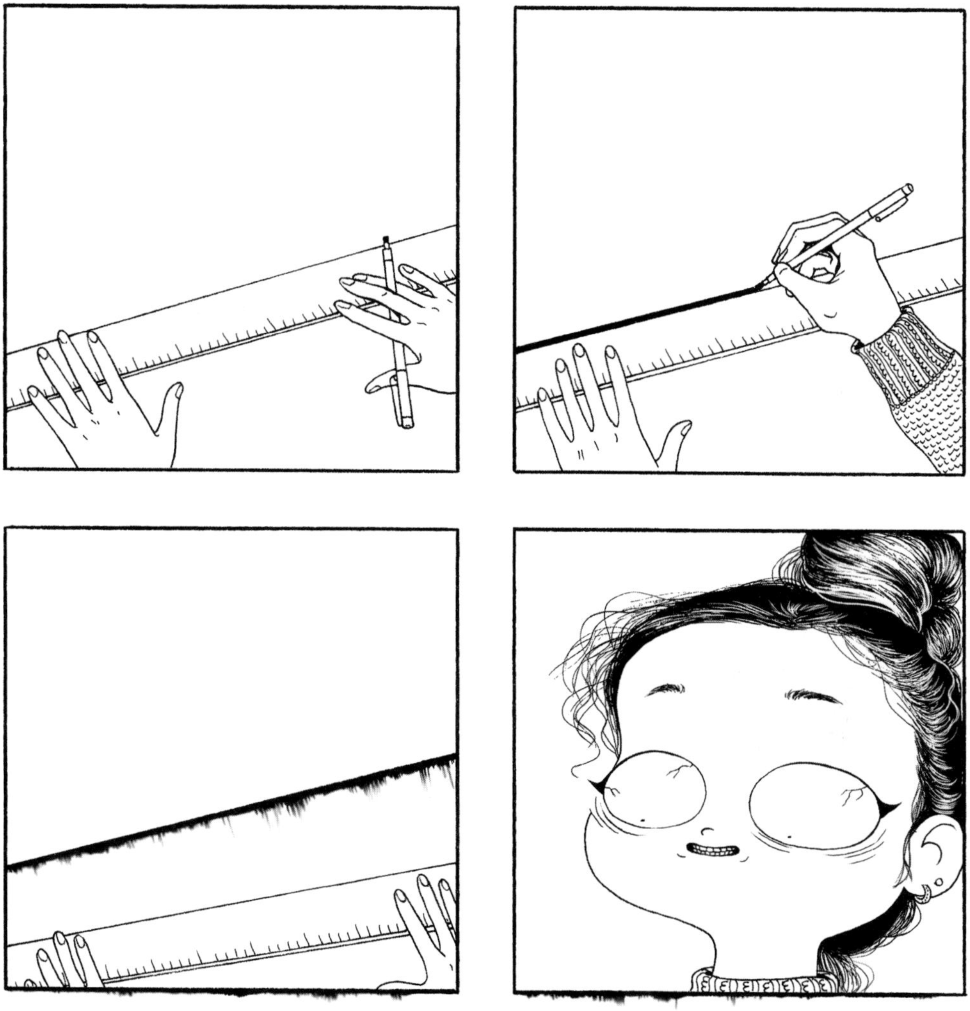

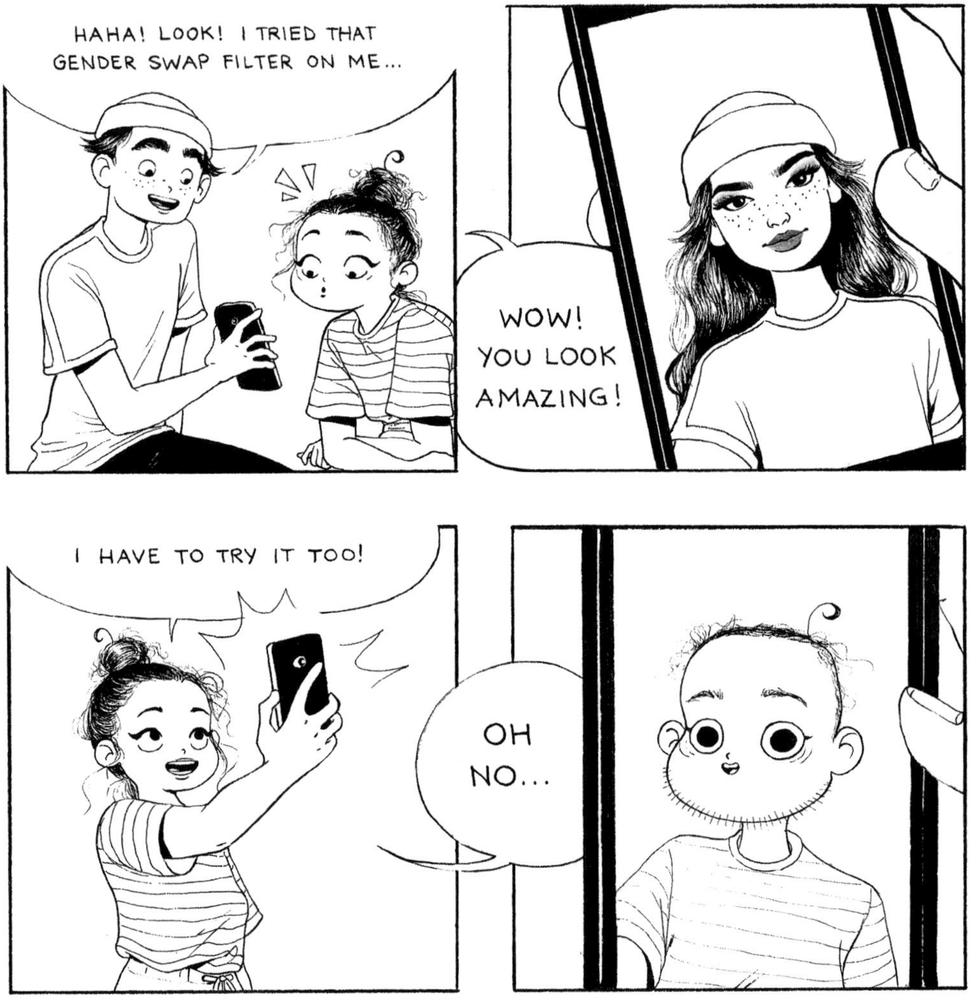
HAHA! LOOK! I TRIED THAT GENDER SWAP FILTER ON ME...
WOW! YOU LOOK AMAZING!
I HAVE TO TRY IT TOO!
OH NO...

STRAIGHT BROWS

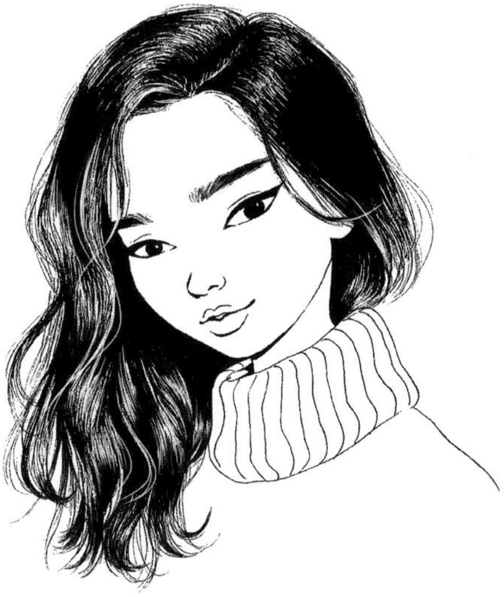

EXPECTATIONS

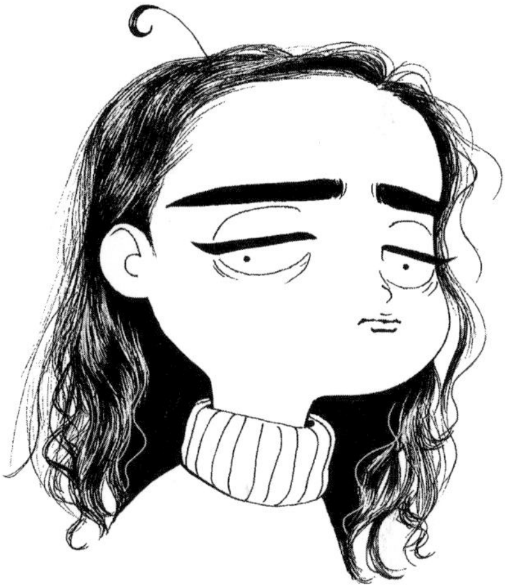

REALITY

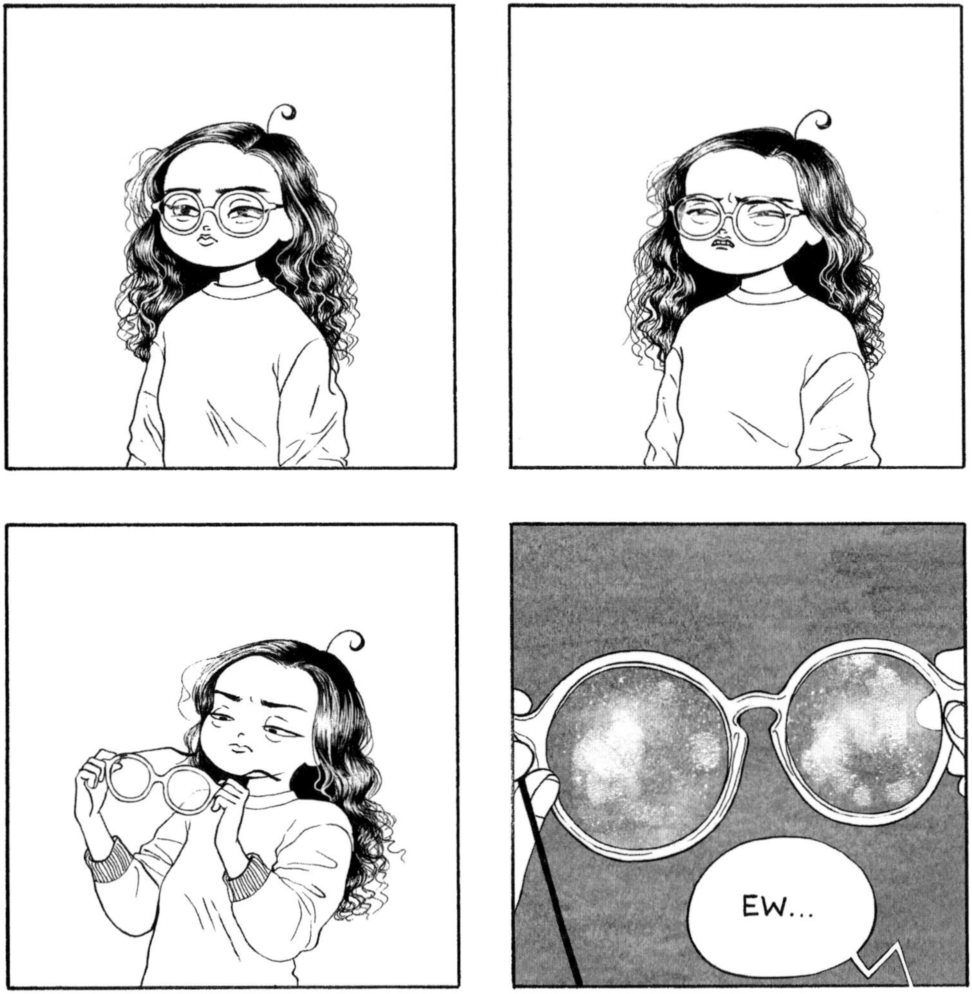
EW...

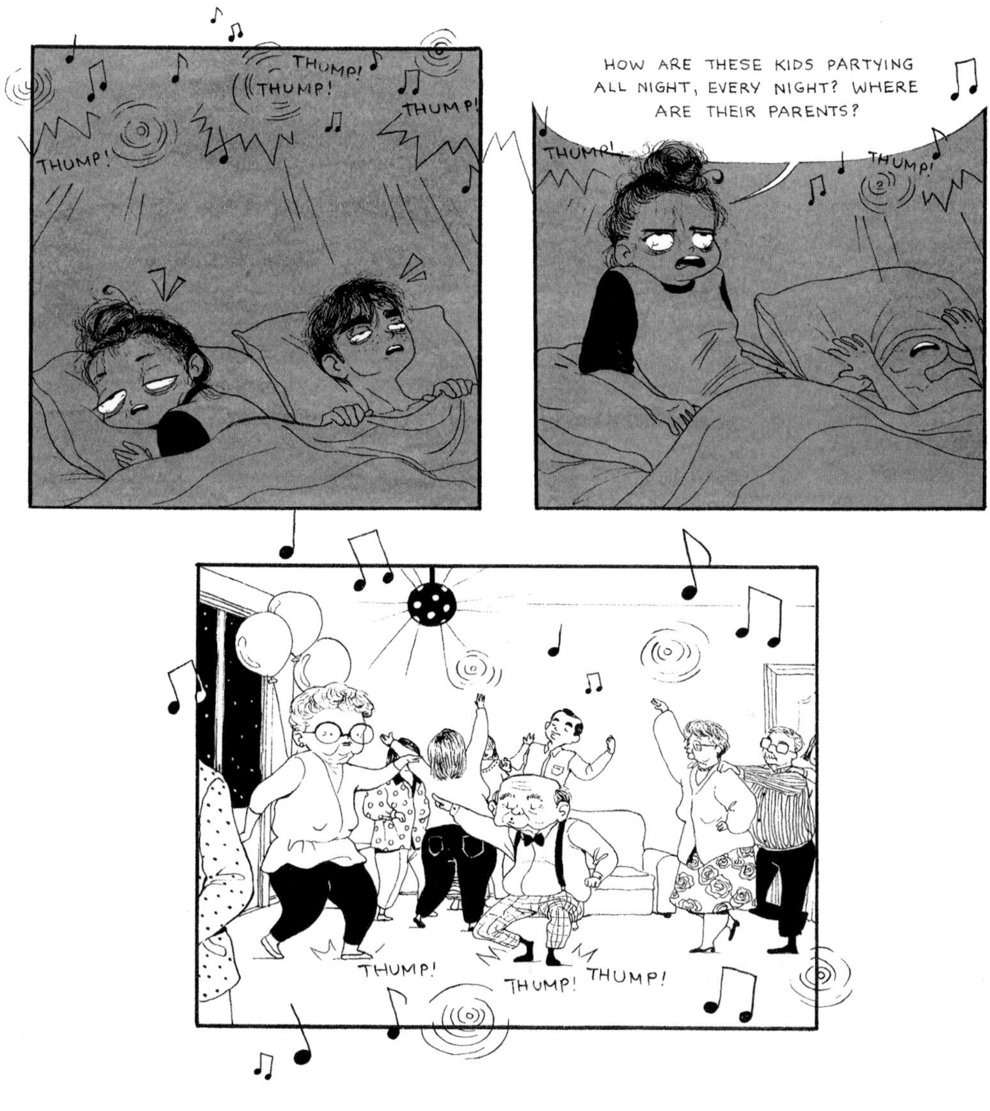
THUMP!
THUMP!
THUMP!
THUMP!
HOW ARE THESE KIDS PARTYING ALL NIGHT, EVERY NIGHT? WHERE ARE THEIR PARENTS?
THUMP!
THUMP!
THUMP!
THUMP!
THUMP!

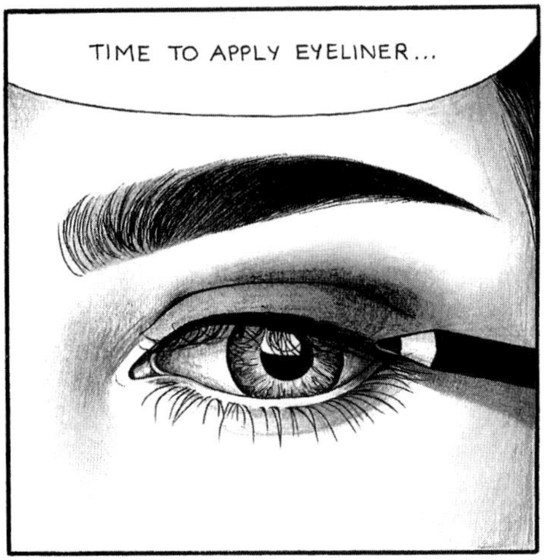
TIME TO APPLY EYELINER...

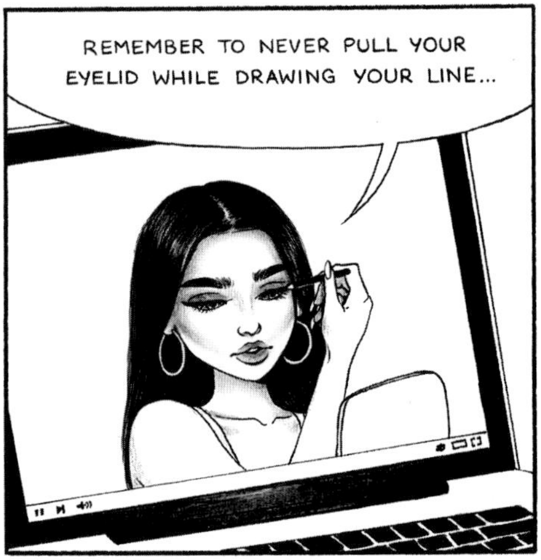
REMEMBER TO NEVER PULL YOUR EYELID WHILE DRAWING YOUR LINE...

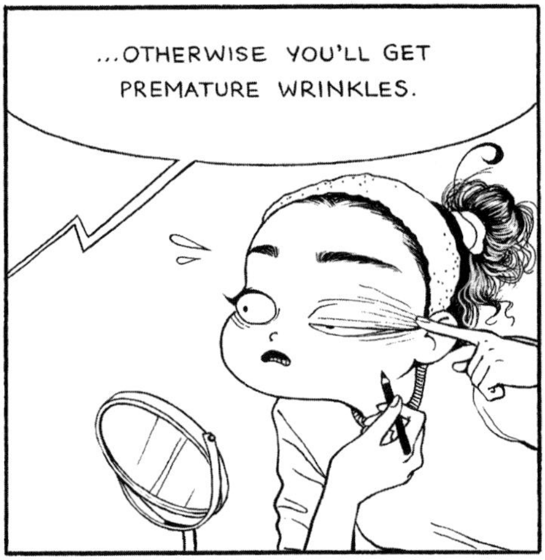
...OTHERWISE YOU'LL GET PREMATURE WRINKLES.

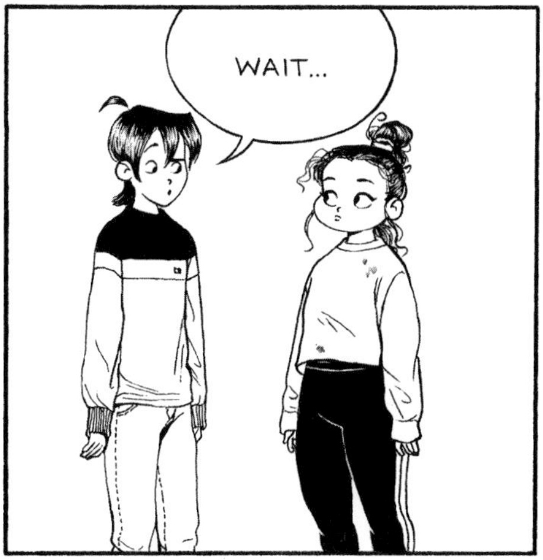
WAIT...

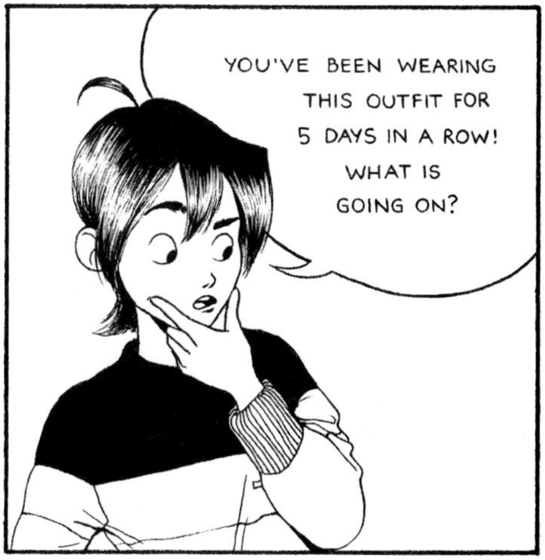
YOU'VE BEEN WEARING THIS OUTFIT FOR 5 DAYS IN A ROW! WHAT IS GOING ON?

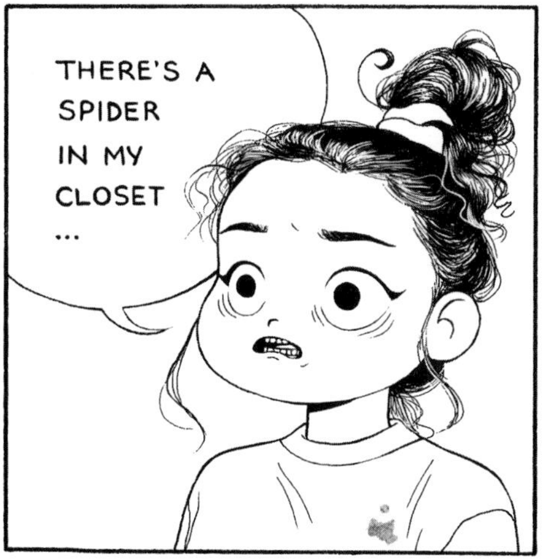
THERE'S A SPIDER IN MY CLOSET ...

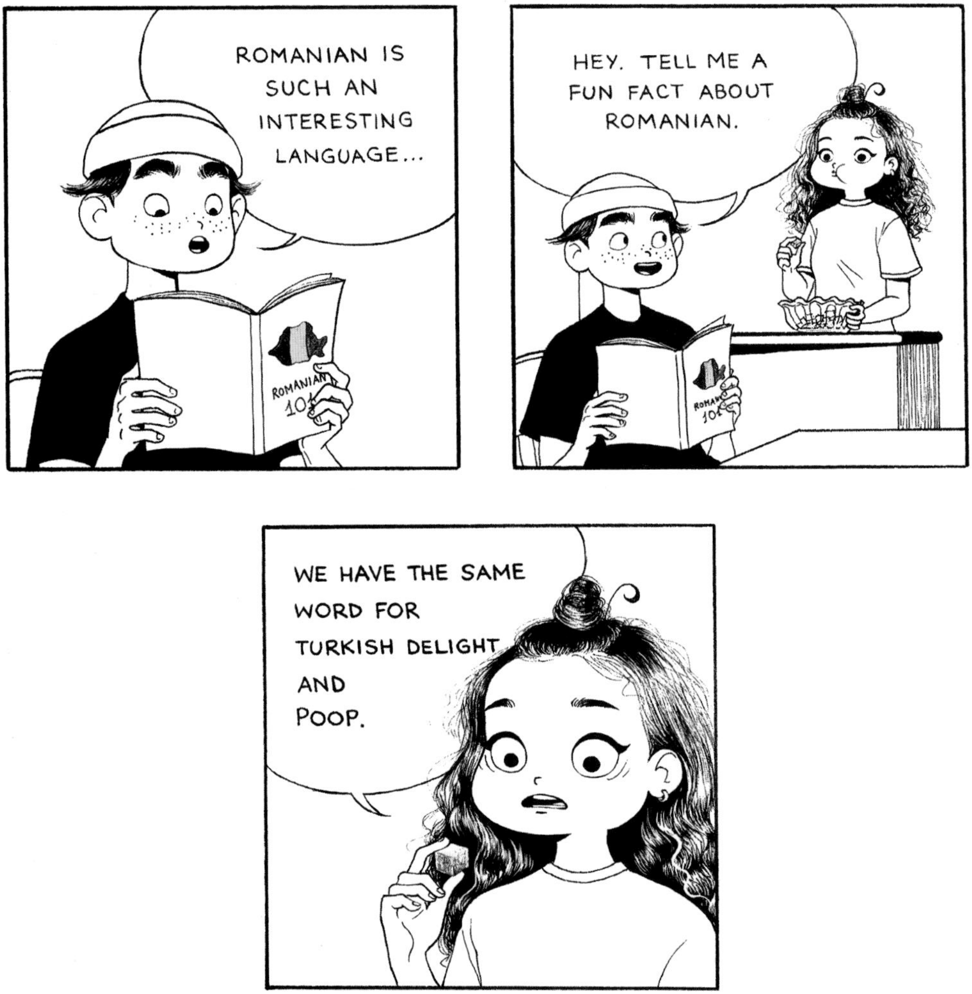
ROMANIAN IS SUCH AN INTERESTING LANGUAGE...
ROMANIAN 101
HEY. TELL ME A FUN FACT ABOUT ROMANIAN.
WE HAVE THE SAME WORD FOR TURKISH DELIGHT AND POOP.

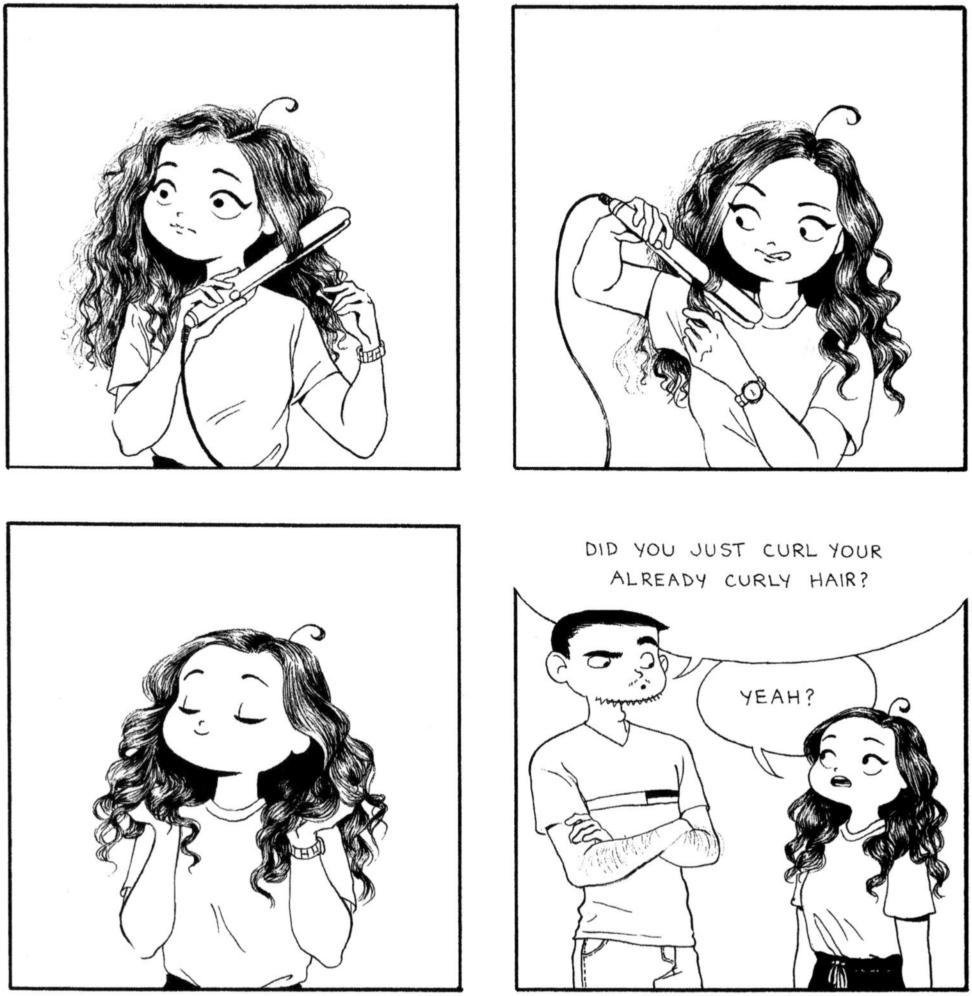
DID YOU JUST CURL YOUR ALREADY CURLY HAIR?
YEAH?

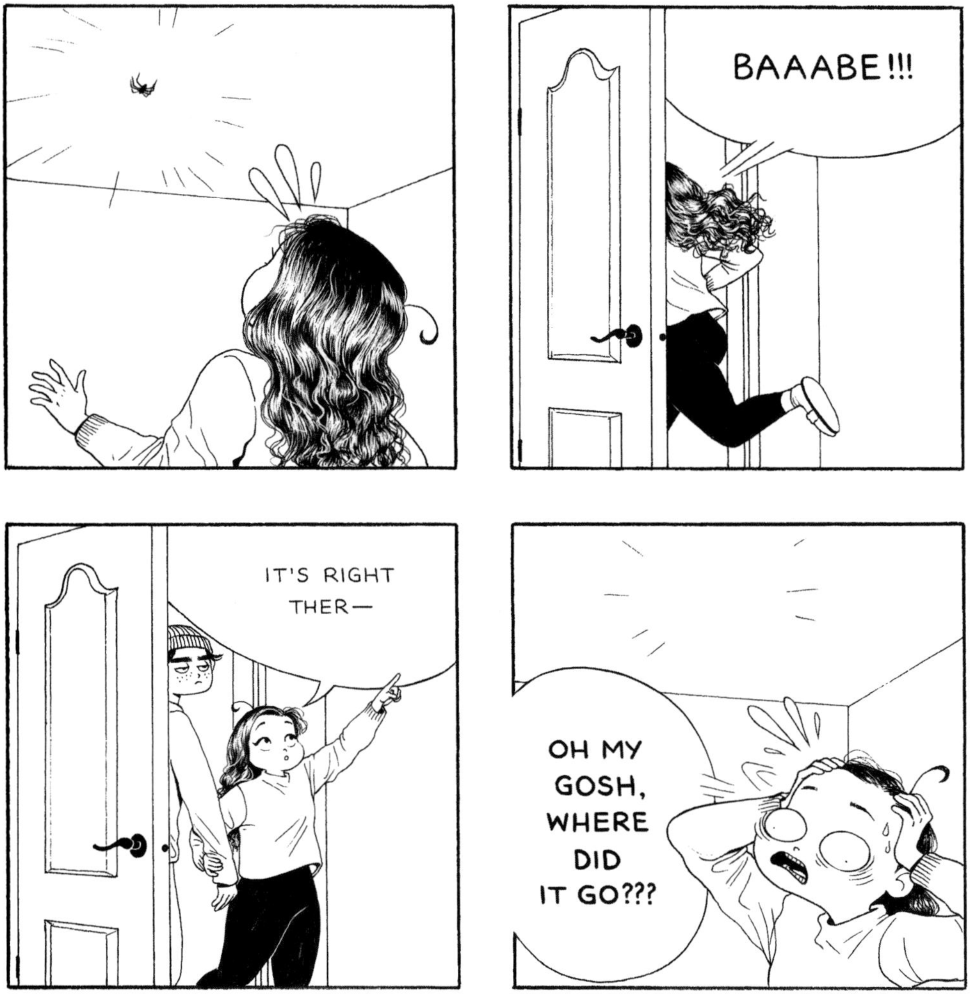
BAAABE!!!
IT'S RIGHT THER—
OH MY GOSH, WHERE DID IT GO???

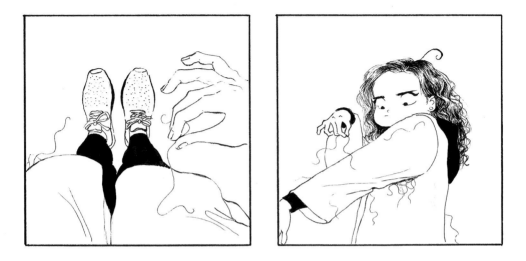

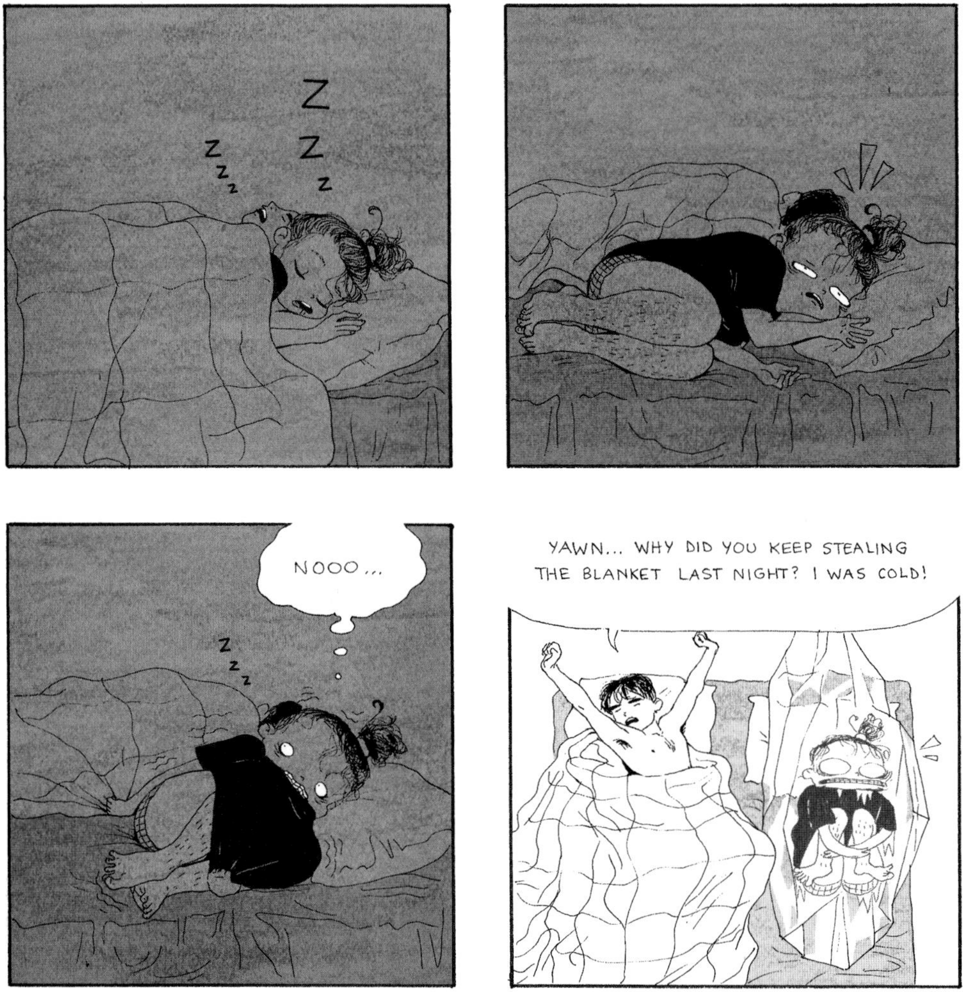
Z Z Z
Z Z Z
Z Z Z
NOOO...
YAWN... WHY DID YOU KEEP STEALING THE BLANKET LAST NIGHT? I WAS COLD!

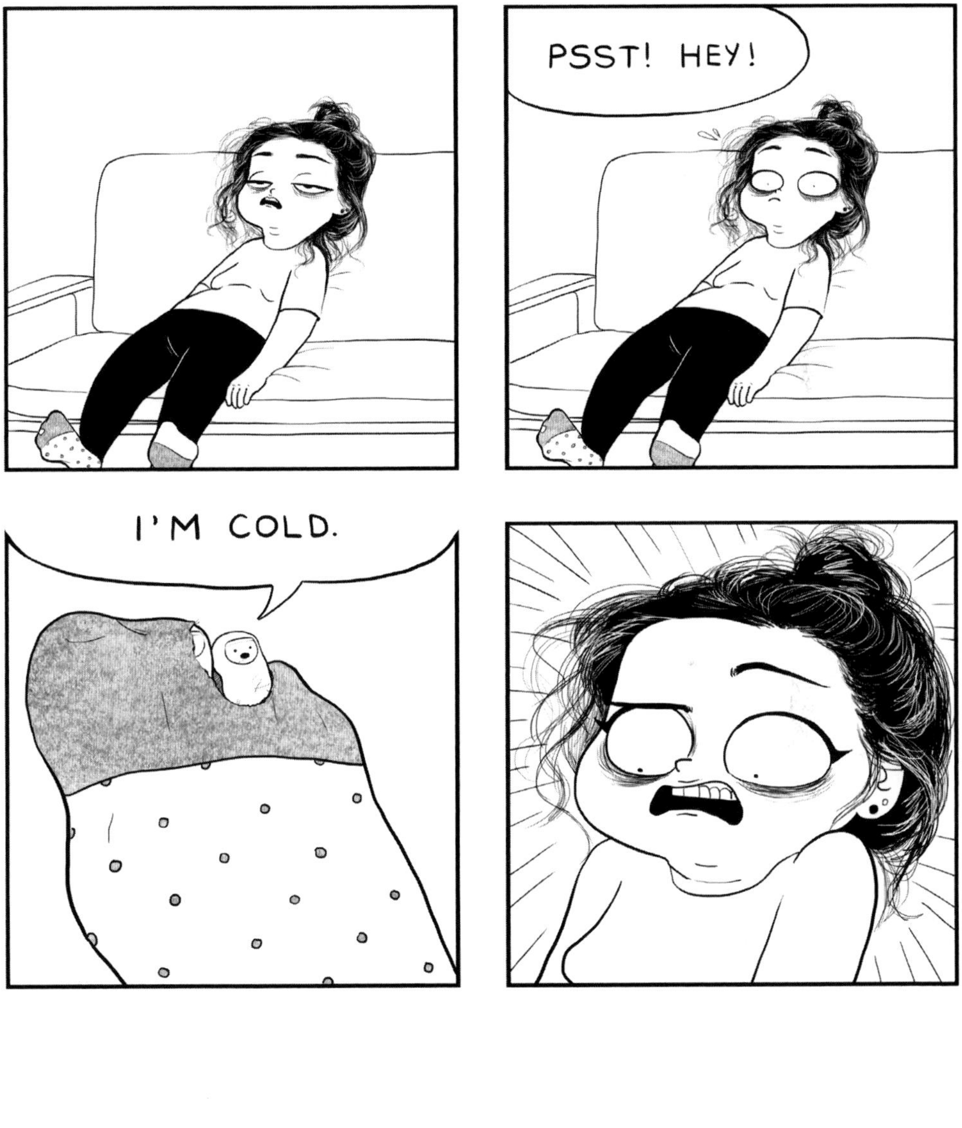
PSST! HEY!
I'M COLD.

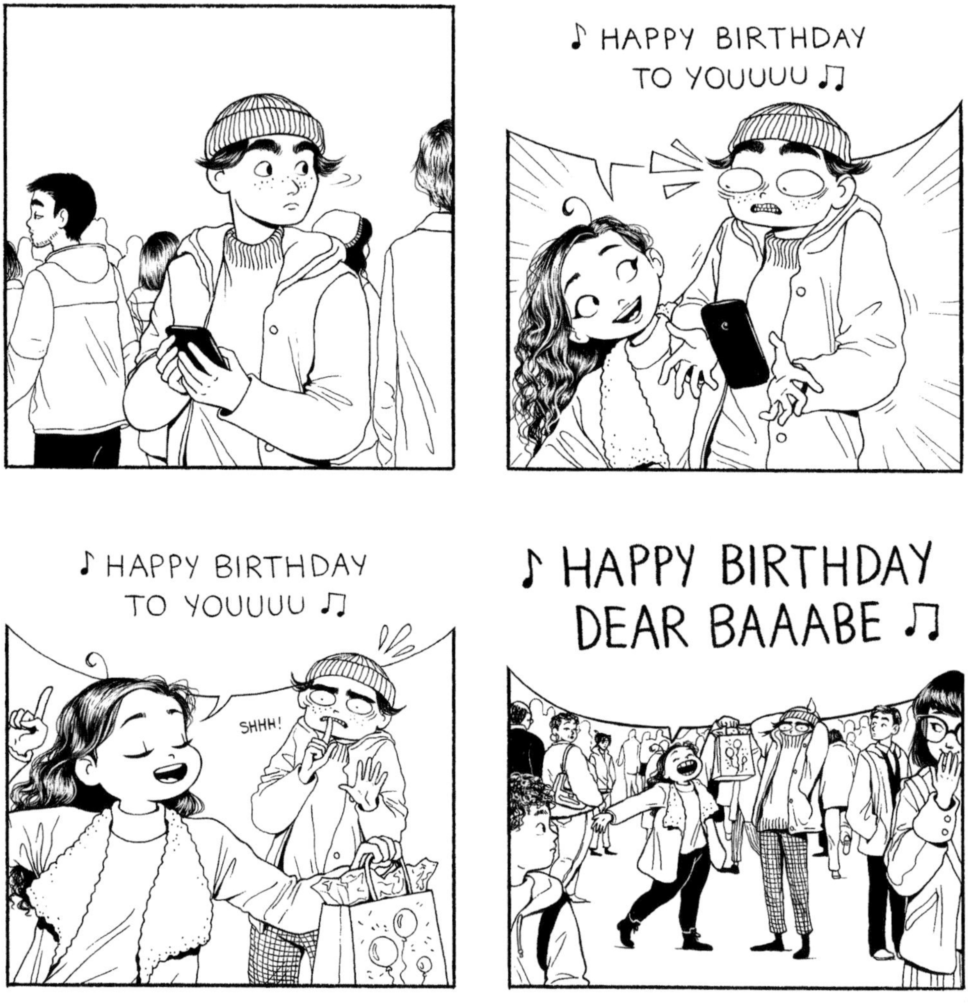
♪ HAPPY BIRTHDAY
TO YOUUUU ♫
♪ HAPPY BIRTHDAY
TO YOUUUU ♫
SHHH!
♪ HAPPY BIRTHDAY
DEAR BAAABE ♫

BEANIE

EXPECTATIONS   REALITY

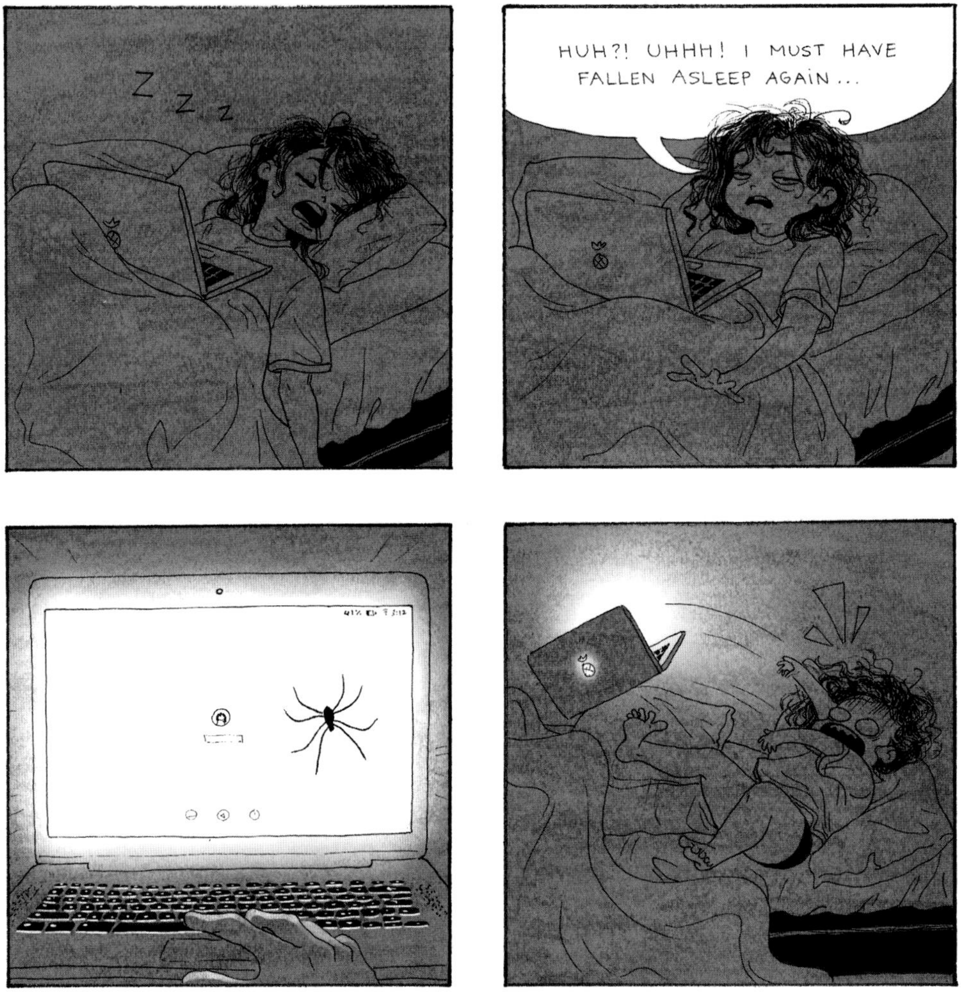
Z Z Z
HUH?! UHHH! I MUST HAVE FALLEN ASLEEP AGAIN...

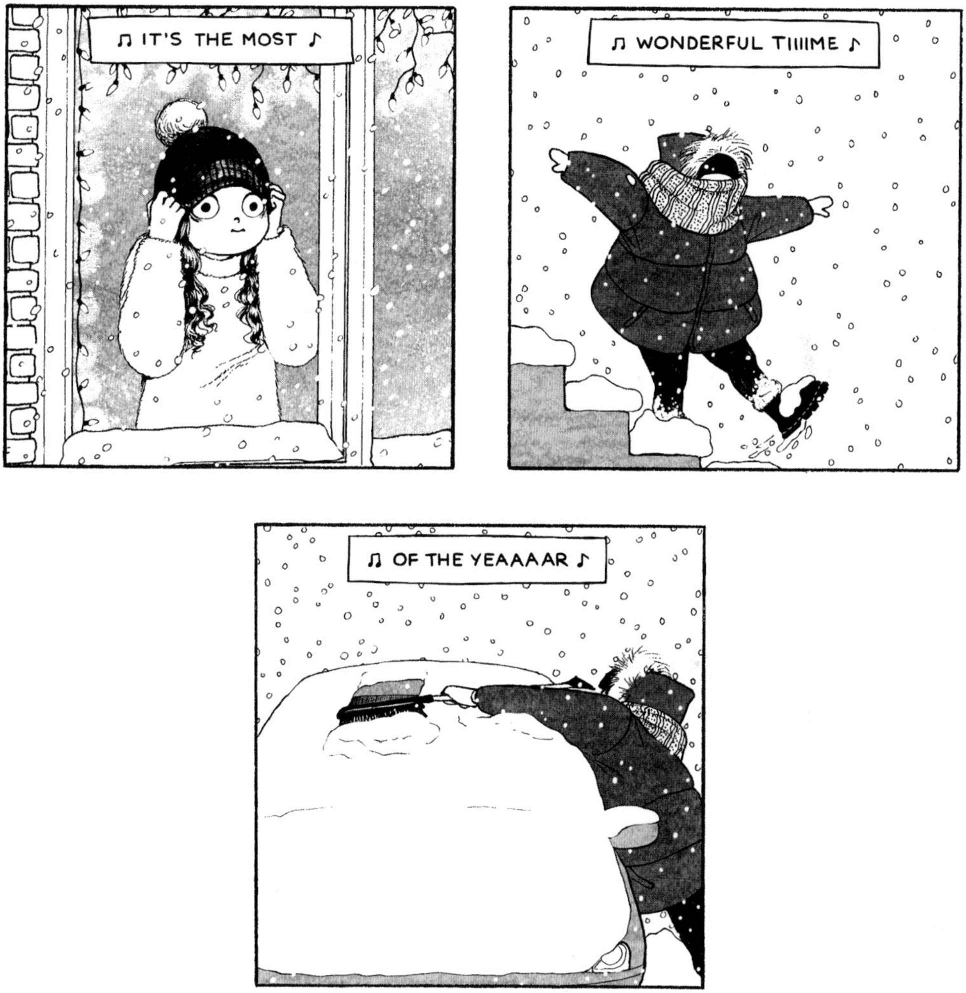
♫ IT'S THE MOST ♪
♫ WONDERFUL TIIIIME ♪
♫ OF THE YEAAAAR ♪

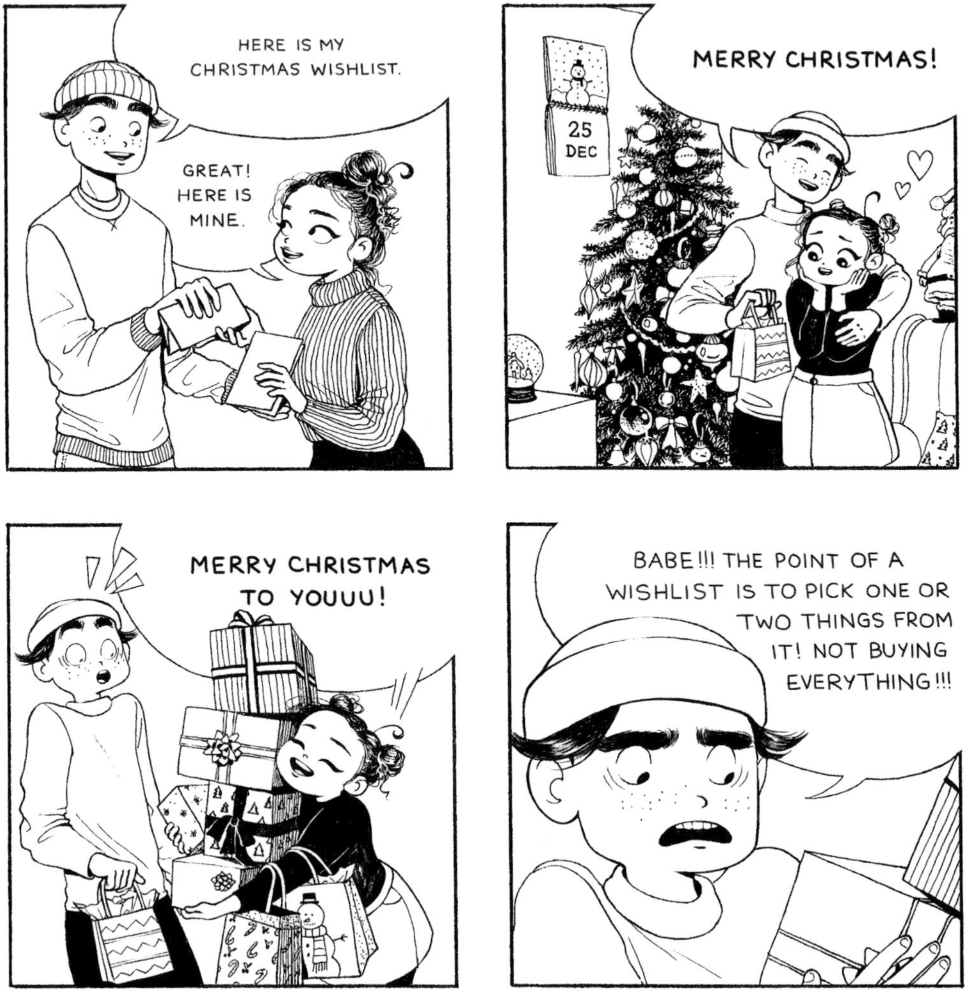
HERE IS MY CHRISTMAS WISHLIST.
GREAT! HERE IS MINE.
25 DEC
MERRY CHRISTMAS!
MERRY CHRISTMAS TO YOUUU!
BABE!!! THE POINT OF A WISHLIST IS TO PICK ONE OR TWO THINGS FROM IT! NOT BUYING EVERYTHING!!!

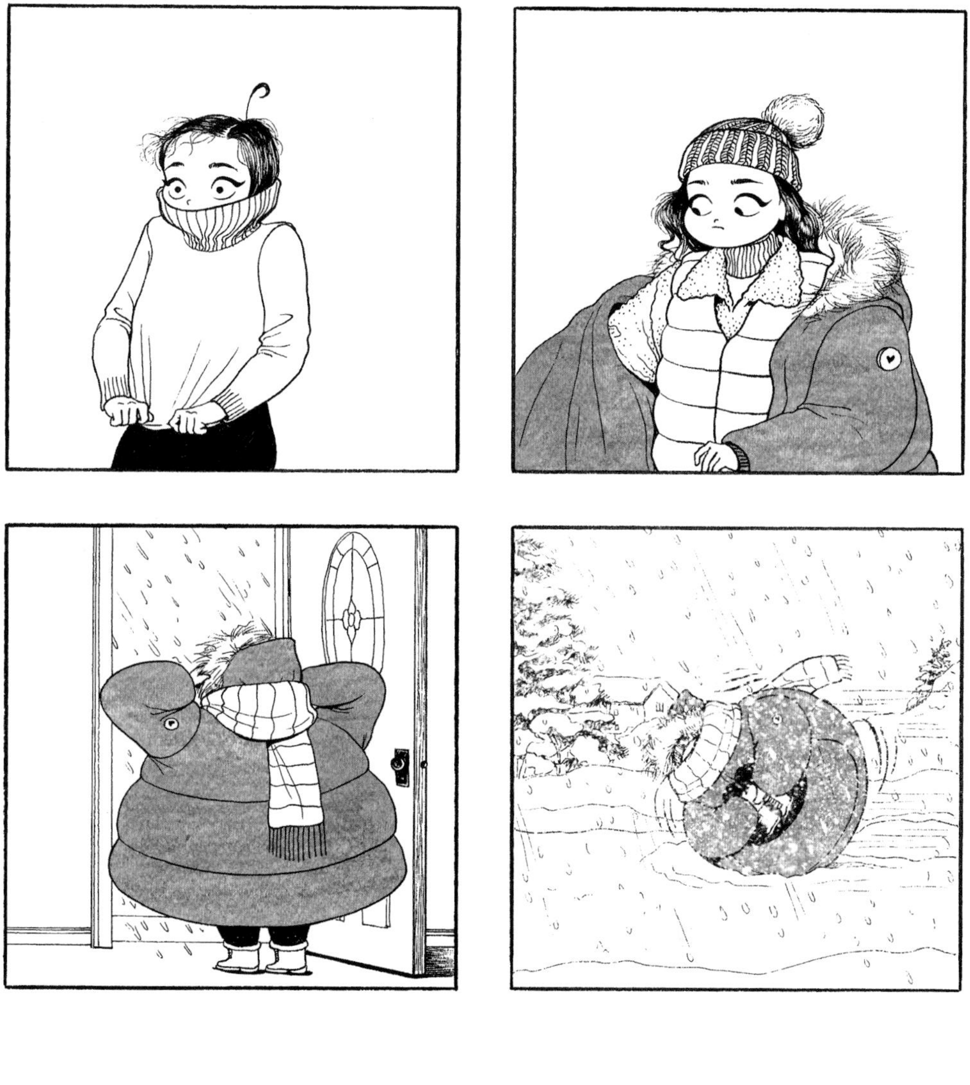

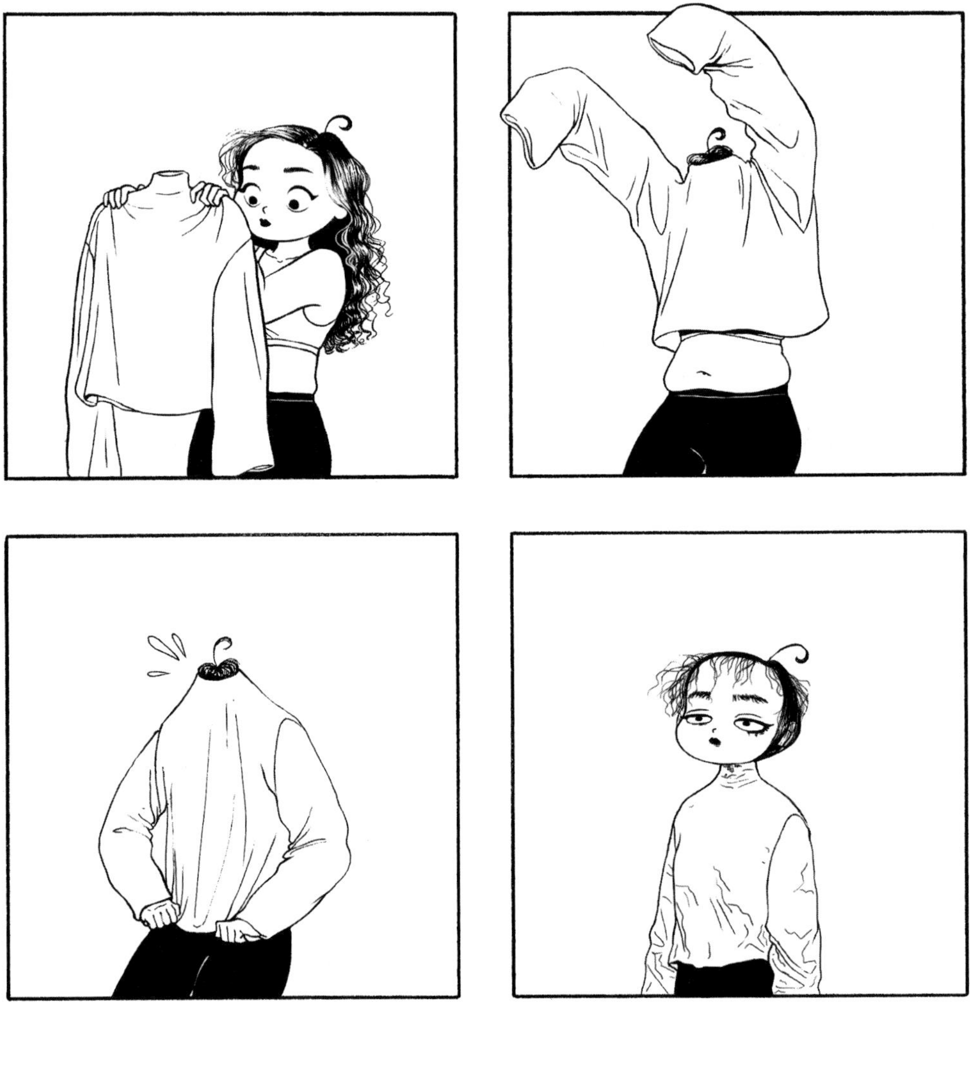

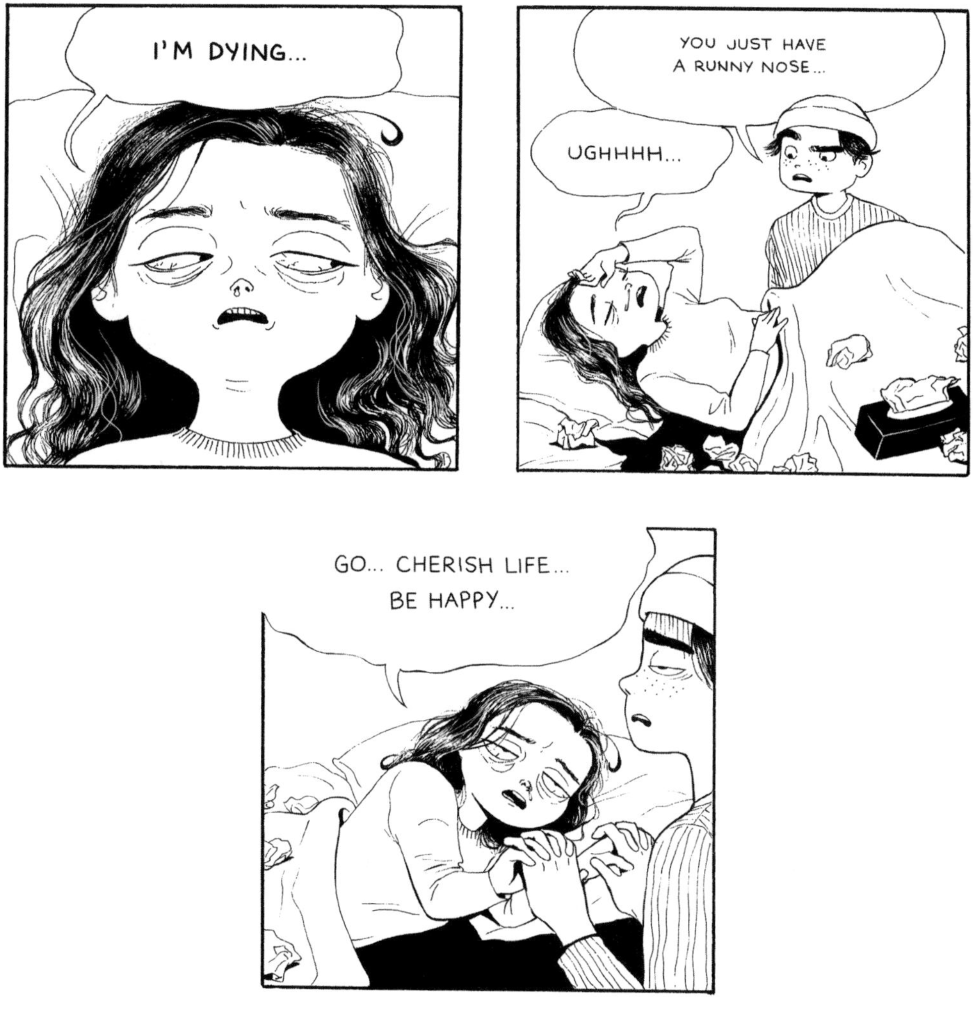
I'M DYING...
YOU JUST HAVE A RUNNY NOSE...
UGHHHH...
GO... CHERISH LIFE... BE HAPPY...

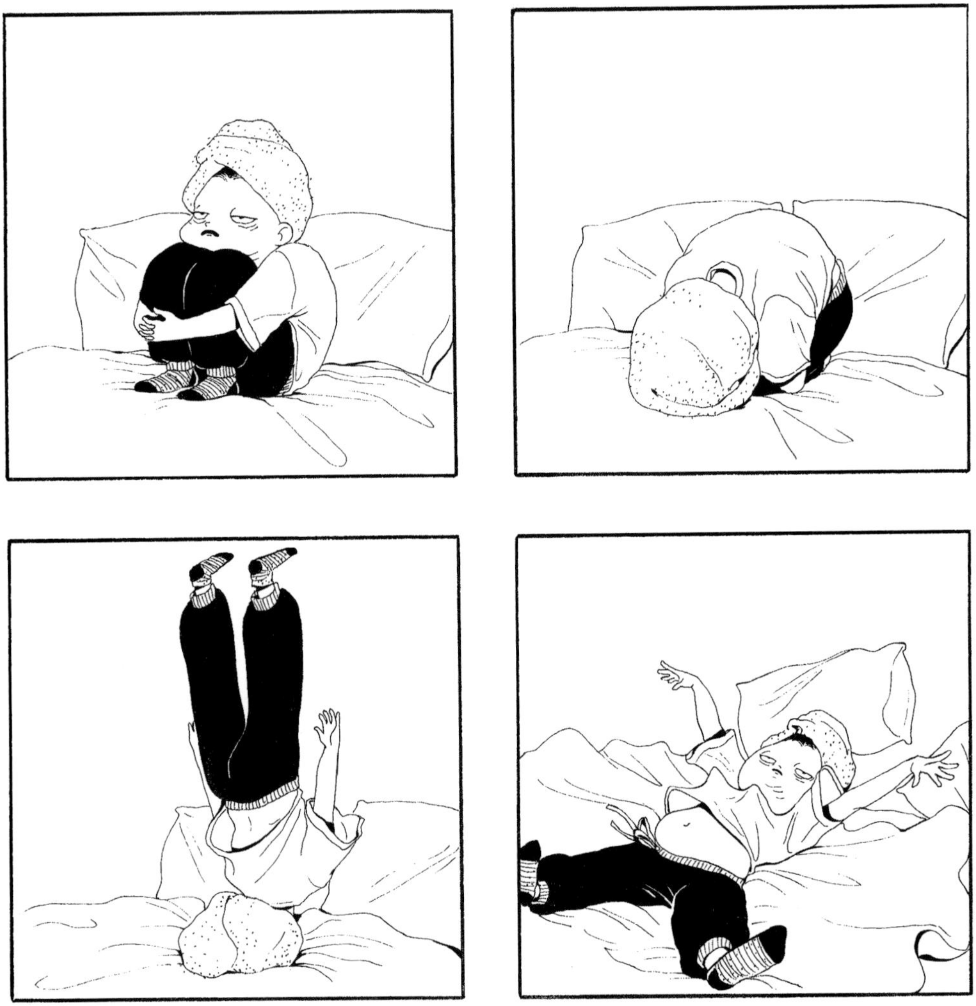

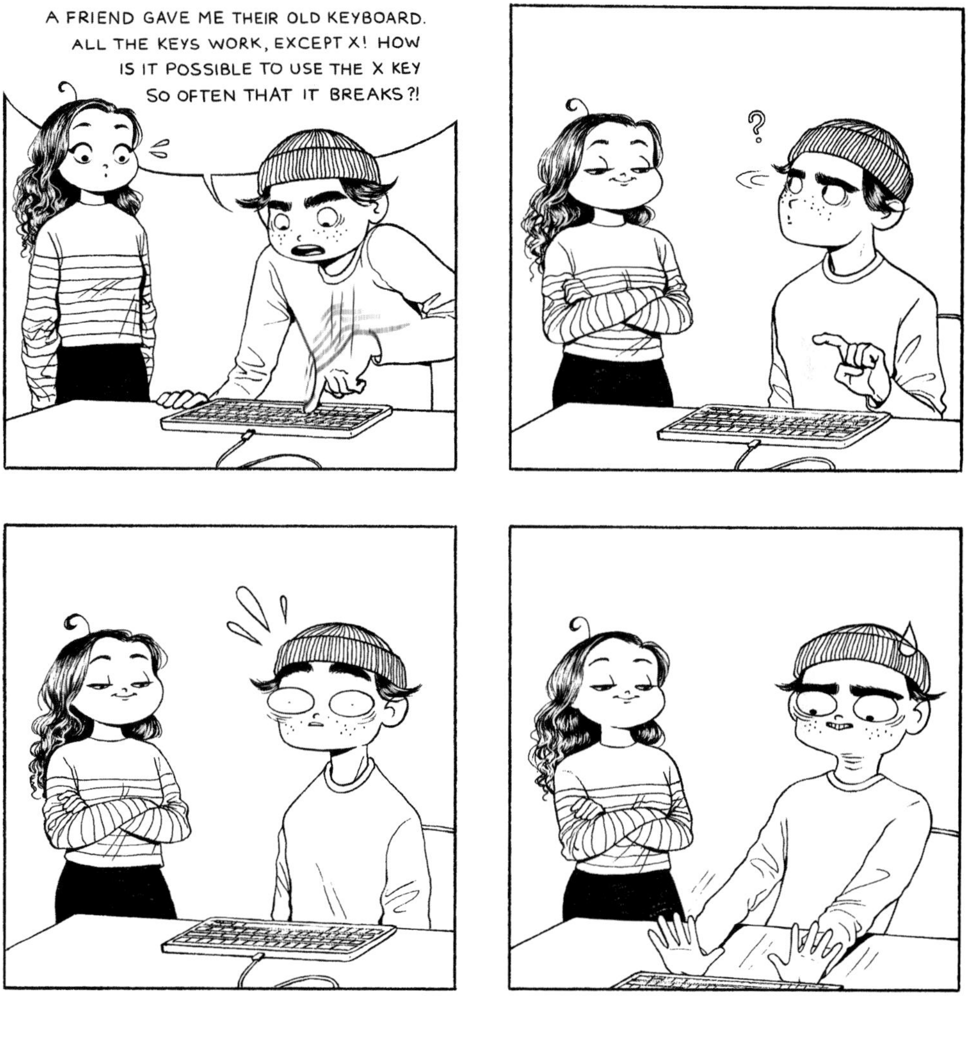
A FRIEND GAVE ME THEIR OLD KEYBOARD. ALL THE KEYS WORK, EXCEPT X! HOW IS IT POSSIBLE TO USE THE X KEY SO OFTEN THAT IT BREAKS?!
?

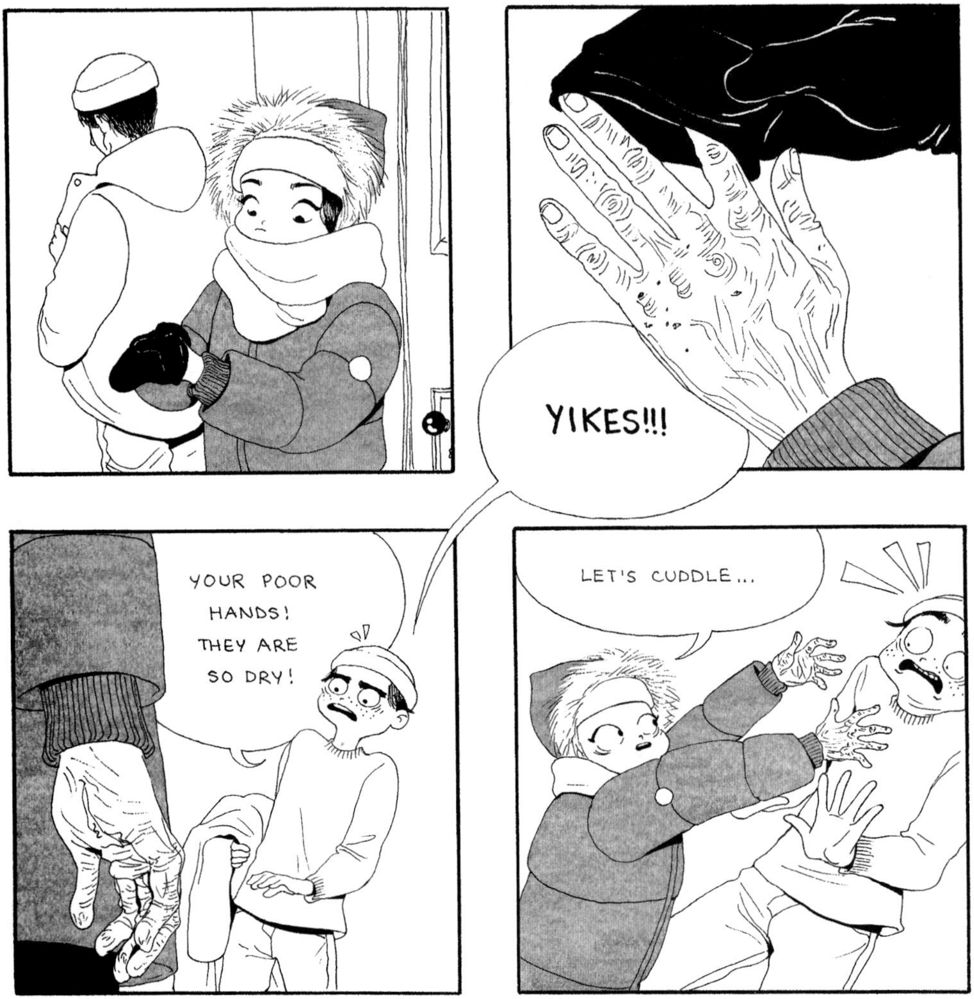
YIKES!!!
YOUR POOR HANDS! THEY ARE SO DRY!
LET'S CUDDLE...

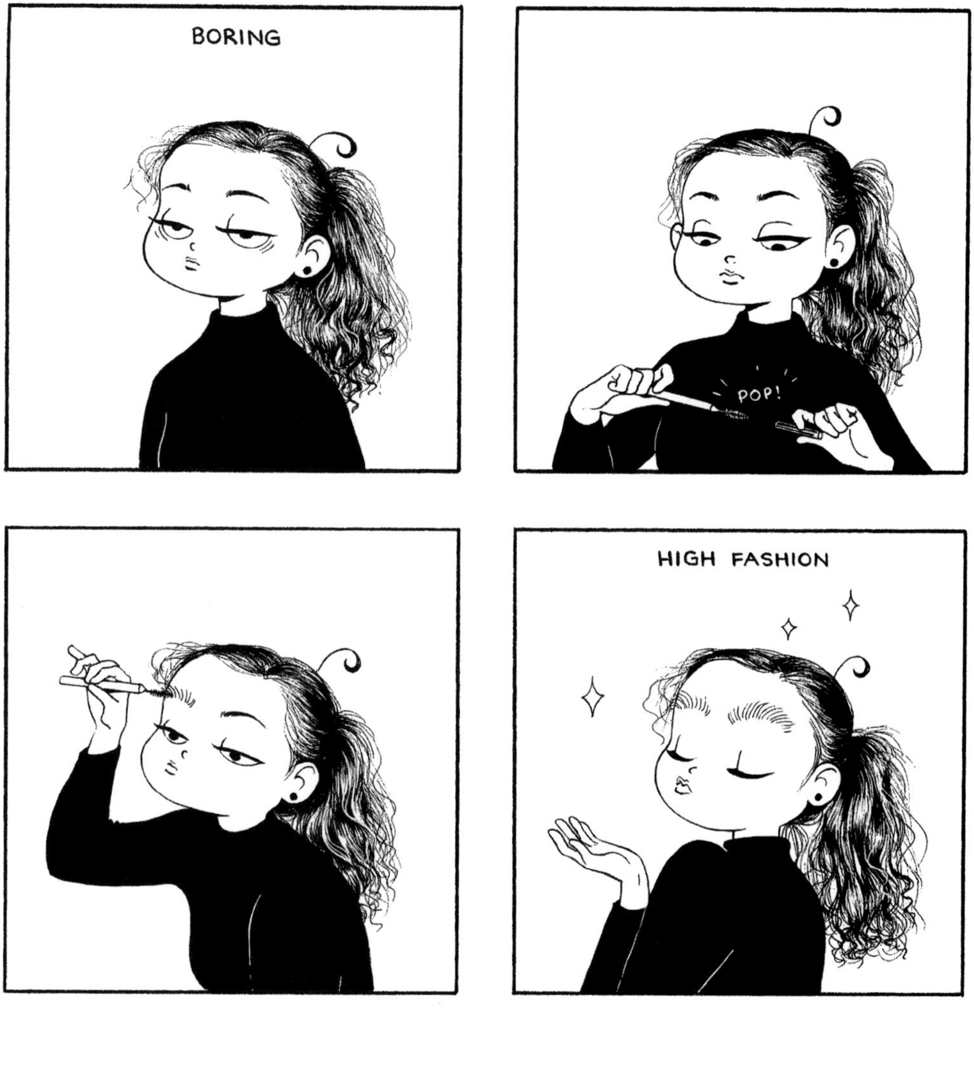
BORING
POP!
HIGH FASHION

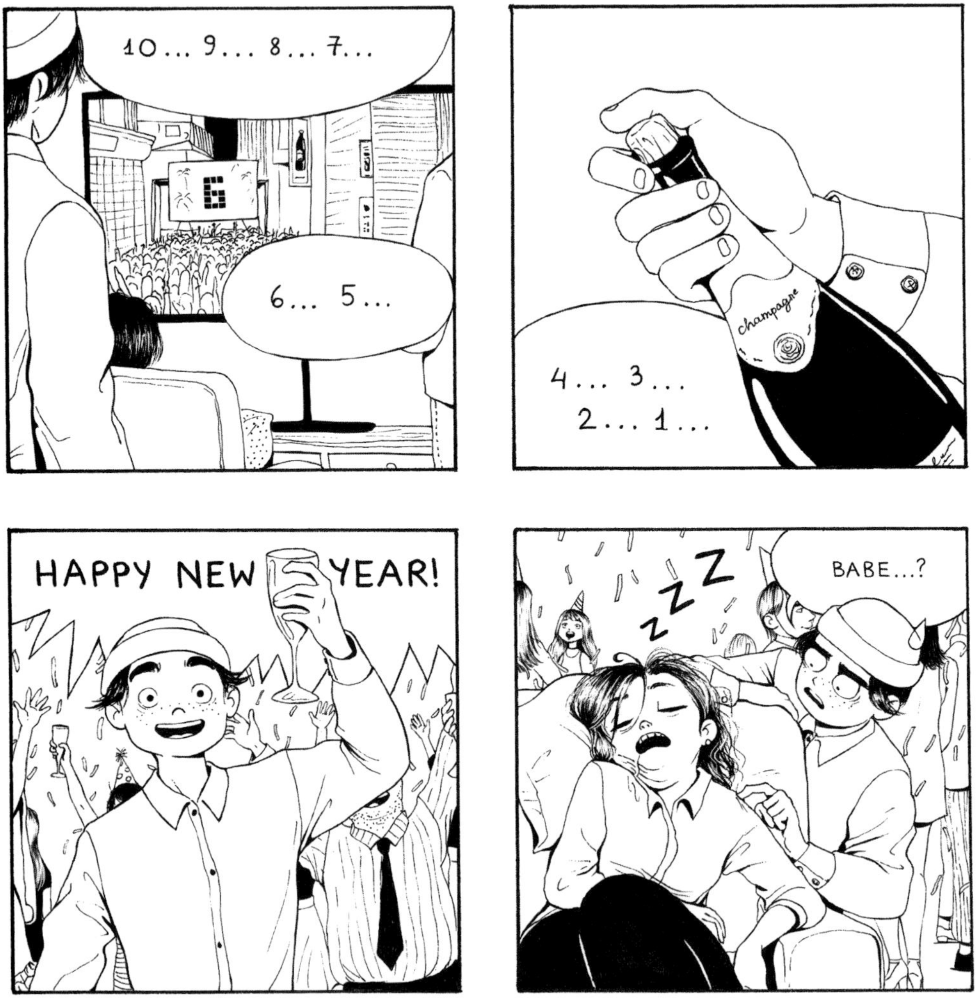
10... 9... 8... 7...
6... 5...
champagne
4... 3...
2... 1...
HAPPY NEW YEAR!
zZZ
BABE...?

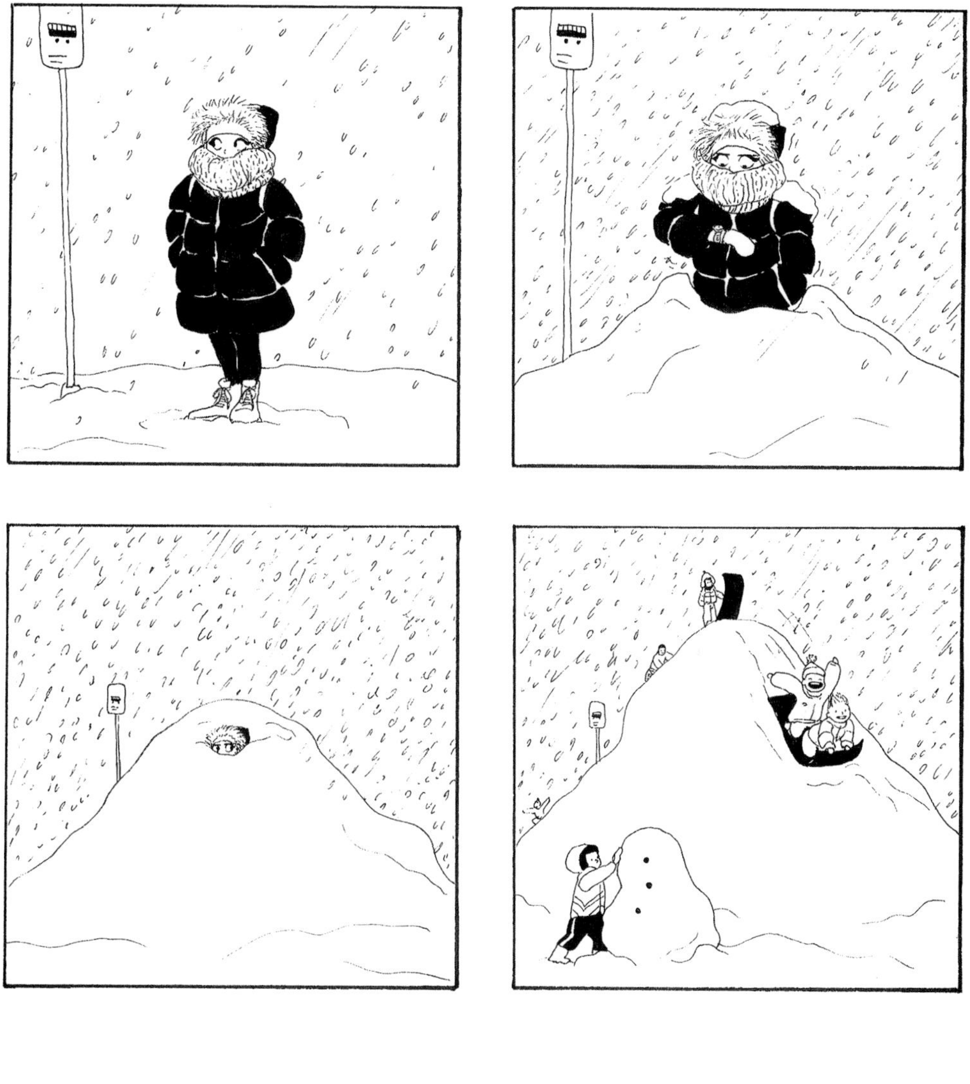

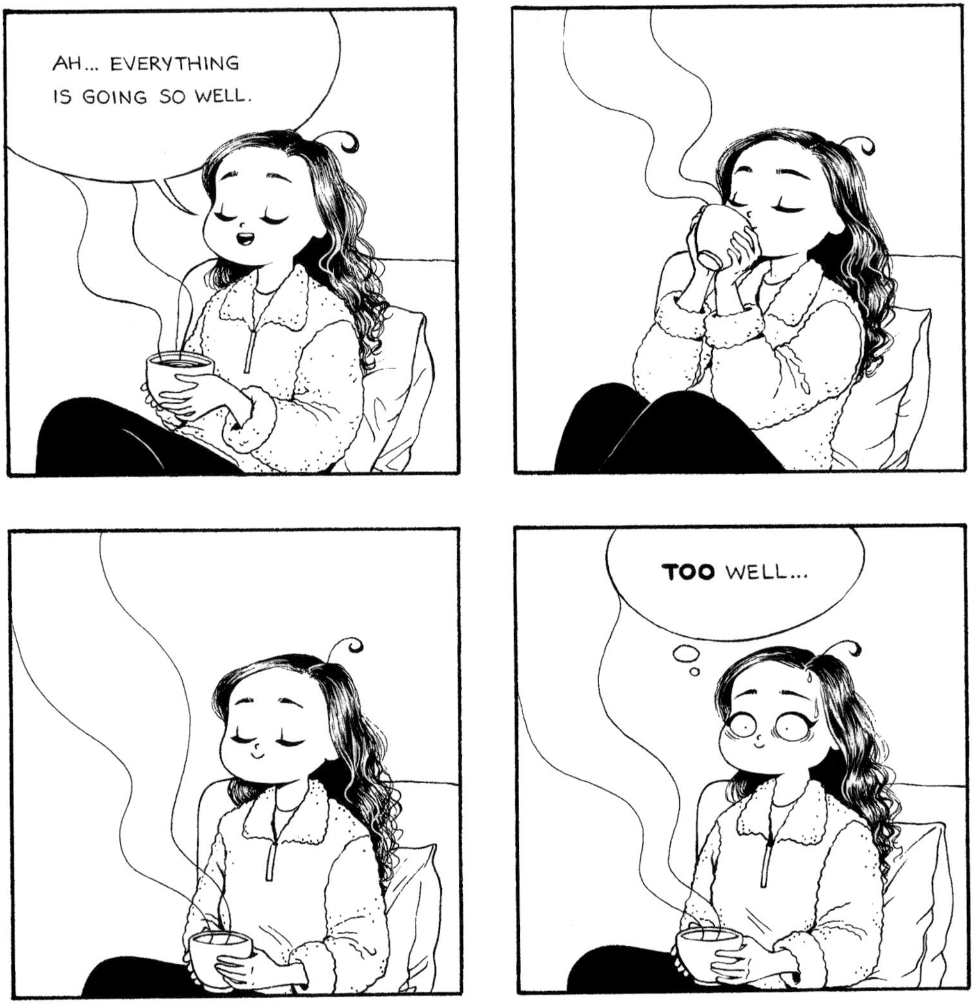
AH... EVERYTHING IS GOING SO WELL.
TOO WELL...

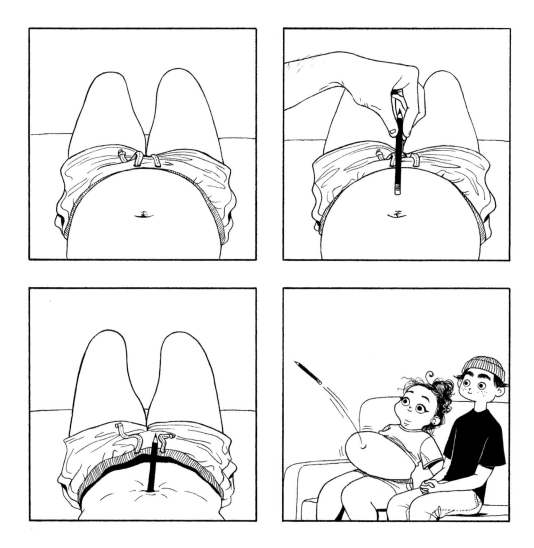

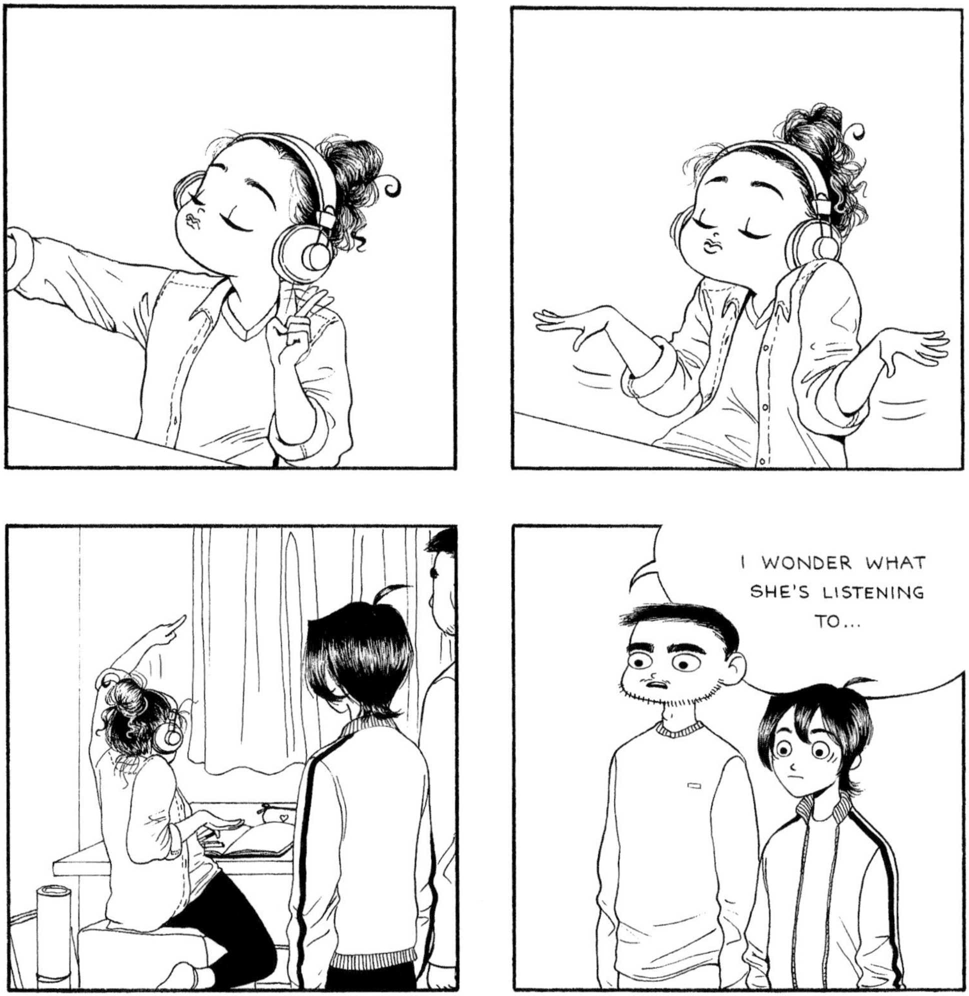
I WONDER WHAT SHE'S LISTENING TO...

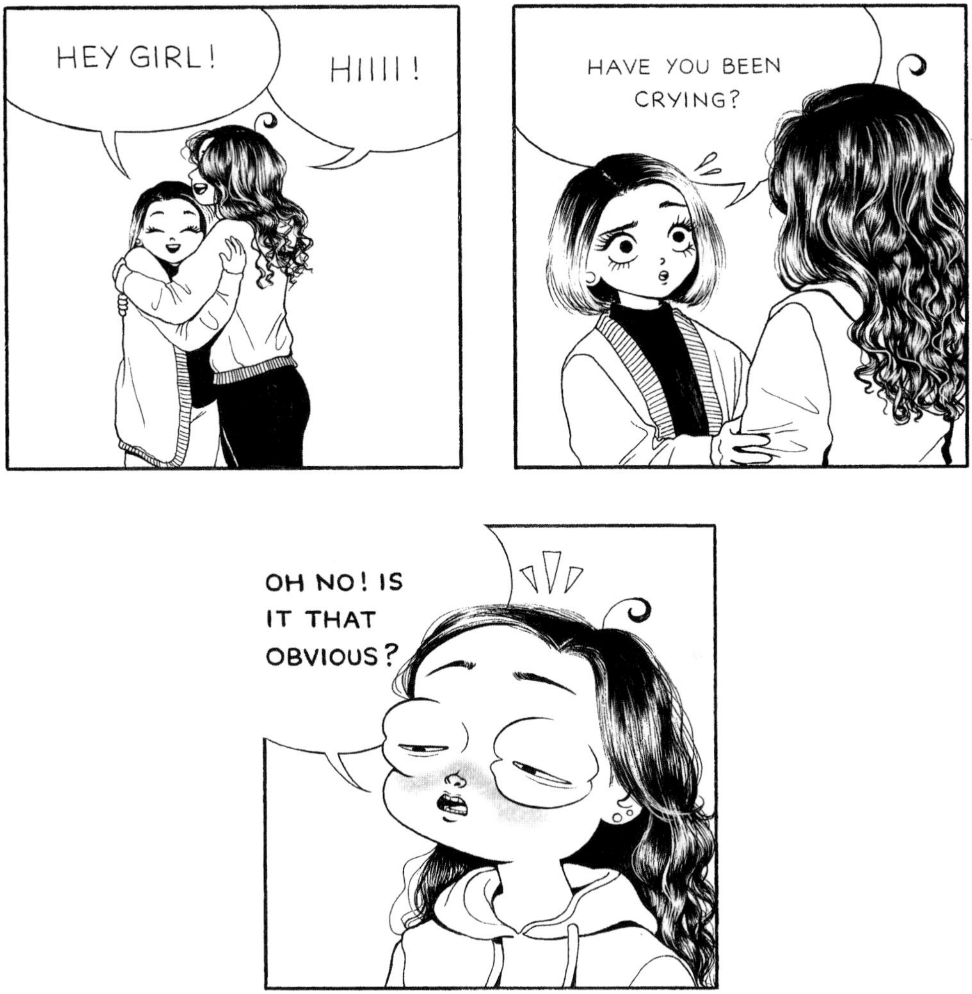
HEY GIRL!
HIIII!
HAVE YOU BEEN CRYING?
OH NO! IS IT THAT OBVIOUS?

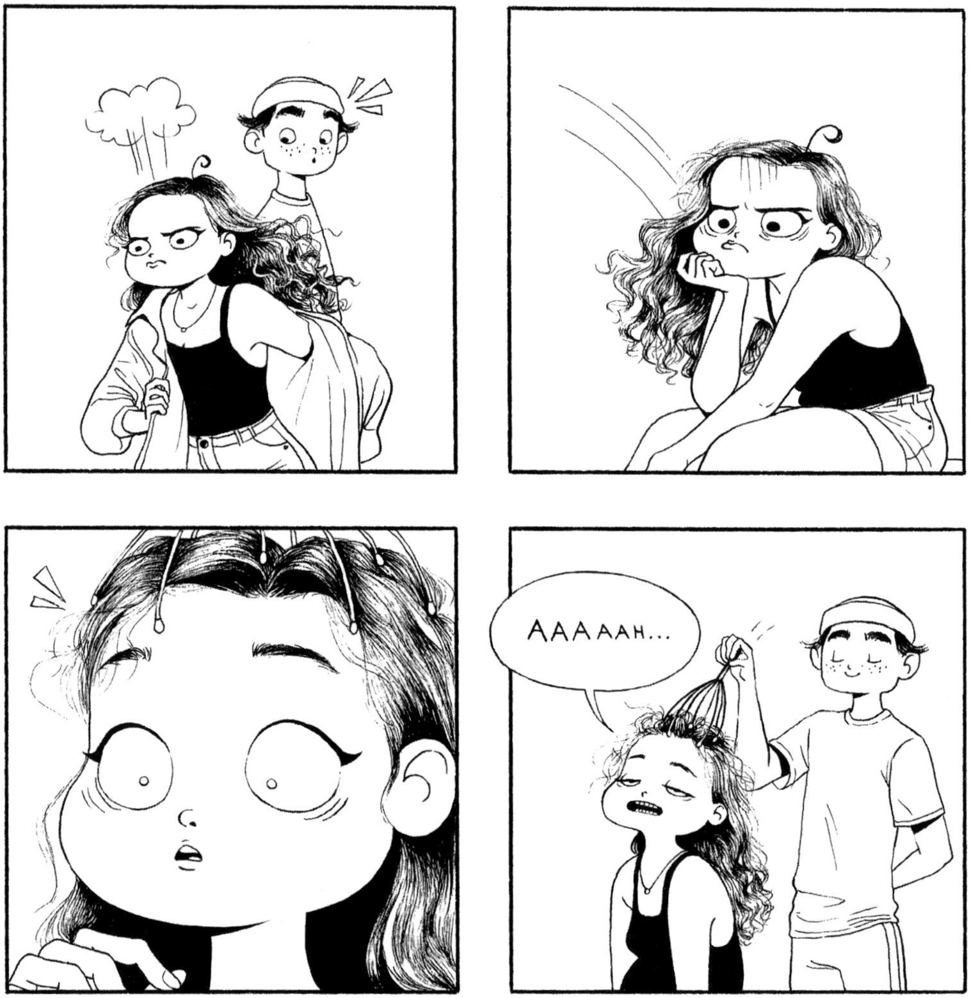
AAAAAH...

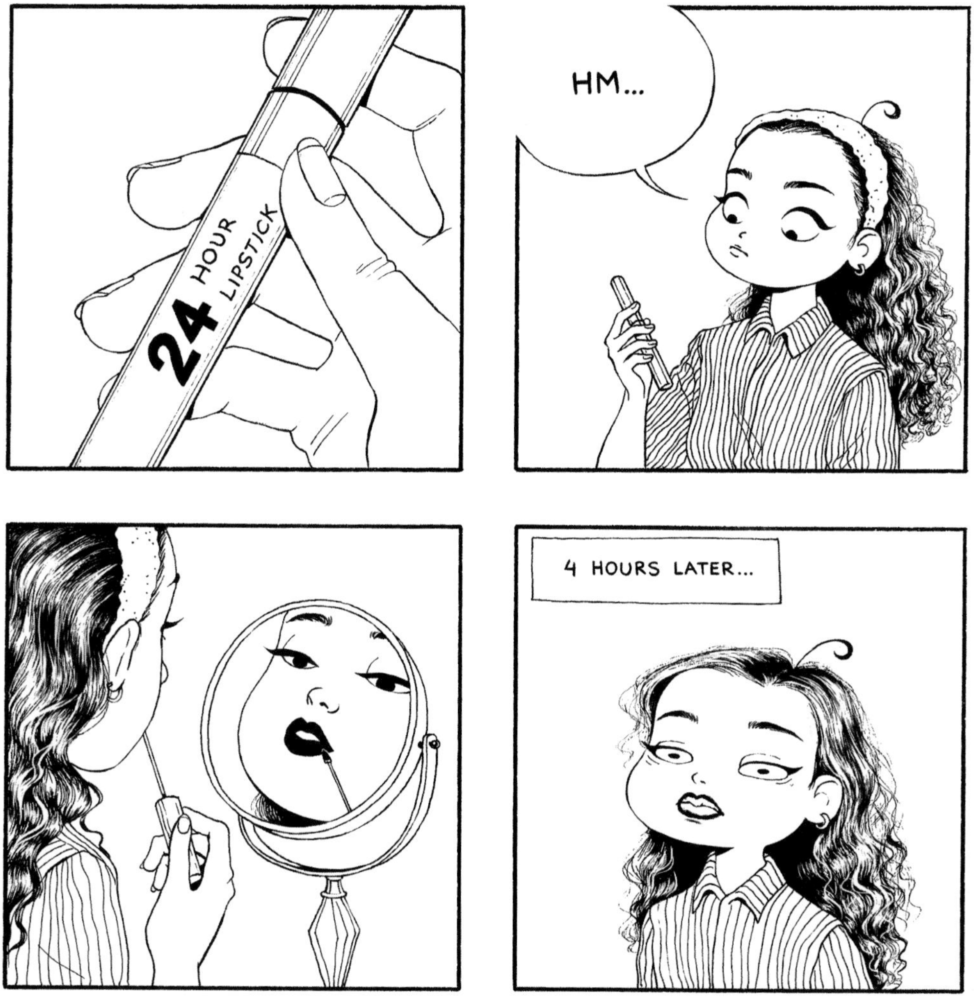
24 HOUR LIPSTICK
HM...
4 HOURS LATER...

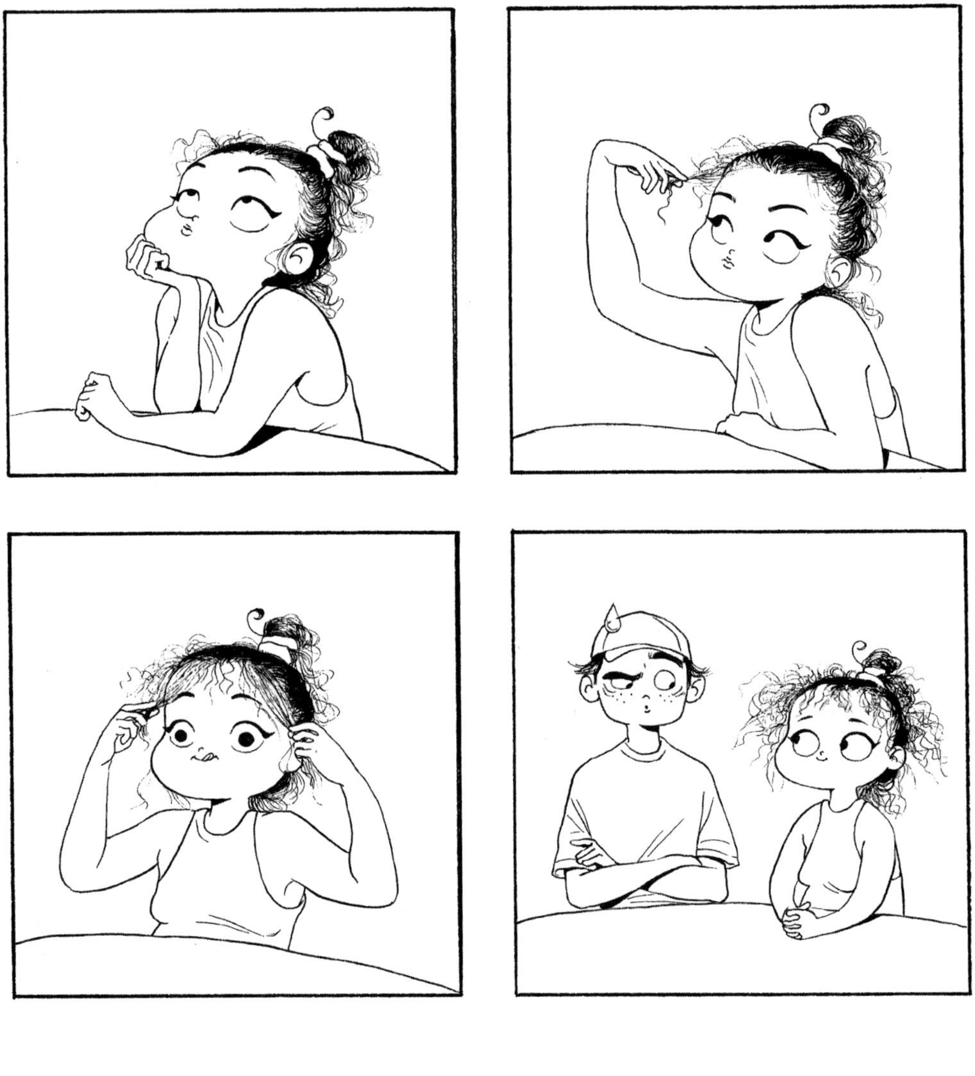

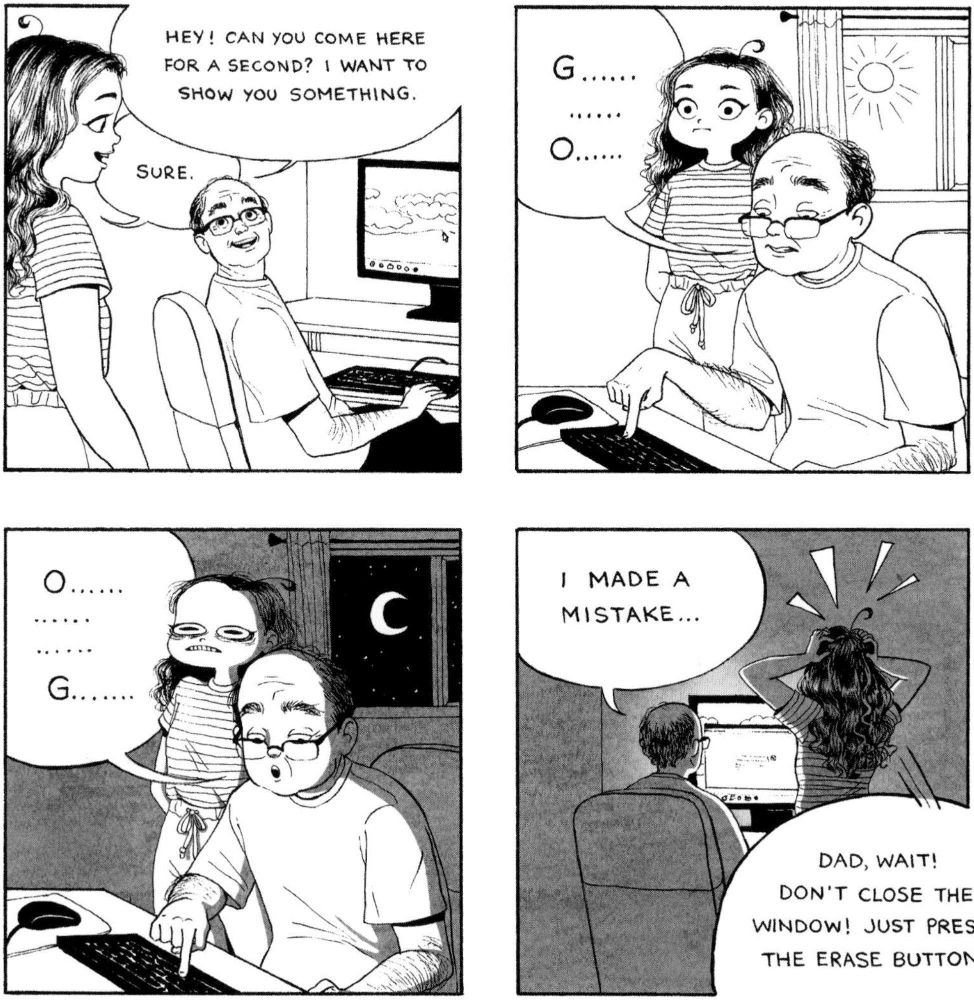
HEY! CAN YOU COME HERE FOR A SECOND? I WANT TO SHOW YOU SOMETHING.
SURE.
G...... ...... O......
O...... .... G.......
I MADE A MISTAKE...
DAD, WAIT! DON'T CLOSE THE WINDOW! JUST PRESS THE ERASE BUTTON!

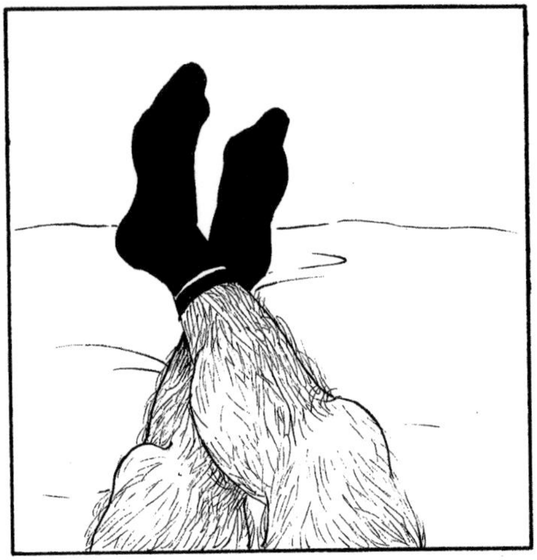
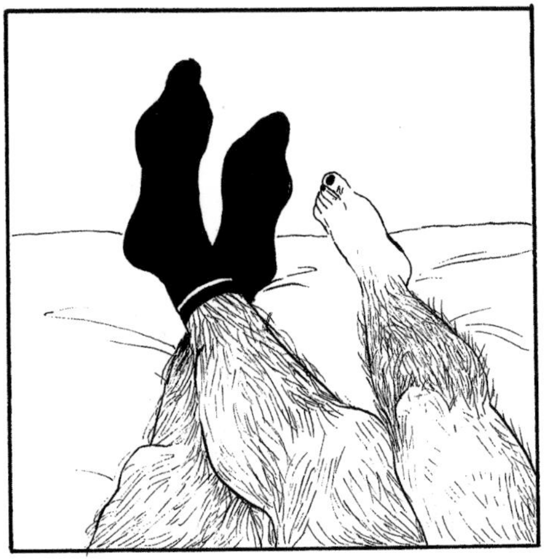
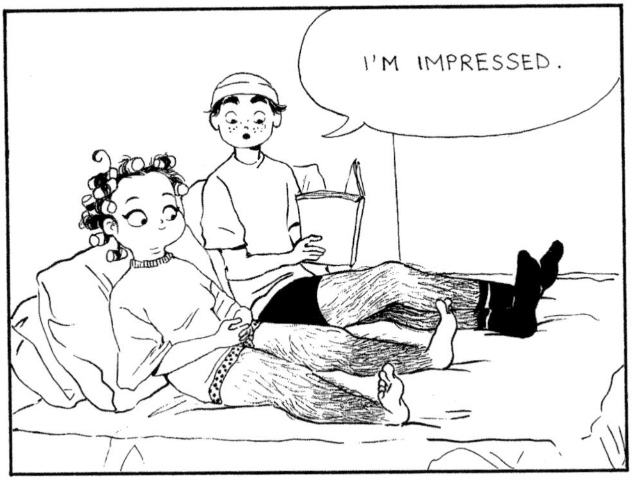
I'M IMPRESSED.

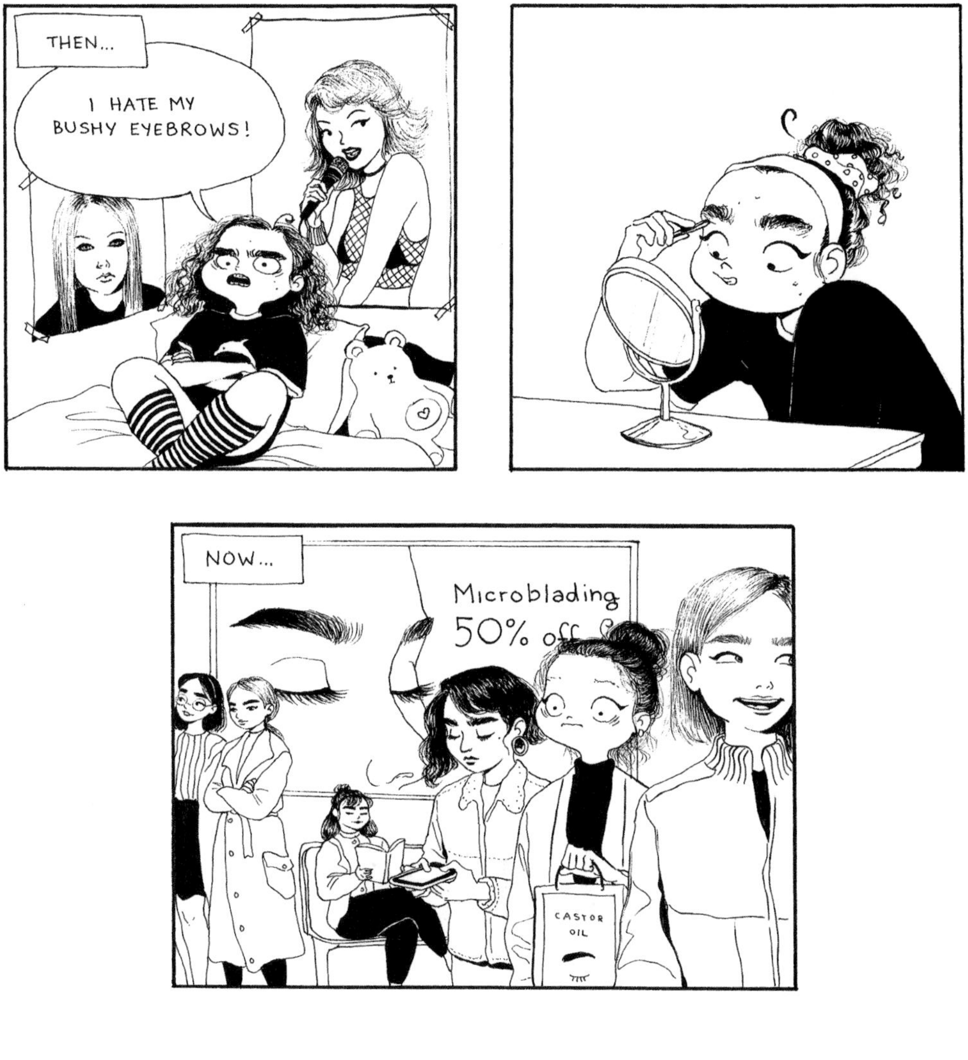
THEN...
I HATE MY BUSHY EYEBROWS!
NOW...
Microblading 50% off
CASTOR OIL

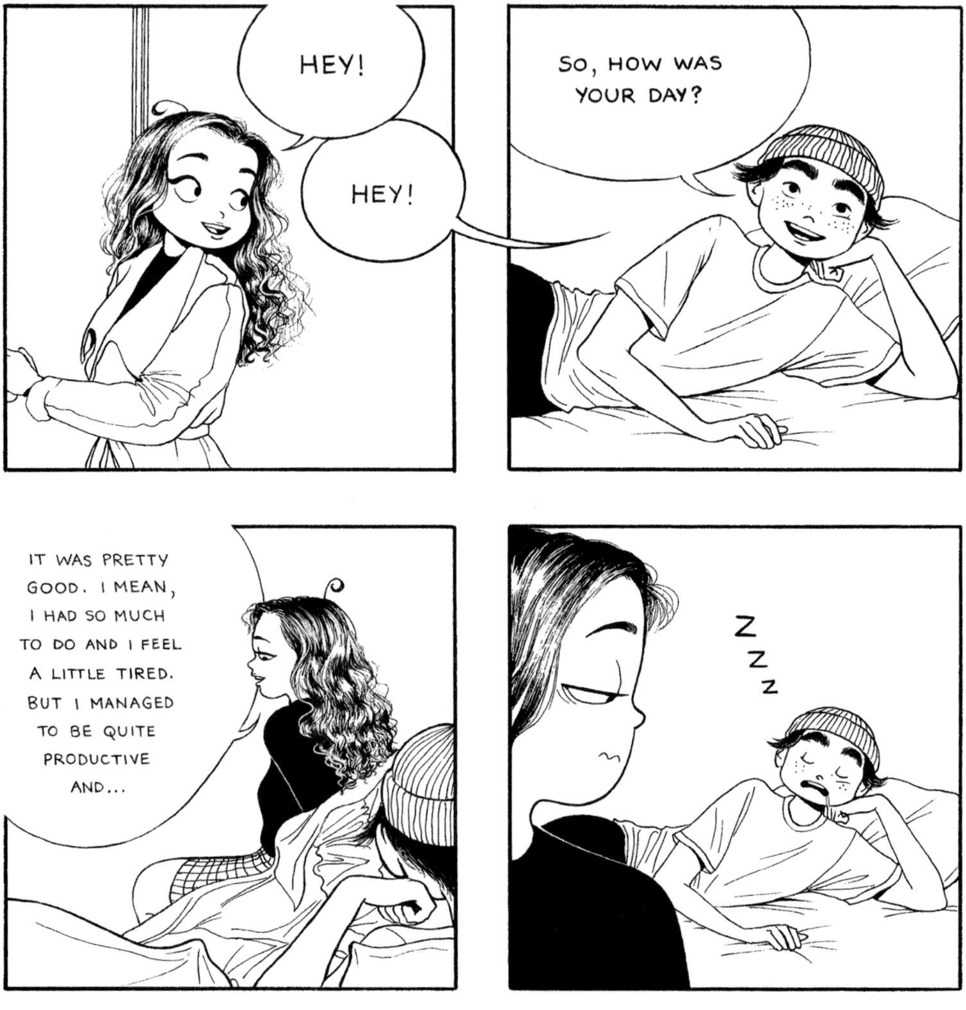
HEY!
HEY!
SO, HOW WAS YOUR DAY?
IT WAS PRETTY GOOD. I MEAN, I HAD SO MUCH TO DO AND I FEEL A LITTLE TIRED. BUT I MANAGED TO BE QUITE PRODUCTIVE AND...
Z Z Z

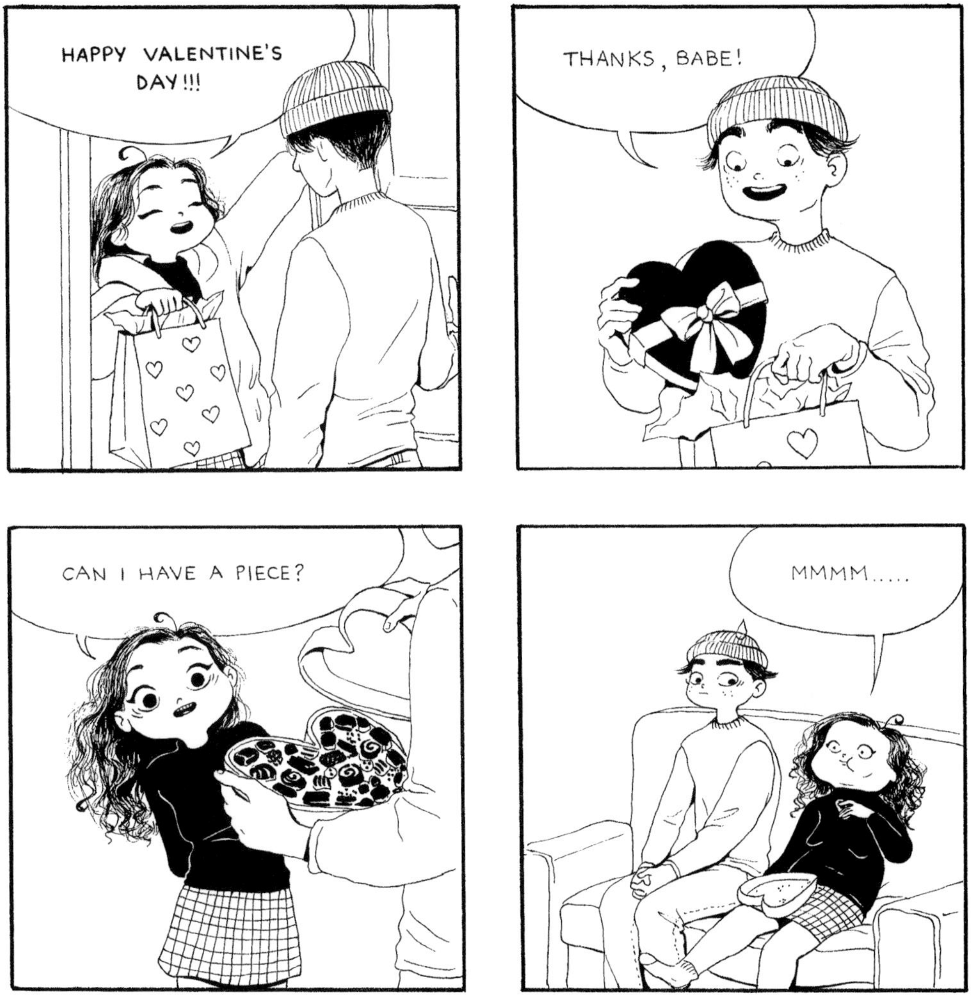
HAPPY VALENTINE'S DAY!!!
THANKS, BABE!
CAN I HAVE A PIECE?
MMMM.....

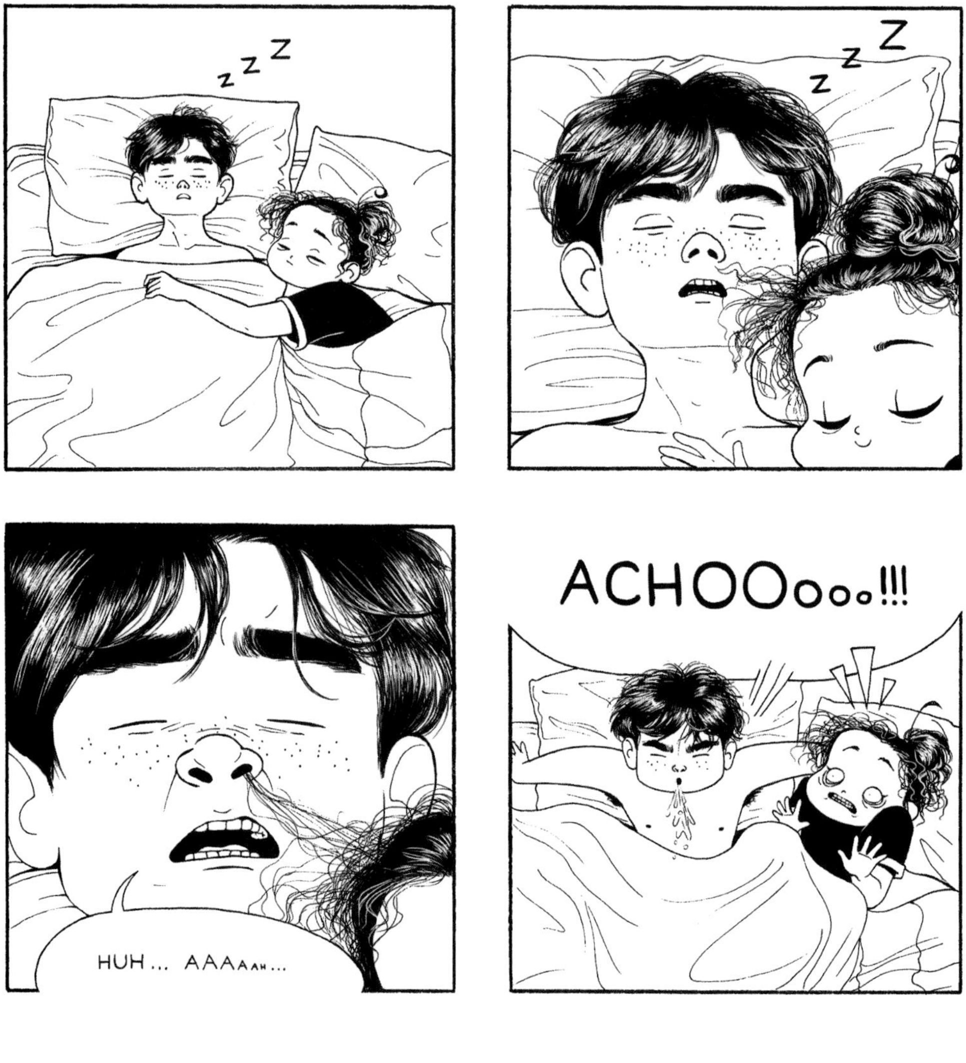
z z Z
z z Z
HUH... AAAaah...
ACHOOooo!!!

LOW CUT SWIMSUIT

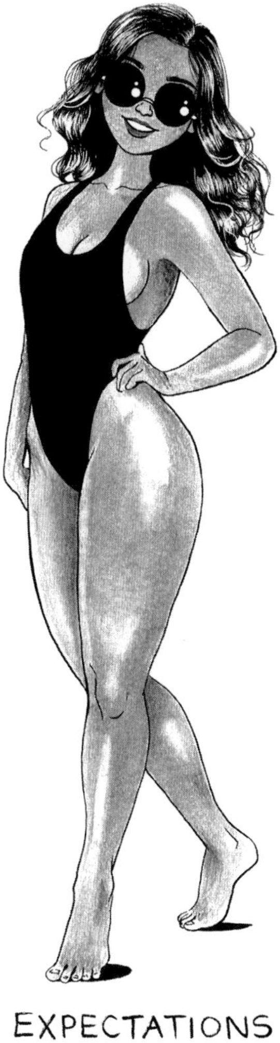

EXPECTATIONS

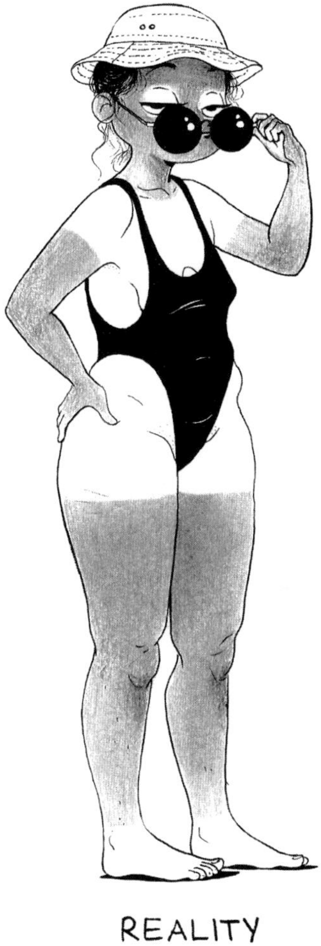

REALITY

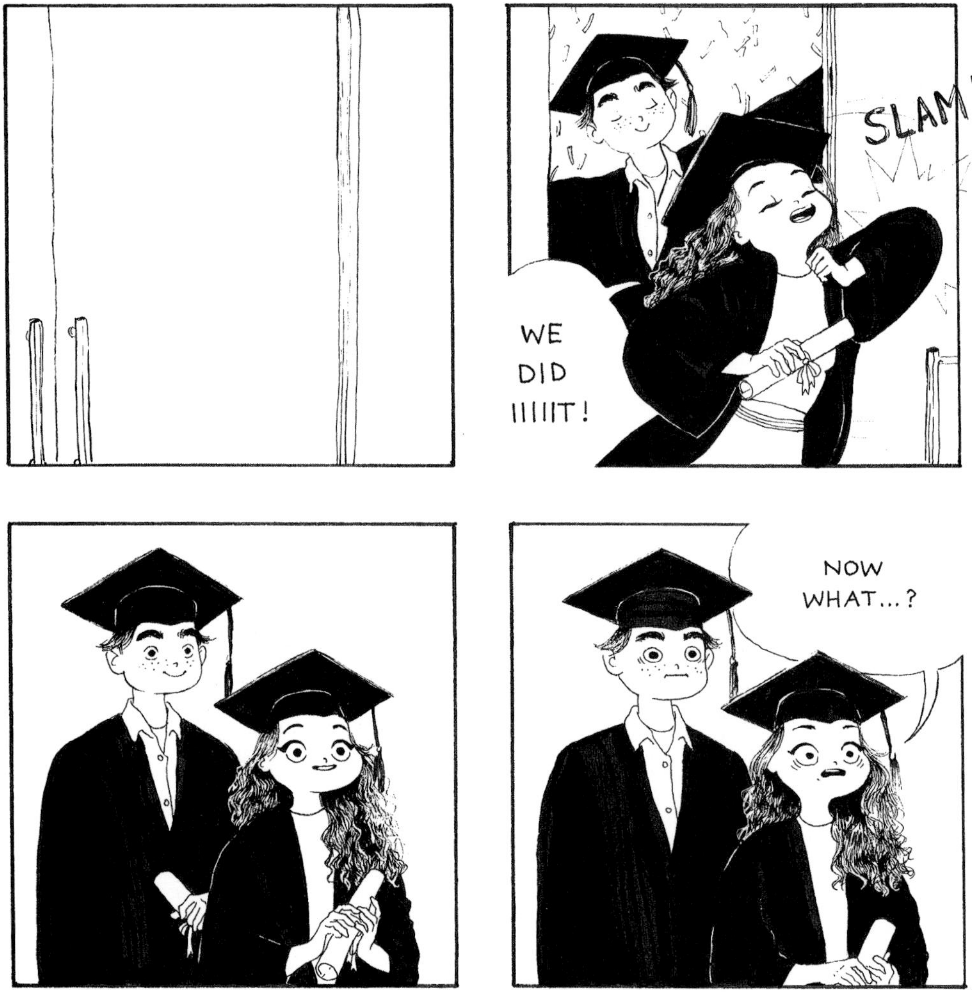
SLAM!
WE DID IIIIIT!
NOW WHAT...?

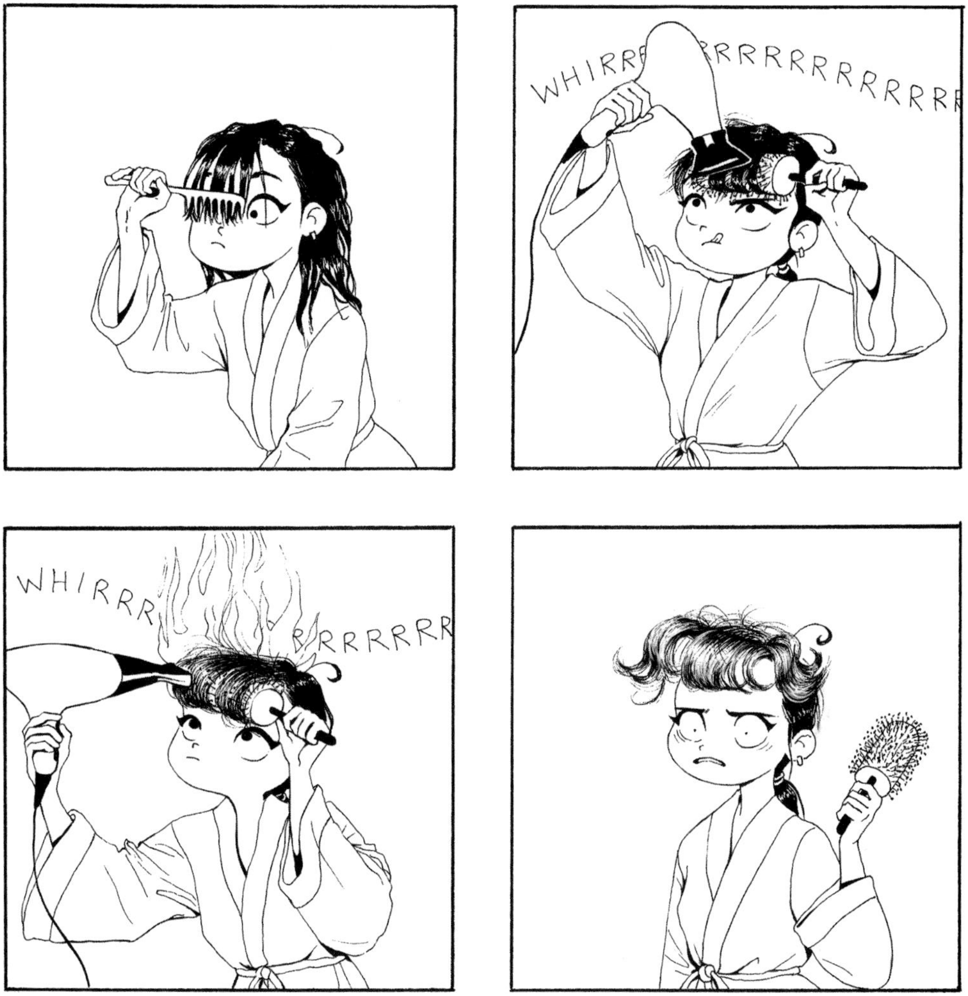
WHIRRRRRRRRRRRRRR
WHIRRR RRRRRRR

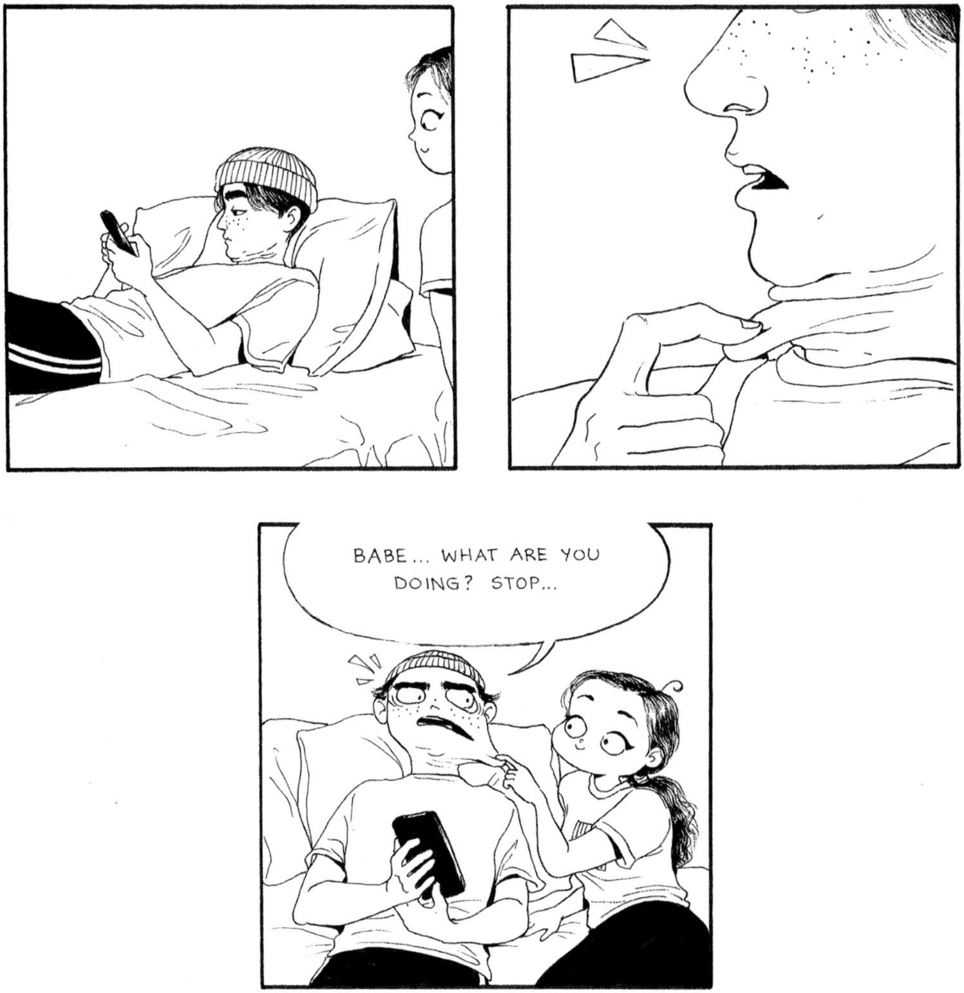
BABE... WHAT ARE YOU DOING? STOP...

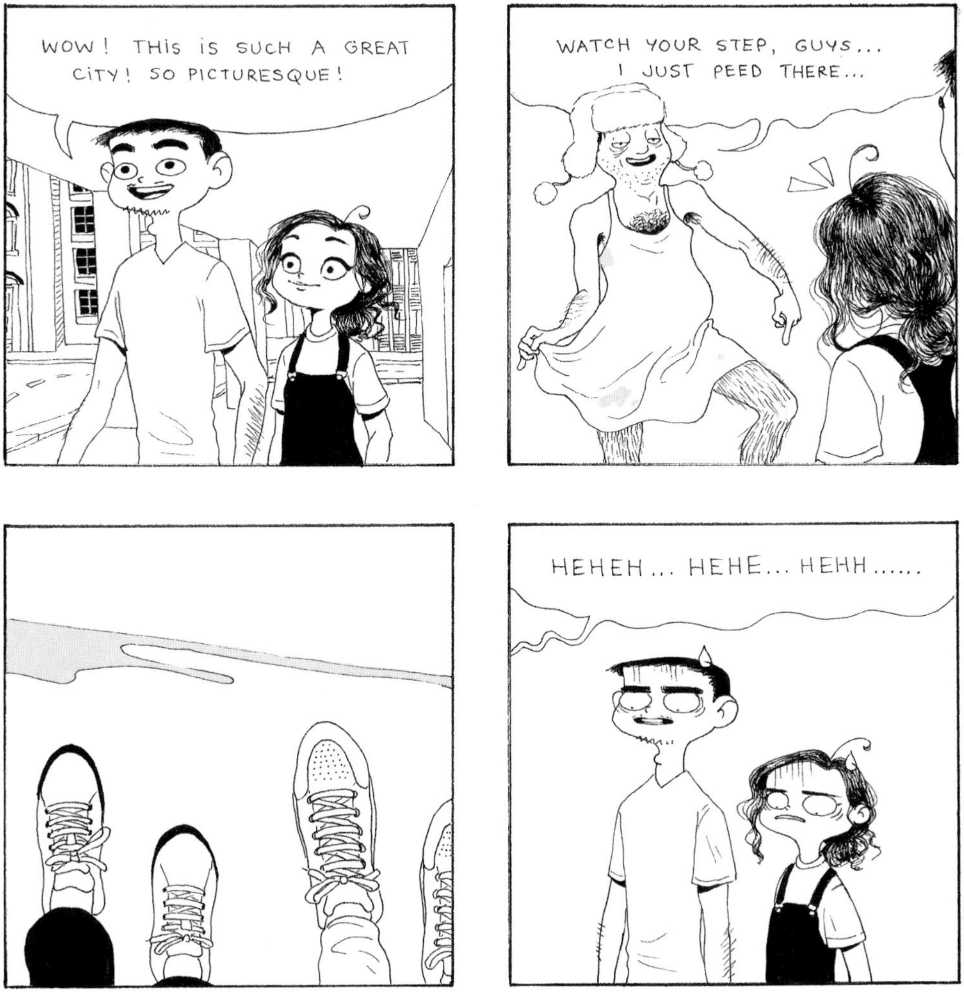
WOW! THIS IS SUCH A GREAT CITY! SO PICTURESQUE!
WATCH YOUR STEP, GUYS... I JUST PEED THERE...
HEHEH... HEHE... HEHH......

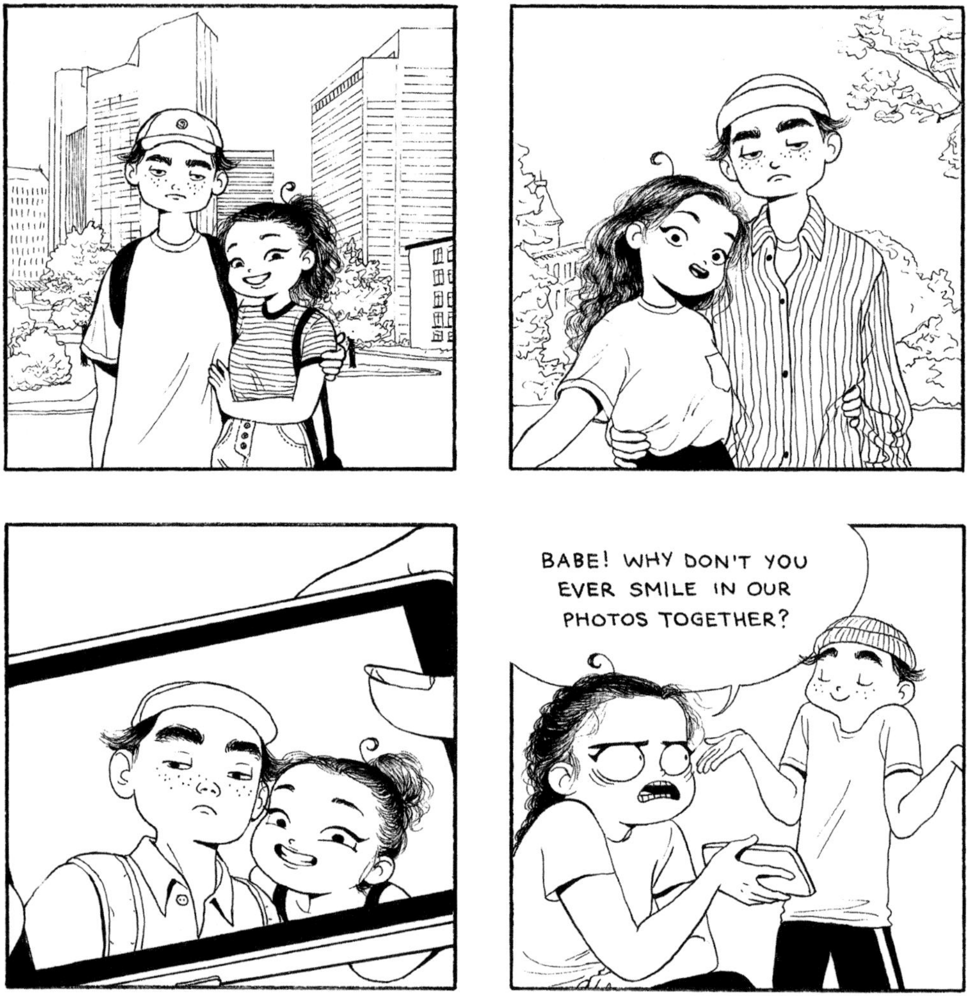
BABE! WHY DON'T YOU EVER SMILE IN OUR PHOTOS TOGETHER?

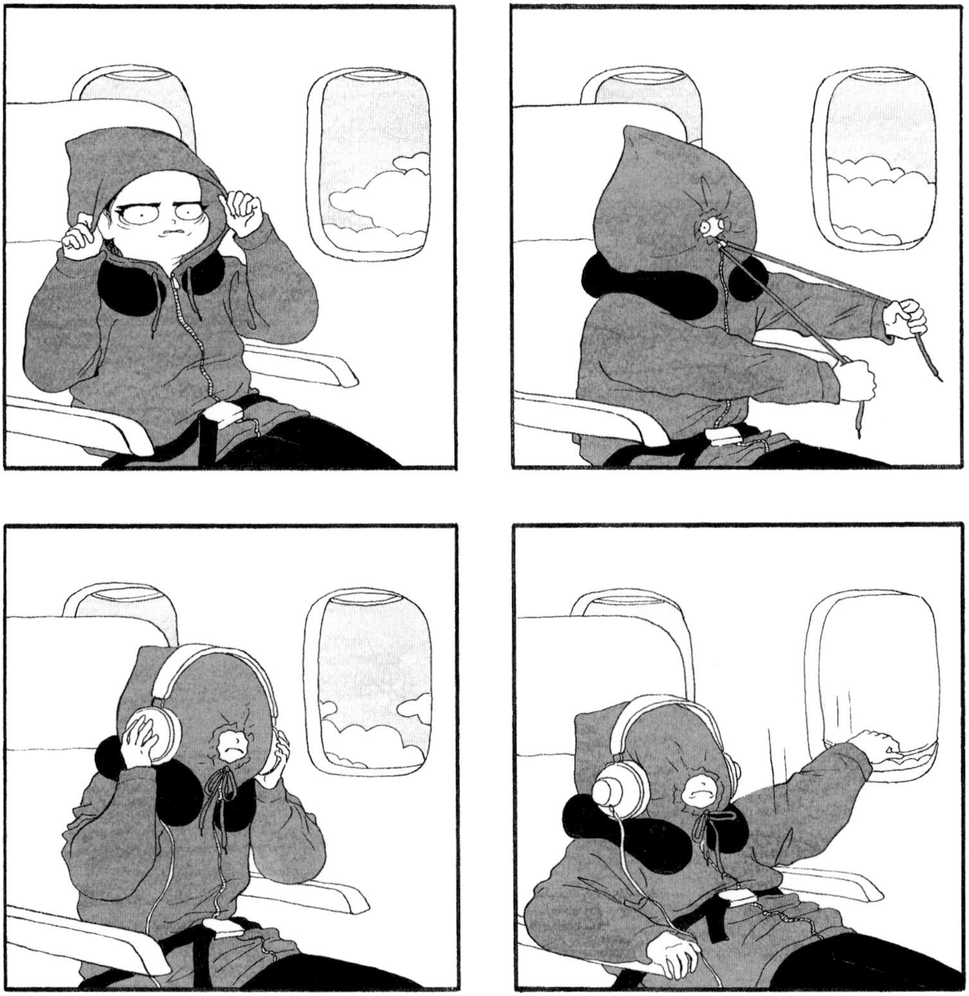

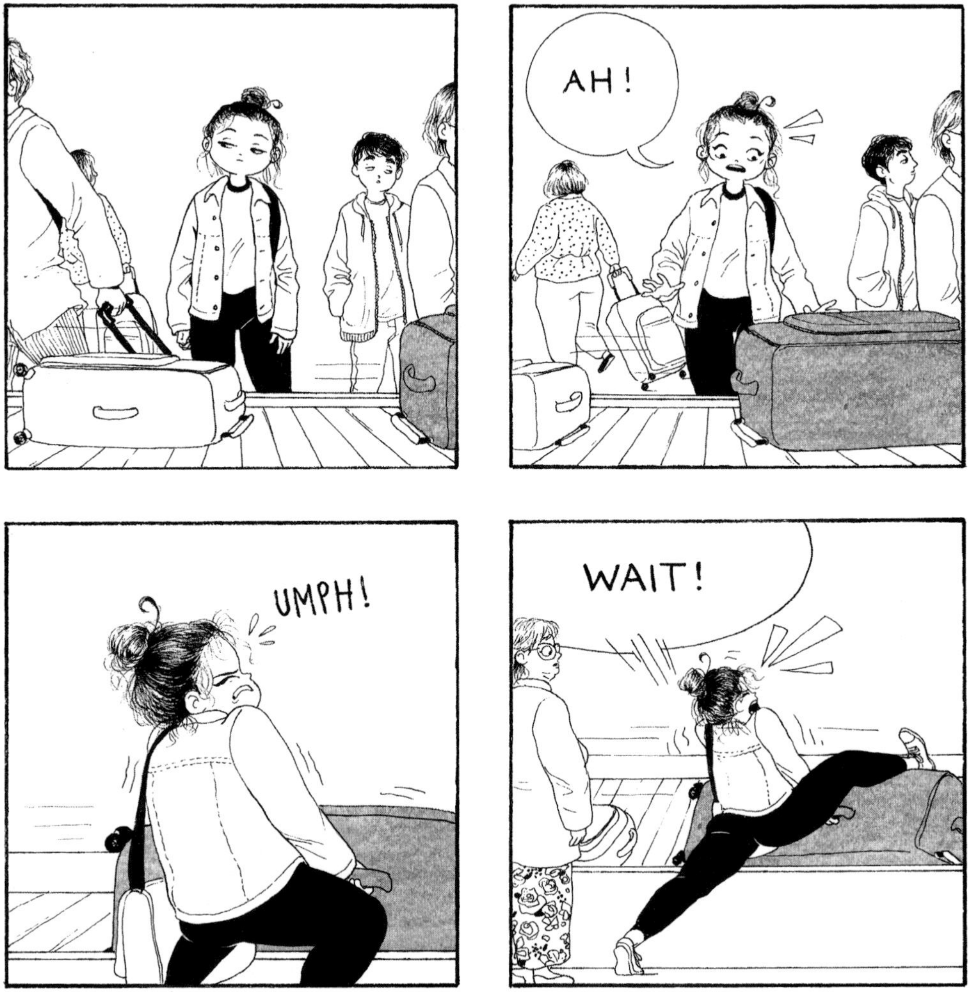
AH!
UMPH!
WAIT!

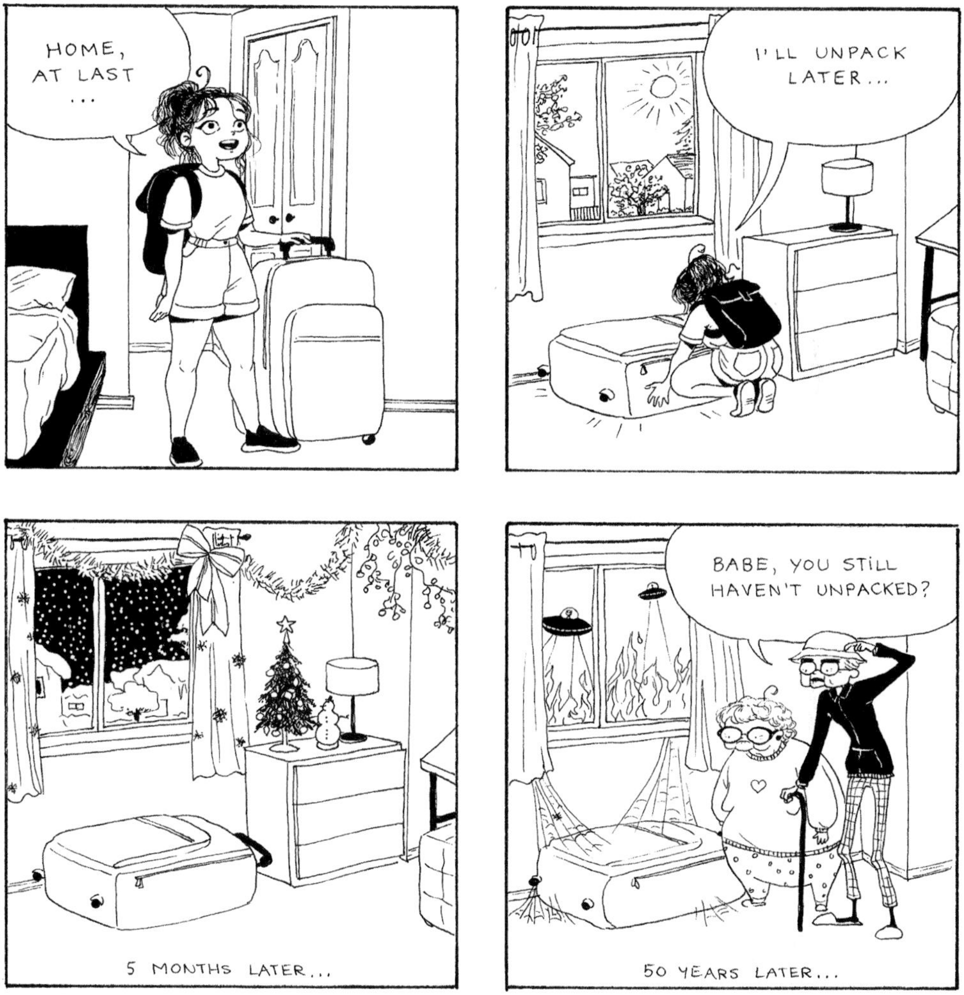
HOME, AT LAST ...
I'LL UNPACK LATER...
5 MONTHS LATER...
BABE, YOU STILL HAVEN'T UNPACKED?
50 YEARS LATER...

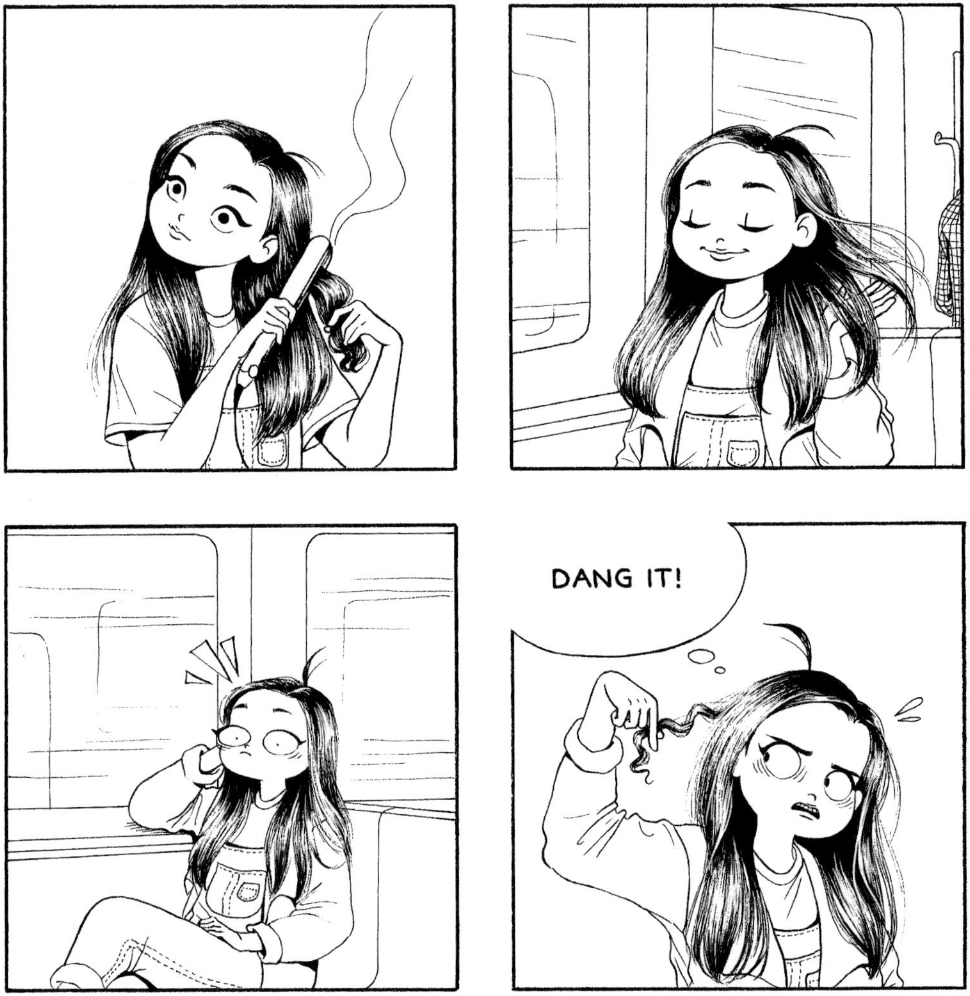
DANG IT!

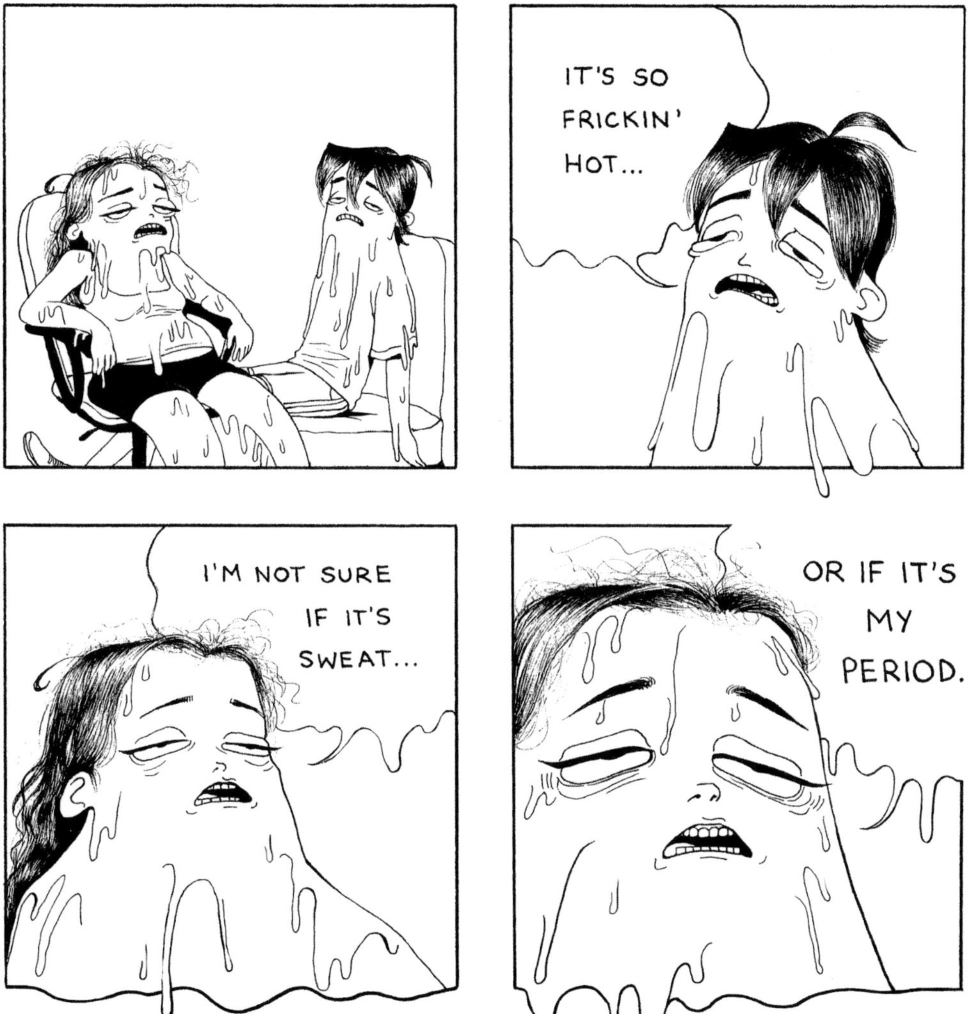
IT'S SO FRICKIN' HOT...
I'M NOT SURE IF IT'S SWEAT...
OR IF IT'S MY PERIOD.

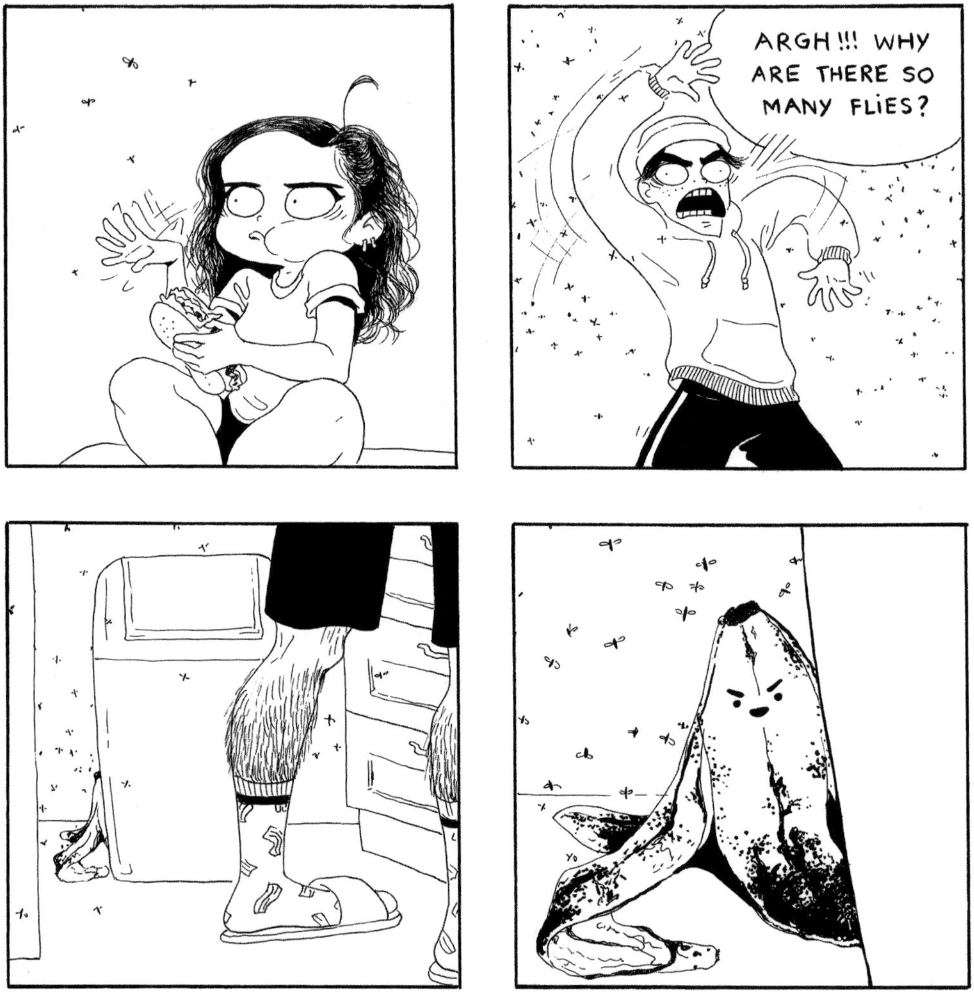
ARGH!!! WHY ARE THERE SO MANY FLIES?

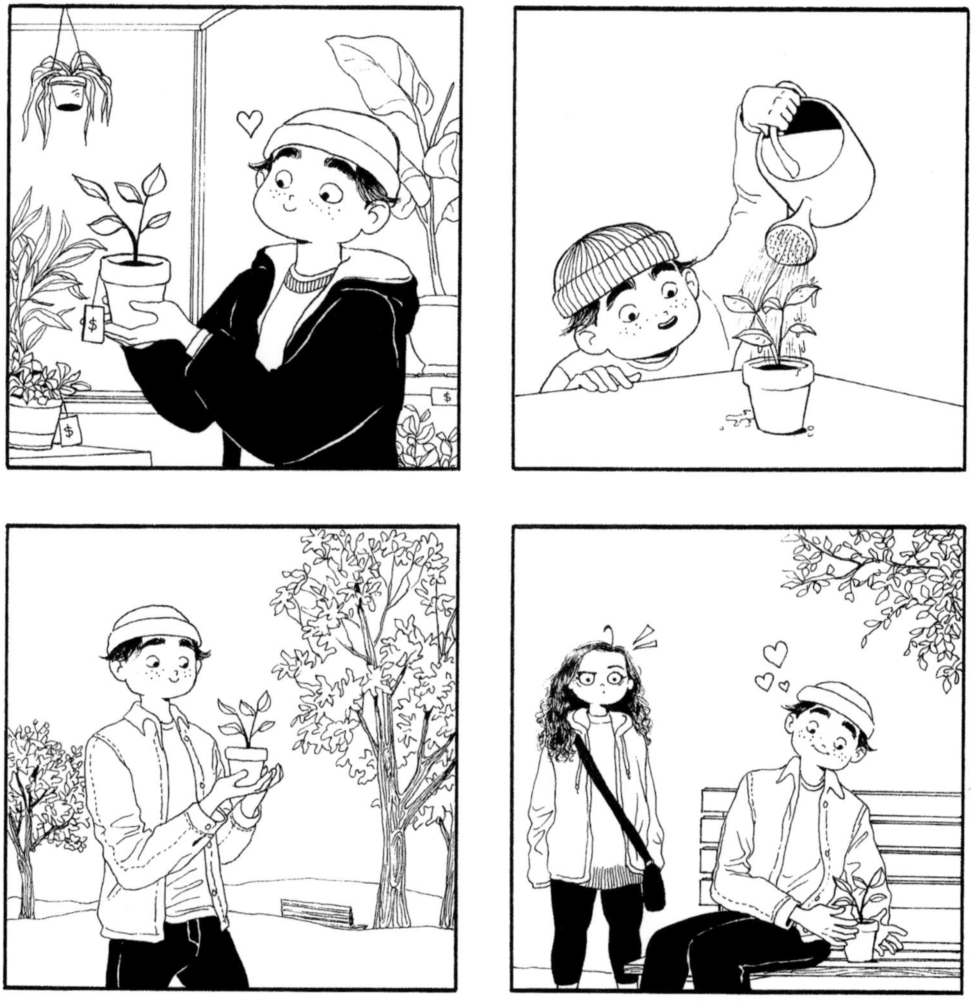
$
$
$

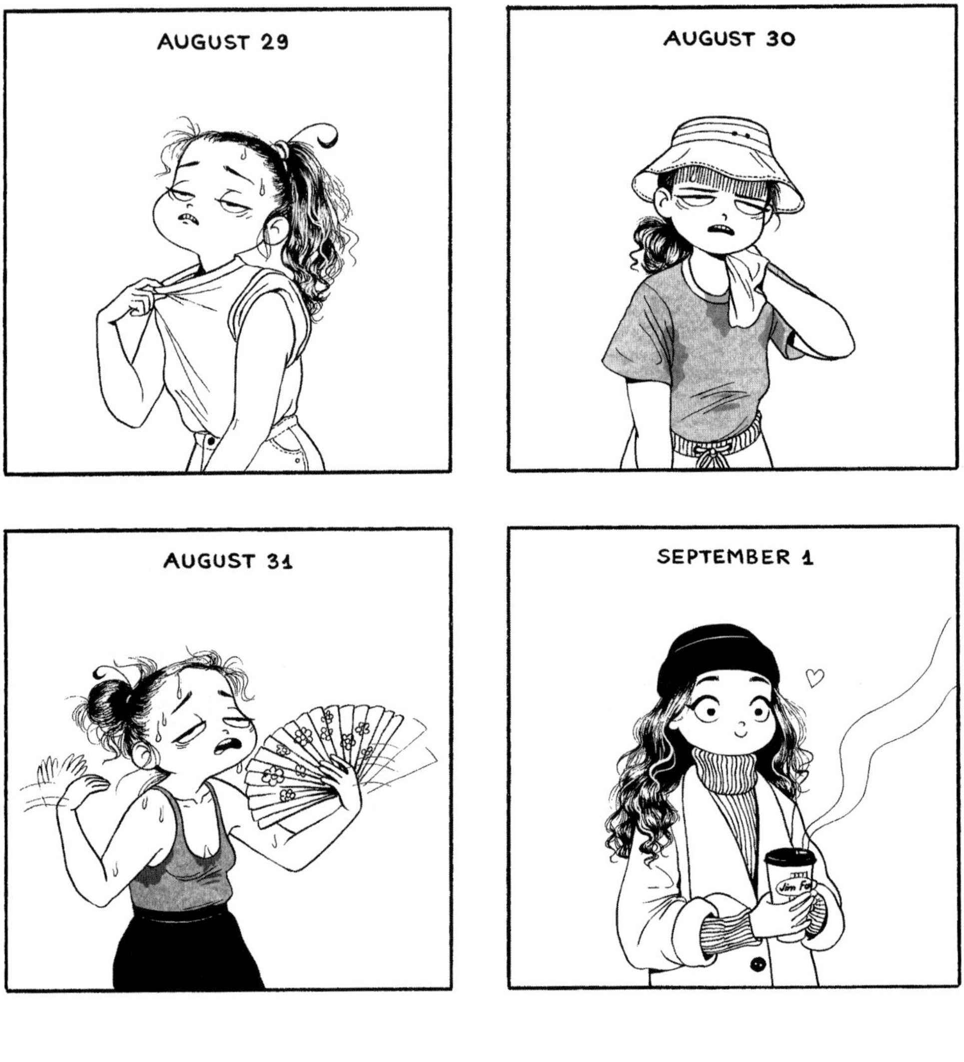
AUGUST 29
AUGUST 30
AUGUST 31
SEPTEMBER 1

SPANISH CHIGNON

EXPECTATIONS   REALITY

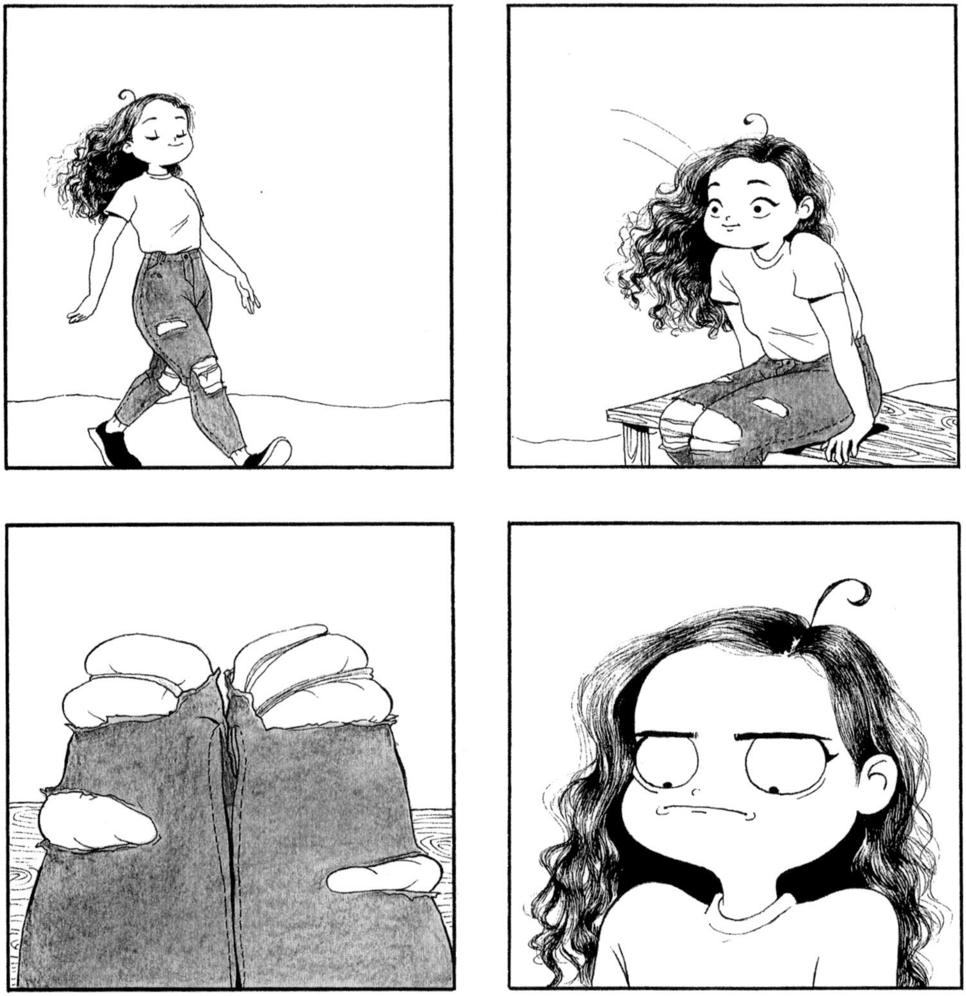

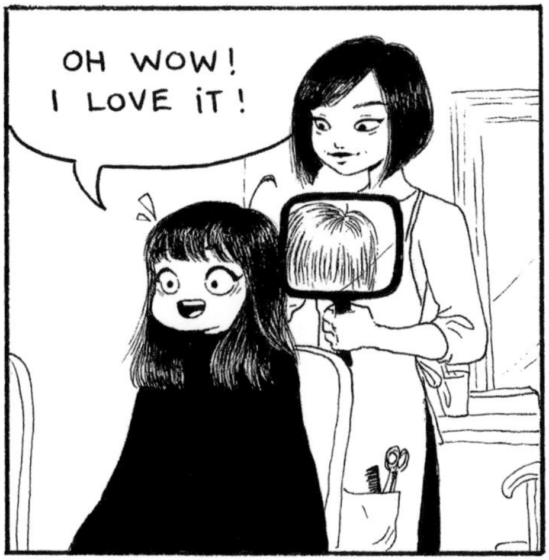
OH WOW! I LOVE IT!

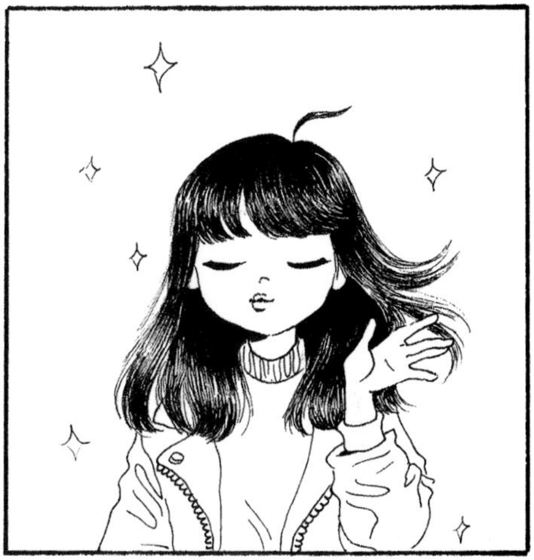

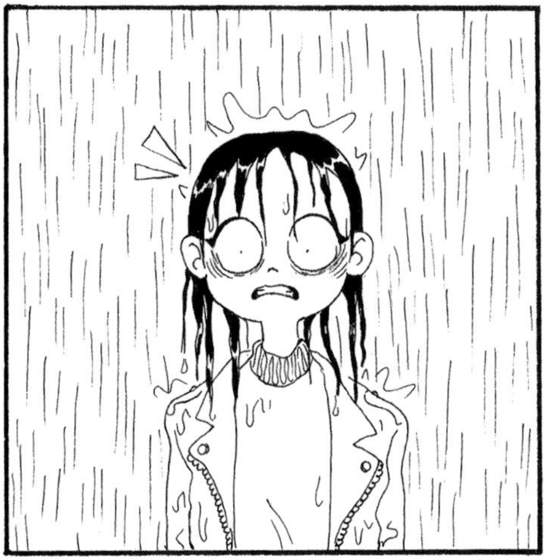

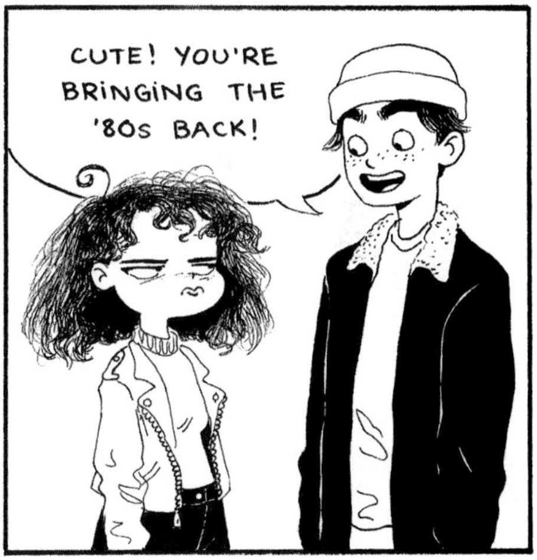
CUTE! YOU'RE BRINGING THE '80S BACK!

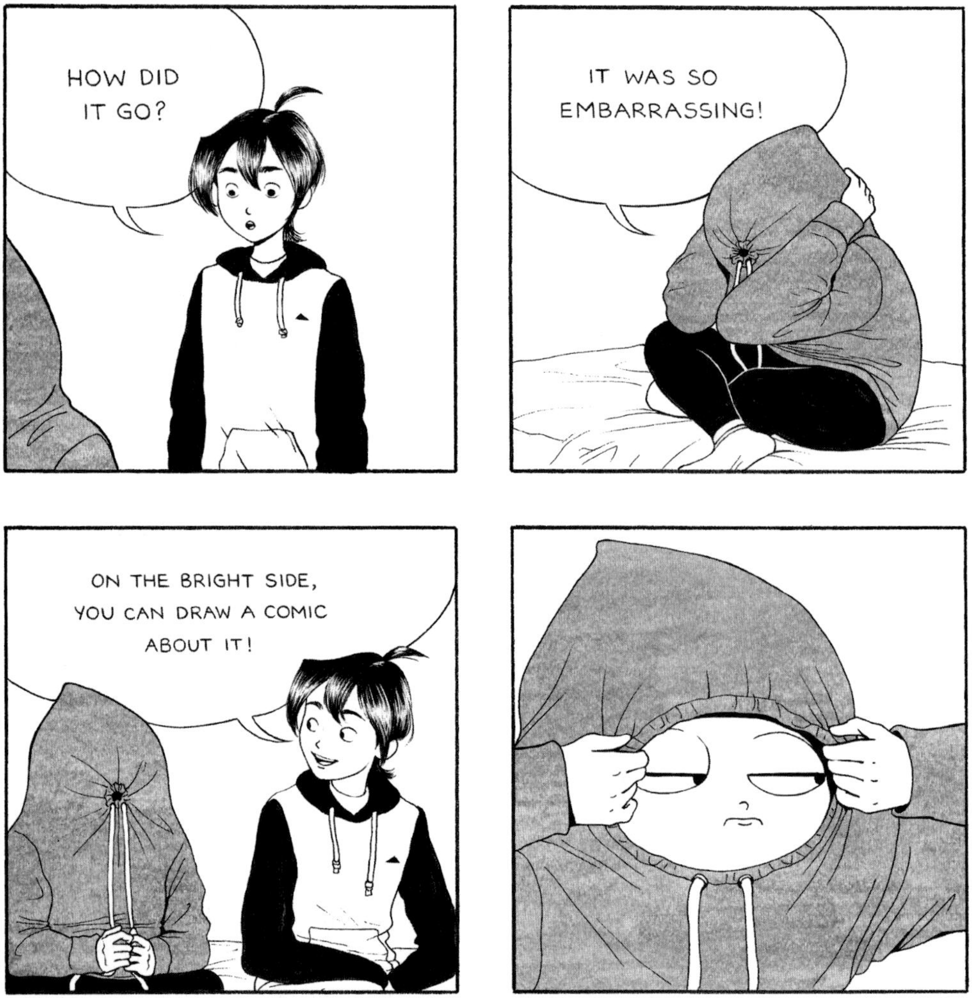
HOW DID IT GO?
IT WAS SO EMBARRASSING!
ON THE BRIGHT SIDE, YOU CAN DRAW A COMIC ABOUT IT!

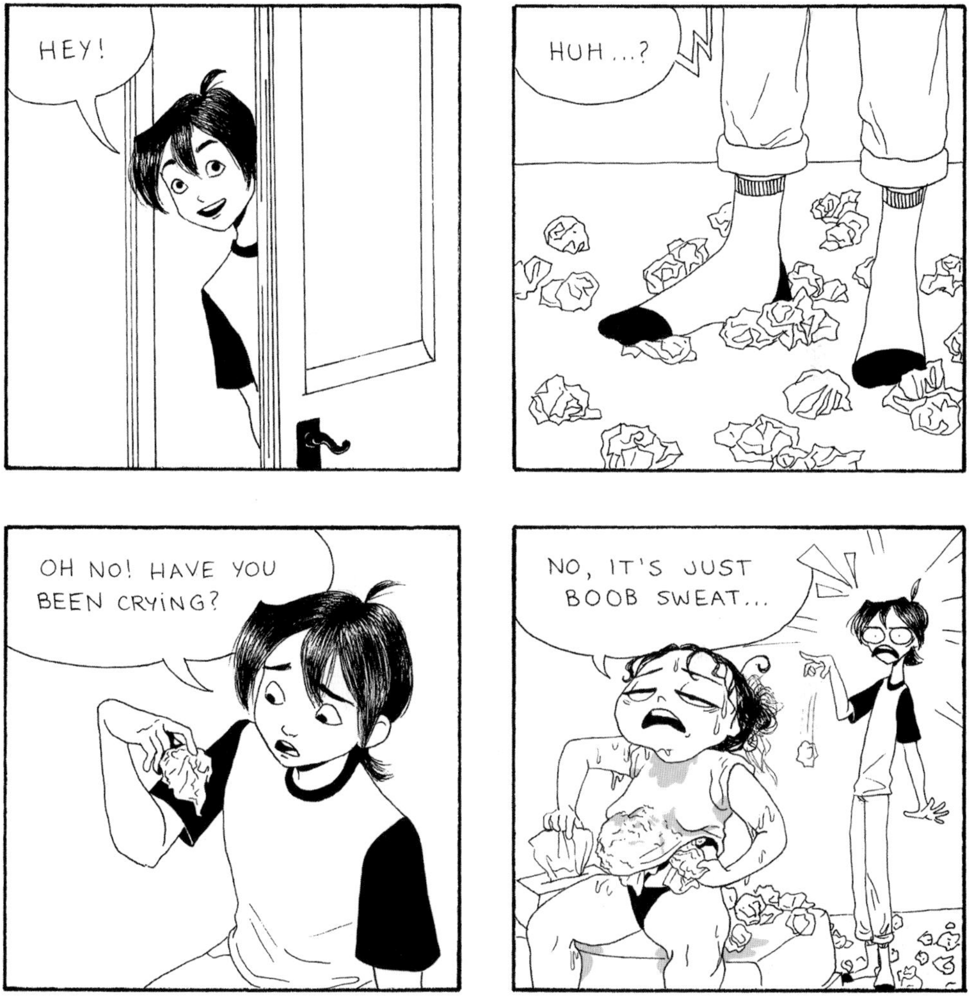
HEY!
HUH...?
OH NO! HAVE YOU BEEN CRYING?
NO, IT'S JUST BOOB SWEAT...

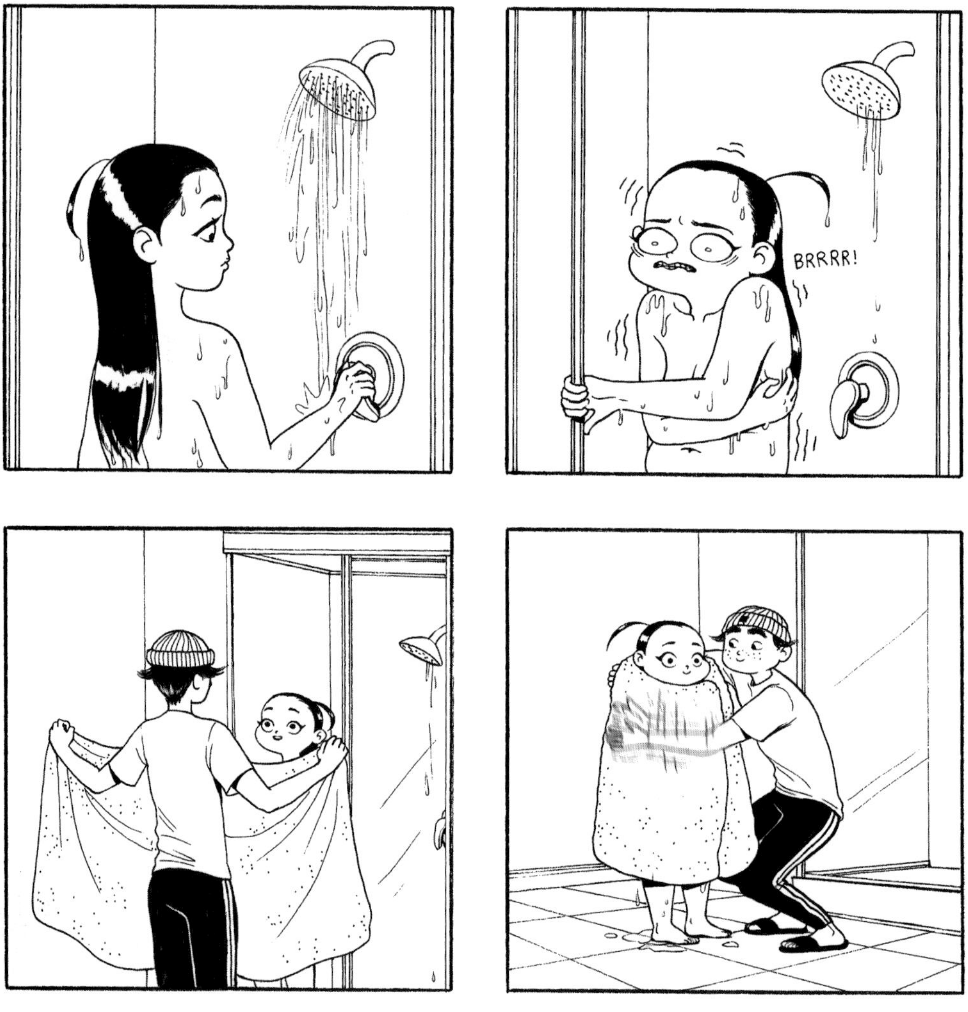
BRRRR!

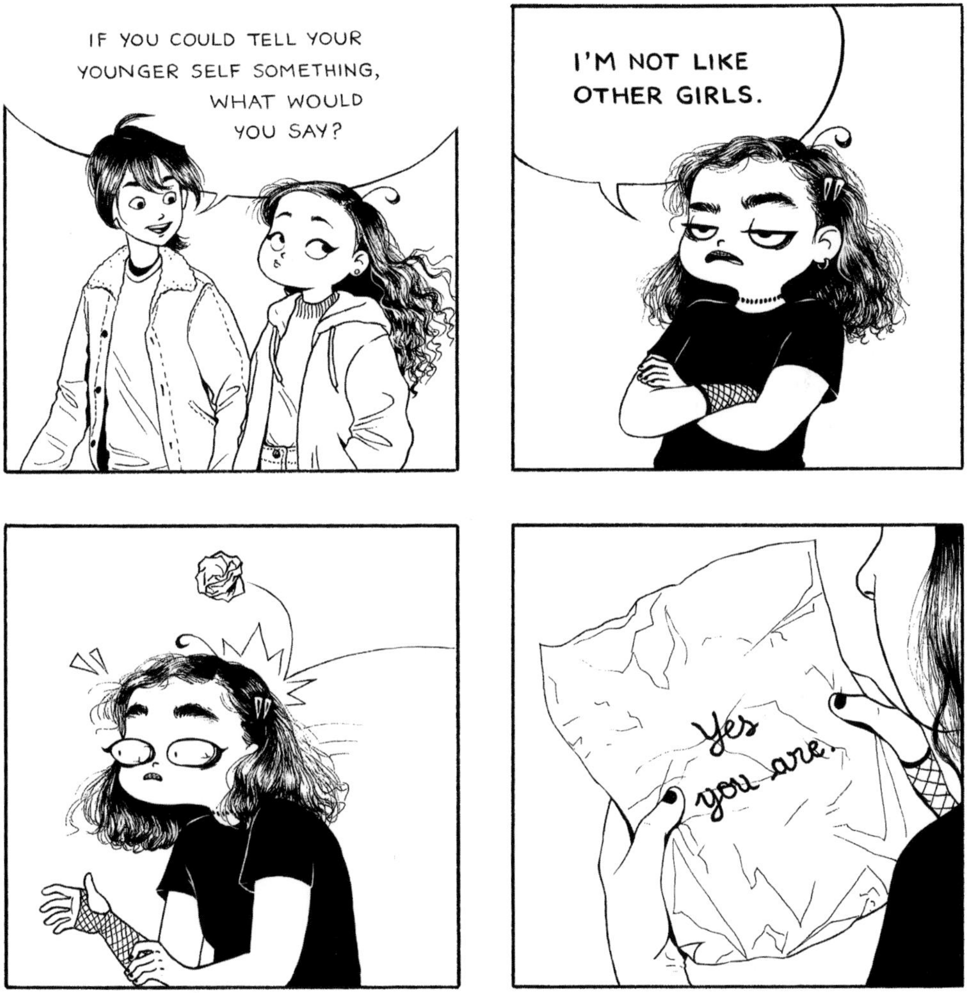
IF YOU COULD TELL YOUR YOUNGER SELF SOMETHING, WHAT WOULD YOU SAY?
I'M NOT LIKE OTHER GIRLS.
Yes you are.

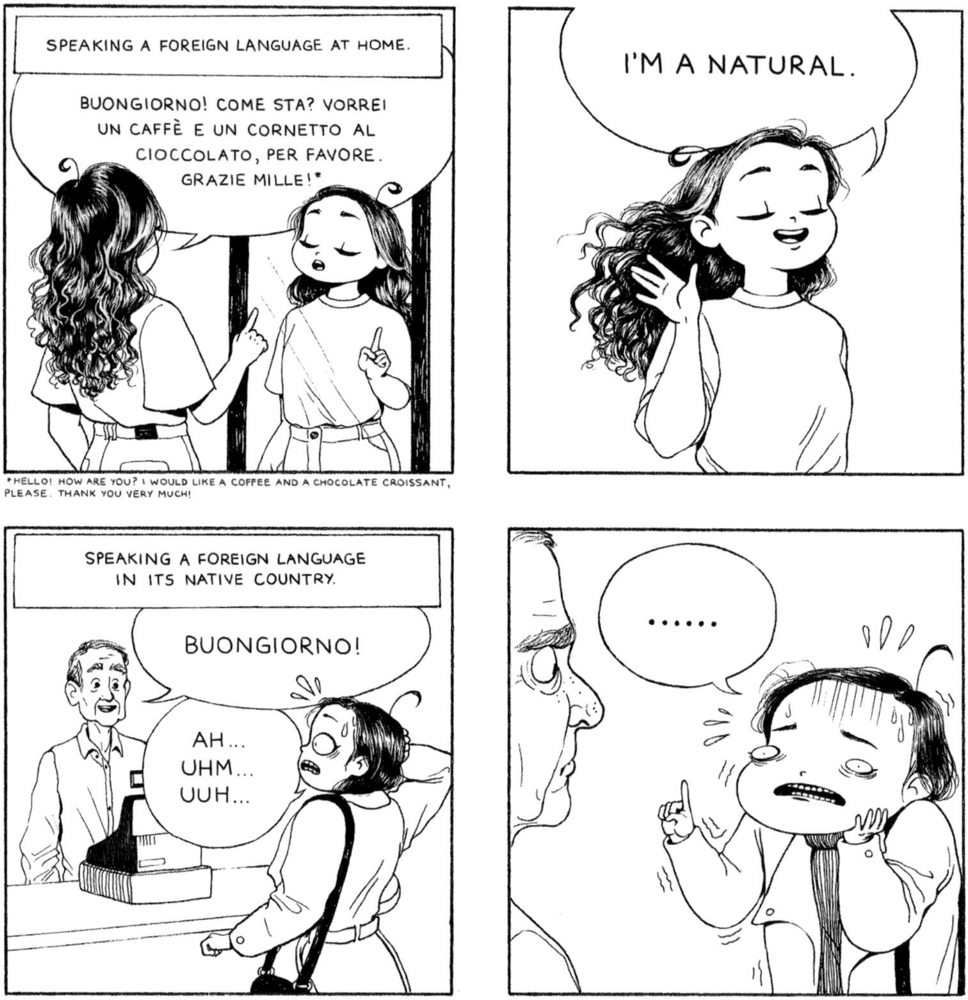
SPEAKING A FOREIGN LANGUAGE AT HOME.
BUONGIORNO! COME STA? VORREI UN CAFFÈ E UN CORNETTO AL CIOCCOLATO, PER FAVORE. GRAZIE MILLE!*
I'M A NATURAL.
SPEAKING A FOREIGN LANGUAGE IN ITS NATIVE COUNTRY.
BUONGIORNO!
AH... UHM... UUH...
......

*HELLO! HOW ARE YOU? I WOULD LIKE A COFFEE AND A CHOCOLATE CROISSANT, PLEASE. THANK YOU VERY MUCH!

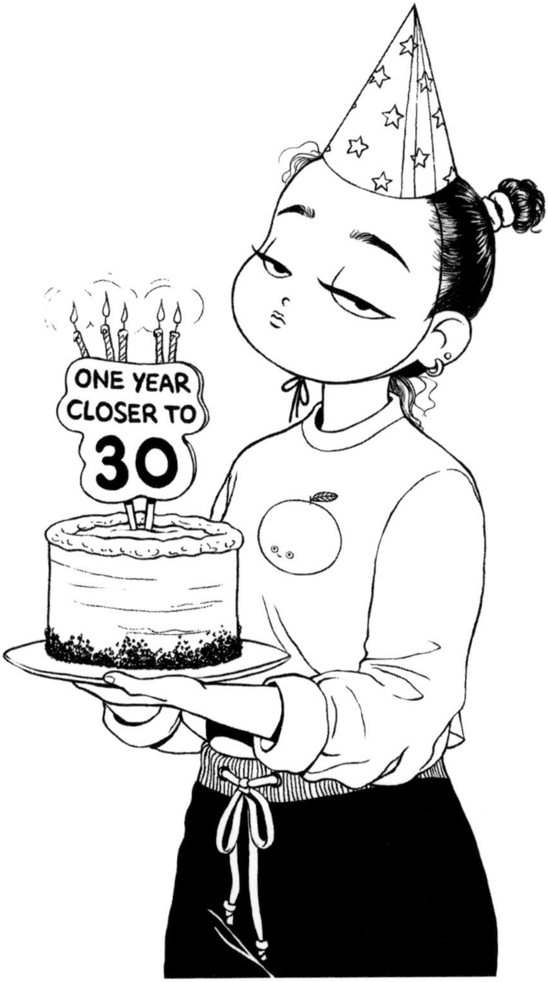
ONE YEAR CLOSER TO 30

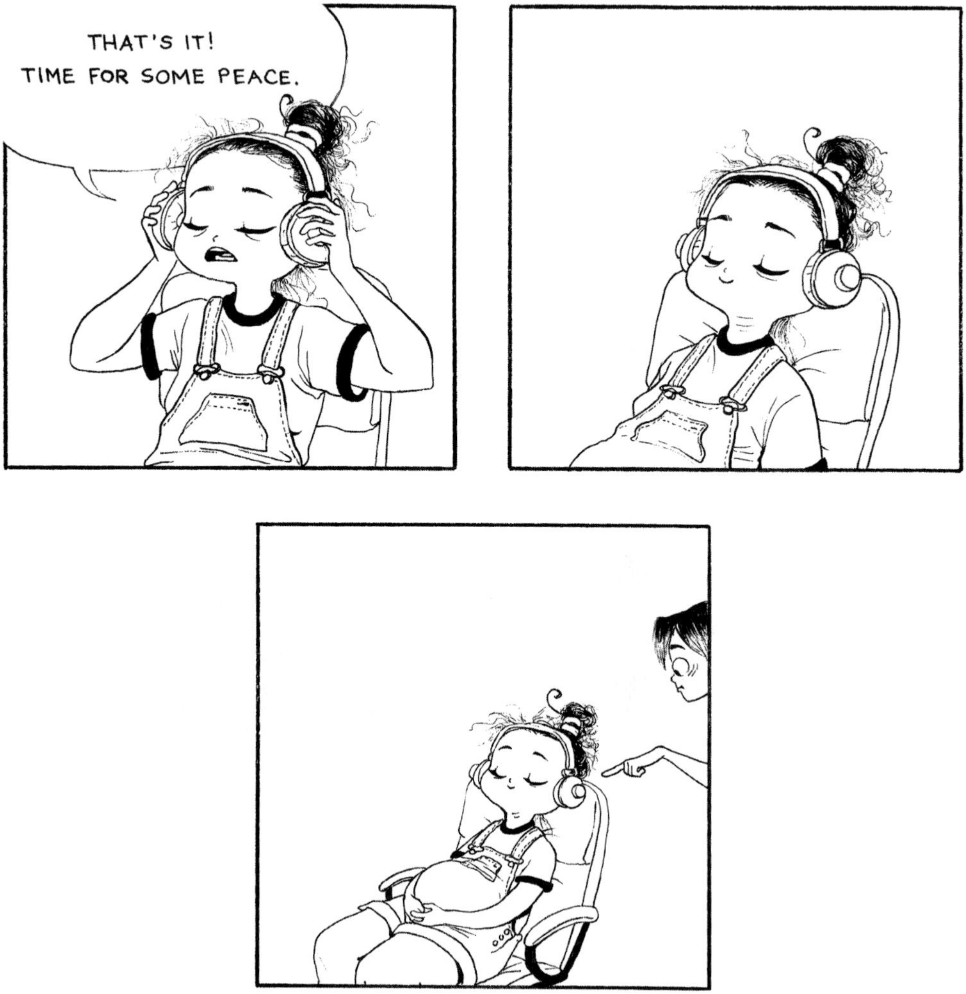
THAT'S IT!
TIME FOR SOME PEACE.

CONTOURING

EXPECTATIONS   REALITY

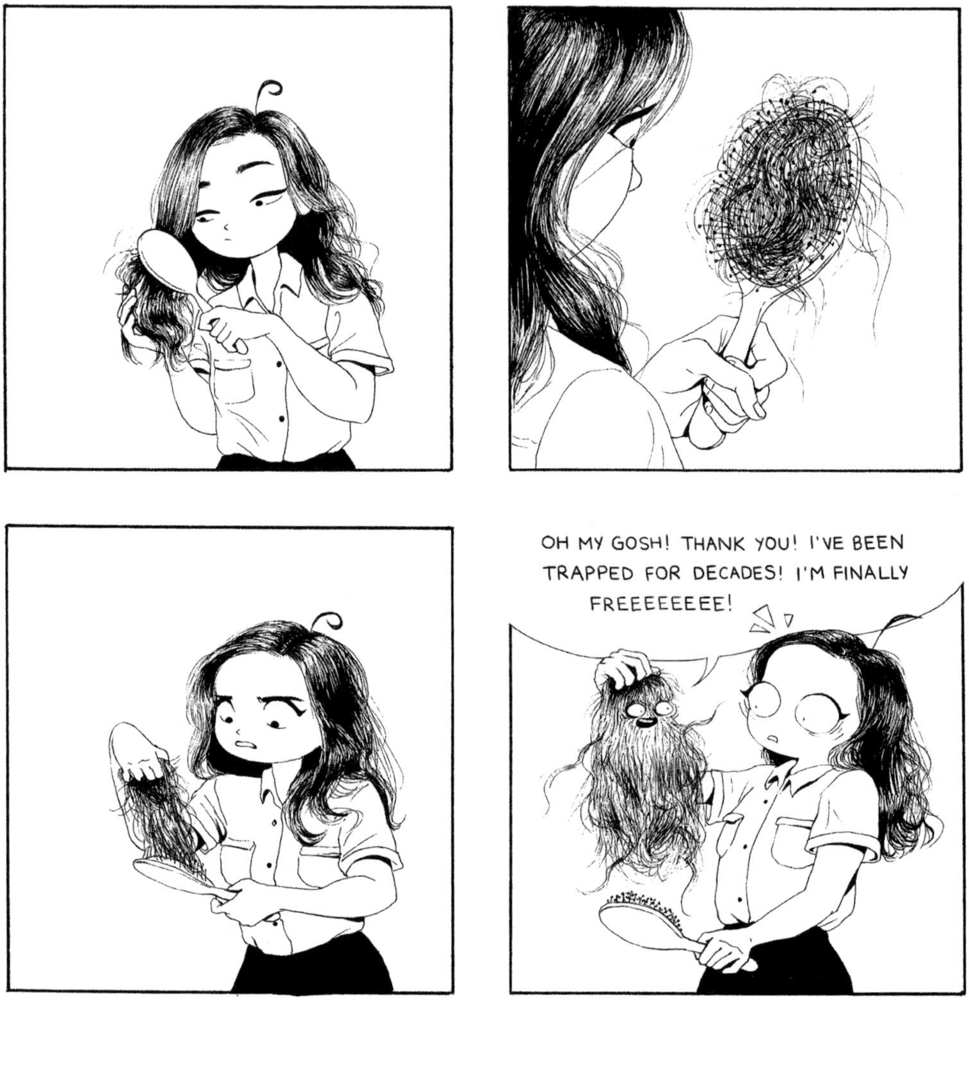
OH MY GOSH! THANK YOU! I'VE BEEN TRAPPED FOR DECADES! I'M FINALLY FREEEEEEEE!

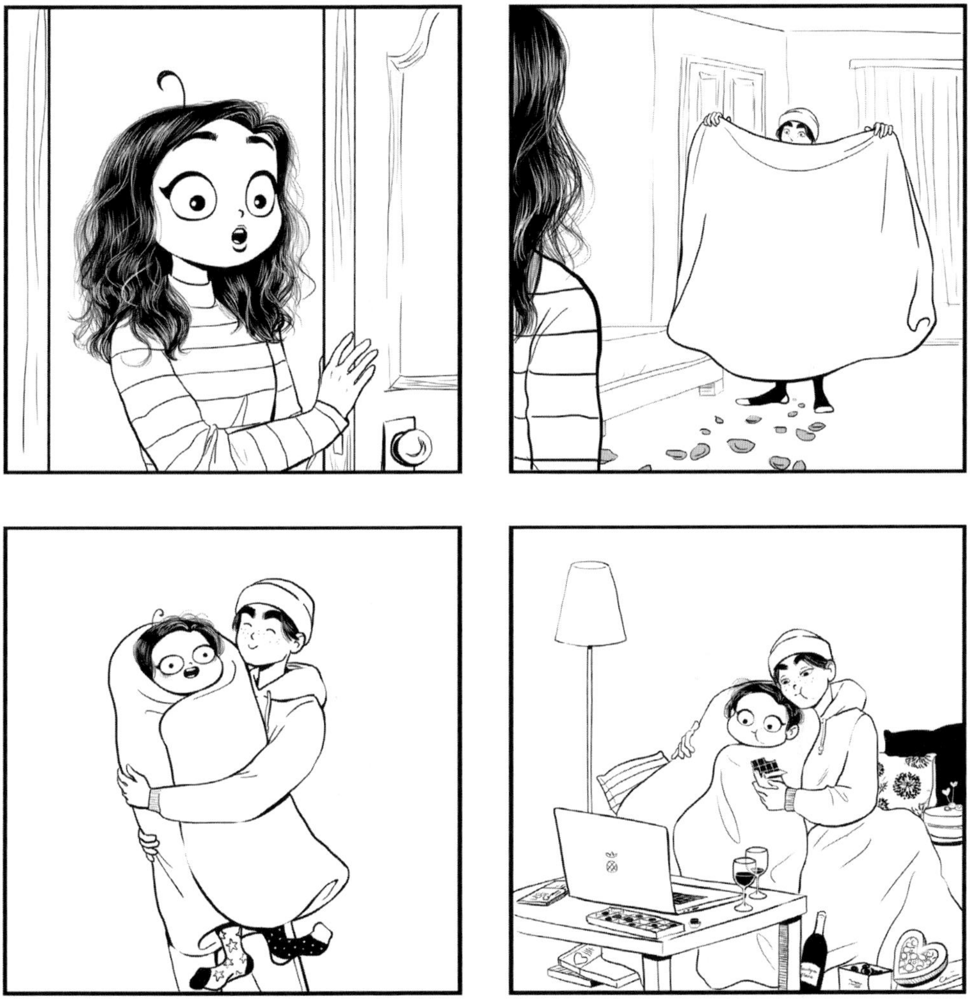

I left the house today!

Andrews McMeel Publishing
a division of Andrews McMeel Universal
1130 Walnut Street, Kansas City, Missouri 64106

20 21 22 23 24 RR2 10 9 8 7 6 5 4 3 2

ISBN: 978-1-5248-5557-4

Library of Congress Control Number: 2019957191

Editor: Lucas Wetzel
Art Director: Spencer Williams
Production Editor: Meg Daniels
Production Manager: Tamara Haus

www.andrewsmcmeel.com
www.cassandracalin.com

ATTENTION: SCHOOLS AND BUSINESSES

Andrews McMeel books are available at quantity discounts with bulk purchase for educational, business, or sales promotional use. For information, please e-mail the Andrews McMeel Publishing Special Sales Department: specialsales@amuniversal.com.